Minicomputer and Microprocessor Interfacing

Minicomputer and Microprocessor Interfacing

J.C. Cluley

Crane Russak • *New York*
Edward Arnold • *London*

Minicomputer and
Microprocessor Interfacing

Published in the United States by
Crane, Russak & Company, Inc.
3 East 44th Street
New York, New York 10017
ISBN 0-8448-1400-8
LC 82-8003

Published in Great Britain by
Edward Arnold (Publishers) Ltd.
41 Bedford Square
London WC1B 3DQ
ISBN 0 7131 3474 7

Printed in the United States of America

Contents

Preface

Since the first edition was published the development of VLSI techniques has enabled complex logic networks comprising tens of thousands of transistors to be fabricated on a single slice of silicon.

Apart from storage packages, the major application of these techniques has been the fabrication of the central processors for small computer systems. These are now produced in such large quantities that it is now economical to fabricate some of the standard peripheral interfaces using the same technology. These are functionally similar to the interface boards built for conventional minicomputers, but necessarily differ in some respects due to the constraints of high volume production and a limited number of pins for external connections.

In preparing this second edition I have extended its scope to include a brief description of microprocessor architecture, and the characteristics of their interface packages.

I have also included some description of microprocessor bus arrangements, and the rather different design techniques needed when programs are held in read-only storage.

Since the boundary between microprocessors and minicomputers is ill-defined and continually changing I think that they are best treated as a continuum.

I have tried to indicate the common features of their operation and interfacing and hope that the new edition will prove useful to students and practicing engineers.

Chapter 1

Introduction

Although the majority of electronic digital computers are at present used for data processing in government, commerce, and industry, an expanding market has appeared in recent years for small computers to control industrial plants and processes. The development of semiconductor devices, and particularly integrated circuits, has been the main technological advance which permitted this expansion, since it led to cheaper and much more reliable computers than were previously available.

This book is concerned with computers in the second category which are used, for example, to control or monitor some system and are closely linked to it. Before beginning a study in detail, we will consider the relation of such operations to other computing activities; the essential components of a small computer; and the additional features required for computers used in these control and supervisory applications.

1.1. OFF-LINE COMPUTING

All early computers operated in what is now classed as the "off-line" mode. This description is applied to systems in which computer input and output occurs via a physical medium such as punched cards or paper tape, and the electrical circuits of the computer do not extend beyond the peripherals adjacent to the central processor.

Although many small data-processing computers are still operated in this fashion, there are many applications in which remote data terminals, visual display units, teleprinters, etc., are connected to computers through long distance circuits. With such systems the off-line mode of working, in which the central processor alone controls the flow of work, cannot respond to the varying demands placed on the system by the uncoordinated requests for attention from the outlying terminals. The computer must then be operated as an "on-line" system which no longer works its way rigidly through a queue of jobs but can at any moment direct its attention to the most pressing task awaiting it. Systems such as this are used for airline ticket reservation, and for handling bank accounts and insurance premium payments.

1.2. ON-LINE WORKING

The distinctive feature of on-line working is that the central processor is no longer autonomous but must attend to requests for service from the remote devices. Since there are generally more than one of these, the computer requires two facilities not needed for basic off-line operation.

The first of these is a priority system in which each device has a level of priority assigned to it. Thus, when more than one device is requesting attention, the computer can check their priority levels and attend to the most urgent task — indicated by the highest priority level — first.

The second essential feature is a method of allowing a high-priority task to interrupt a lower-priority task. This involves a procedure for storing the current state of the lower-priority calculation, transferring control to a program dealing with the higher-priority request, and then returning to complete the lower-priority task.

The engineering task of connecting many devices to the computer is simplified if a standardized form of connection can be made to a common data highway or bus. The interconnection usually involves both logic and storage elements and is called an "interface."

1.3. COMPUTER STRUCTURE

From the previous section we may conclude that on-line and off-line computers have essentially similar features, but that the structure of the off-line machine will be somewhat more complex in order to provide the necessary input-output and interrupt facilities. Thus, before considering on-line computer structure, it is useful to examine the main components of an off-line computer and their interaction.

A simplified diagram showing the flow of data and control signals is given in Fig. 1.1. This represents a small computer without magnetic tape or disc backing store and with only a teleprinter for input and output. Data and program are held in the main store and can be extracted a number or an instruction at a time. The unit of information, a "word," is generally 12-16 binary digits in small computers, but some machines can also operate on 8-bit units or "bytes." Information from the store is processed in the arithmetic and logic unit (ALU), and the operations of the various components of the system are regulated by the control unit. Information is fed in via the teleprinter keyboard; output is via the printer.

1.4. ARITHMETIC AND LOGIC UNIT

This unit contains a number of registers or single-word stores. The essential register is the accumulator, which always holds the result of any

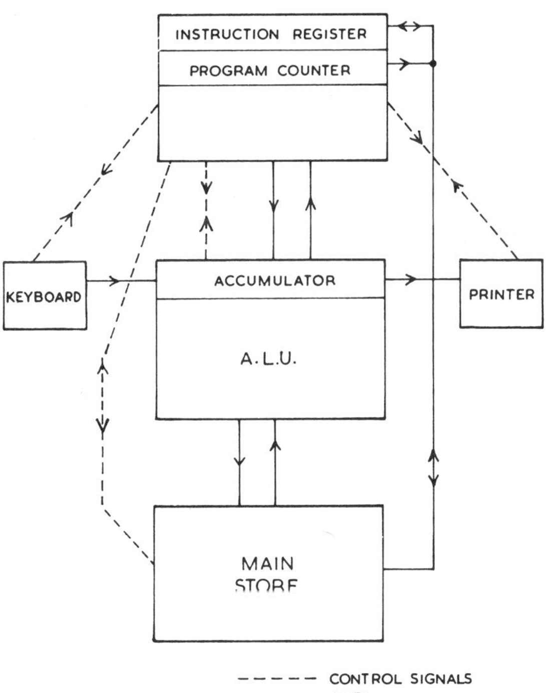

Figure 1.1. Data and control paths in a small computer

operation. In addition, other registers may be needed for other operands and for the other half of a double-length product. For example, the product of two 16-bit numbers may contain 32 bits; the most significant 16 bits would generally be left in the accumulator, and the least significant 16 in another auxiliary register.

The minimum arithmetical operations required are addition, complementing, clearing to zero, and shifting left and right. This basic repertoire also enables the machine to subtract, multiply, and divide, although the last two operations will be slow. Many small machines have extra hardware to perform multiplication and division rapidly, rather than by a program of shifting and addition or subtraction.

The ALU also has facilities for logical operations such as AND and OR on the corresponding bits of two operands, for depositing data from the accumulator into the store, and for loading the accumulator from the store.

1.5. MAIN STORE

A typical small computer has a minimum store size of, generally, 4K words. (Here, 1K is used to denote $2^{10} = 1024$.) The stores of earlier computers used square-loop ferrite cores with cycle times of $^3/_4$ to $1^1/_2\mu s$, each involving a read and re-write operation. Many current minicomputers provide semiconductor main stores either as a standard item or as an option. These use much less power and, as they can perform a non-destructive read, need only execute a read cycle or a write cycle. This feature, added to the inherent high speed of the transistors which form the store, enable cycle times down to 150ns to be obtained.

Semiconductor storage is, of course, volatile (that is, data disappears if the power is removed) but most versions require less power when quiescent than when continually transferring data. Thus, it is simple to arrange automatic changeover to batteries when the main power fails, so preserving the stored data.

Although many on-line computers, particularly if dedicated to a specific task, may require only a few thousand words of storage, some other arrangement is needed if a number of programs are to be stored and executed, or if a large volume of data is being handled.

We can distinguish between the working store needed to handle a particular task and the ''backing store'' for programs to be loaded into the working store as required. The working store must be ''random access,'' that is, any word within it must be accessible in the same time. Access to the backing store is required much less frequently, so that it can be a system which provides access to blocks of data rather than to individual words. Generally, a much longer time to access the data can be tolerated in the backing store, and the designer tries to exploit this feature to reduce the cost per bit of the storage.

The majority of backing stores now use some form of moving magnetic surface in a variety of configurations, for example rigid discs, floppy discs, reel-to-reel tape, cassette tape, drums, etc.

The data on discs is divided into tracks, any item being accessible in a fraction of a second, whereas tape, although cheaper, has a much longer access time. A full reel may hold 2400ft of tape which takes several minutes to pass through the tape transport. In contrast, fast access drums which have a head for each track have an average access time of around 10ms.

A possible replacement for the disc store is the magnetic bubble store which avoids the need for the great mechanical precision and clean atmosphere essential for reliable disc operation. The magnetic bubble store is a static device and is currently available in modest-sized units with a capacity of 1 million bytes.

A typical single rigid disc can store several million bytes, and transfer at a faster rate. However, further development of the bubble store should provide a device comparable in storage capacity with a disc store but at a much lower price, and with no moving parts to wear or require maintenance.

1.6. CONTROL UNIT

The operations of the various parts of a computer are organized by the control unit which interprets instructions, issues commands, and ensures that the transmission paths for any data movement are established.

The actions of the control unit can be divided basically into those of fetching an instruction, and then executing it. Examined in rather more detail, several distinct phases can be discerned:

(a) Fetch instruction and increment program counter.

(b) If the instruction requires no access to the main store, but only to internal central processing unit (CPU) registers, it can be executed directly. An example is "clear accumulator." If an operand must be obtained from the main store, execution must be delayed during an extra store cycle to obtain this operand. There may be an extra delay if an extra arithmetic operation is needed to compute the effective address of the operand. This situation occurs with indexed addressing and with addressing relative to the program counter.

(c) If indirect addressing is required, an additional store cycle is needed to obtain the operand.

(d) The instruction can now be executed.

(e) Where the instruction set allows for the result of the operation to be returned to the store, a further storage cycle may be required for this operation.

(f) Before fetching the next instruction, the computer will check whether an interrupt has been signalled (see Chapter 4) and whether the interrupt feature is enabled. If both of these conditions are true it will divert its attention to a service program and abandon temporarily its previous sequence of operations. In some minicomputers and nearly all microprocessors the "fetch" state may be prolonged since an instruction may comprise 1–4 words and require a corresponding number of store cycles to extract it from the store. Also in microprocessors, some instructions handle data two words in length. These operands will consequently require two cycles to transfer them to or from the store.

Two registers are usually incorporated in the control unit, the instruction register (IR) and the program counter (PC). The instruction register stores the instruction which is being executed, and which will define some machine operation and 0, 1, or 2 operands. Instructions such as SKIP or HALT involve no operands, operations on the accumulator contents such as SHIFT or COMPLEMENT require only the operand stored in the accumulator, and the usual arithmetic processes such as ADD and SUBTRACT require two operands. Since by convention one operand in a process is always taken as the contents of the accumulator, a simple computer never requires more than one operand to be specified in the instruction code. The instruction thus has in general only two components, a portion indicating the function or operation to be performed, and an address specifying the location of the second operand.

In order to obtain more effective use of the system, however, most machines allow other information to be specified in the instruction. One bit is usually allocated to indicate indirect addressing. Thus, if this particular bit is set to 1, the location specified in the instruction does not contain the operand but the address of the operand. A further useful facility is that of address modification or indexing. A few bits of the instruction may specify one of a number of index registers. When executing the instruction the computer adds the address specified in the instruction to the contents of the index register in order to obtain the effective address which is selected by the store.

An additional feature in more complex computers is the use of multiple registers in the central processor. This means that the result of any operation can be routed to any one of perhaps a dozen registers instead of being left in the accumulator, and also that any of these registers can be used to specify one operand in an operation. We thus have in effect a number of accumulators instead of one. This arrangement avoids much swapping of data between store and ALU, and so speeds computation.

The second register in the control unit is the program counter. This holds the address of the next instruction to be executed, and is normally incremented by 1 when each instruction is fetched. However, when a JUMP instruction is executed, the contents of the program counter are altered so that the next instruction is fetched from a different part of the store rather than from the next consecutive location. Some machines also have a SKIP instruction which allows the machine to jump over an instruction. In order to perform this operation the program counter must be incremented by 2.

In simple machines the program counter is not directly accessible to the programmer, but in more complex machines containing a number of registers, one of these may be designated as the program counter. It will then be accessible to the programmer along with the other registers in the central processor.

1.7. MICROPROGRAMMING

The description of the control unit given above is adequate for many purposes, but it omits some details of how the control unit is organized in most modern machines. If we examine a typical computer instruction such as

```
ADD     150
```

we find that in order to execute this the control unit must arrange a number of activities in sequence, some of which involve specific time intervals. Thus it becomes convenient to divide the basic machine cycle into a number of smaller intervals, with facilities for organizing data flow and activating various parts of the computer in each of these intervals. For the ADD instruction the steps would be as follows:

(1) Copy address (150) into store address register.
(2) Initiate store read operation.
(3) Increment program counter.

(4) As soon as the contents of location 150 are available in the store data register, transfer them to one input of the adder.
(5) At the same time, copy the contents of the accumulator into the other input of the adder.
(6) Activate the adder unit.
(7) After an appropriate delay, transfer the output of the adder into the accumulator.

It is convenient to design the computer so that its fundamental operations are the execution of small operations such as described above. These are called ''microoperations'' and a sequence of them comprises a ''microprogram'' which will implement one of the machine instructions which the programmer uses. The complete set of microprograms which execute the instruction set of the machine are normally held in a fast ''read-only'' store (the control store) within the control unit. In order to control all of the data paths and gates in the processor a microinstruction may contain 50 or more bits. Each machine instruction will direct the control unit to a particular address in the control store which contains the first microinstruction of its microprogram.

This method of organizing the control unit is generally adopted for most current minicomputers. An added feature is a section of the control store which is writeable. This allows the programmer to define additional instructions which he can design to perform particular operations not provided for in the basic instruction set. As an example: the Data General Corporation ''Eclipse'' range of computers has a 512 word read-only store incorporated to implement the standard instruction set. This can optionally be augmented by 256 words of writeable control store for additional microprograms.

1.8. ON-LINE OPERATION

The foregoing description of the components of a small computer provides only for input and output via a teletype or similar device. For on-line operation we need facilities for transmitting and receiving digital information in electrical form. This involves a direct connection to the central processor, usually via the accumulator. Since there will generally be a number of devices connected to the computer, there must be some means of selecting which of these is communicating with the accumulator at any particular time. Some timing information is also required so that the operation of the on-line device may be synchronized with the operating cycle of the computer. The final group of signals is concerned with signalling the state of the connected device to the computer and sending control signals from the computer to the device.

Nearly all modern computers handle data in the parallel mode, so that an input or output transfer operation involves one word of 8-16 bits sent simultaneously over the same number of wires (1 bit/wire) or data lines.

Thus the connections between the computer and the external device may be grouped as follows: (a) data lines, usually one per bit; (b) device selection lines, typically six to eight in all; (c) timing signals; and (d) control signals. The general arrangement is shown in Fig. 1.2. This is a typical "highway" scheme in which all of the external devices are connected in parallel to the highway.

Early computers used in the off-line mode had few external devices (usually called "peripherals") and a different radial scheme of connection was used. For this, each peripheral had a set of logic and storage elements incorporated in the central processor, a set of connecting cables, and some additional logic and storage at the peripheral device itself. The hardware in the central processor (the "controller") was different for

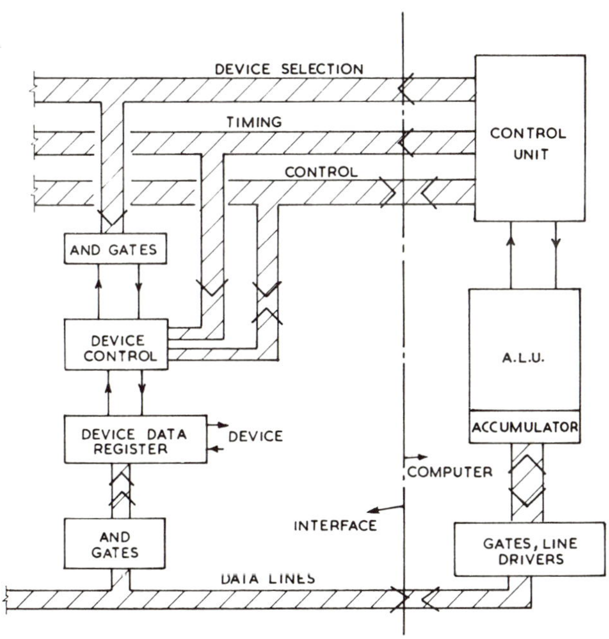

Figure 1.2. Layout of program-controlled interface

each peripheral device, and when a new peripheral was required a considerable amount of rewiring of the central processor was inevitable. This arrangement involves a minimum of hardware at the peripheral device, but if there are many of these the cost of all of the controllers becomes prohibitive.

The data-highway system avoids this expense by using only one set of hardware in the computer, and allowing all of the connected devices access to it one at a time. Since there may be hundreds of devices requiring access to the computer in some on-line systems, the data-highway arrangement is, for economic reasons, the only arrangement possible. When a large number of devices are connected to the data highway, the load imposed on it by all of the connections requires careful consideration by the designer if the system is to perform reliably. A further feature is that some of the lines in the highway may be bidirectional (for example, the data lines may be required for input or output from the computer). This is a requirement not generally encountered elsewhere in digital circuit engineering and one which calls for novel circuit design. This topic is discussed in more detail in Chapter 3.

1.9. DMA TRANSFERS

The input or output transfer process via the accumulator is not very fast since data is normally stored into, or read from, the store. Thus, each incoming word must be transmitted to the data lines, loaded into the accumulator, and then transferred to the store. This requires two instructions, one to perform the transfer and the second to read the word to store. Each of these instructions must be copied from the store into the instruction register, thus requiring two store cycles. In addition, any calculation in progress before the transfer will leave data in the accumulator, data which must be preserved in the store and retrieved afterwards, needing a further two store cycles. Thus, although this mode of transfer, often called a program-controlled transfer, is adequate for slow peripheral devices such as teletypes and paper tape machines, it is far below the maximum possible data rate. We could obviously speed up the transfer process by bypassing the accumulator and transferring data directly to or from the store.

This can be arranged by having access via a further set of data lines to the store data register (sometimes called the store or memory buffer register). We have seen that a store-write operation requires two items of information, the address of the store location being written to and the data to be written. These are sent to the store address register and the store data register. Consequently the device connected in this manner needs two registers which contain the required information. A further register is also needed which allows the device to transfer a specific number of words. Initially this register contains the "word count," that is, the number of words to be transferred. The address register and word-count register are generally loaded by program, but for some fixed systems they may be initialized by hardware. After each word transfer the contents of the address register are increased by one (incremented) and the word count decreased by one (decremented). The process stops when the word count falls to zero. This method of transfer is usually called "direct memory access" (DMA), and can take place at the maximum speed of the core store, typically 1 word/μs. No other computer activity is possible during this time, and the normal operation of the control unit is halted. The general scheme of connection is shown in Fig. 1.3.

This DMA transfer may operate on a word or two at a time, in which case it is sometimes called "cycle-stealing," since the device making the transfer effectively halts the computer's normal activity for a few microseconds and "steals" one or two cycles of the main store. For devices

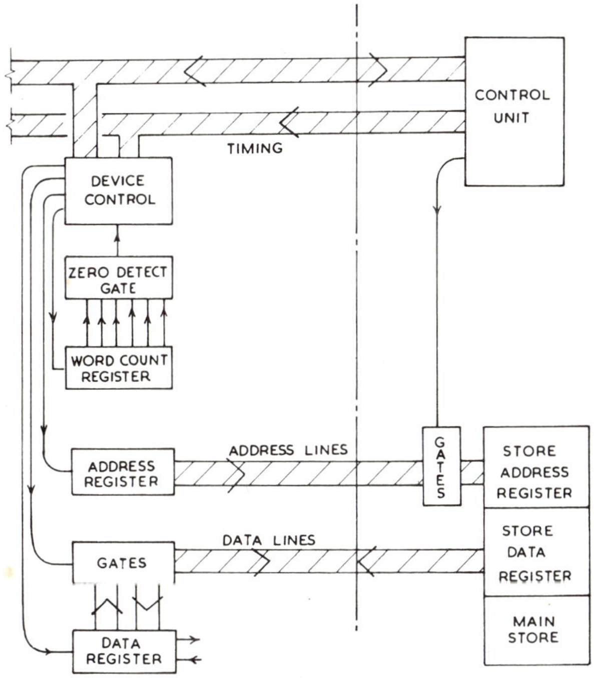

Figure 1.3. DMA interface

with a high data rate, however, a block transfer of a number of words in succession is usually more convenient.

Although DMA transfer is the fastest method of data input or output, it requires a considerable amount of logic and storage hardware at the junction between peripheral device and computer (the interface). The hardware required can be substantially reduced if some of the logic and storage can be provided by the central processor. One possibility is to use two locations in the main store for the address register and the word-count register, and use the arithmetic unit for incrementing and decrementing their contents. The maximum data transfer rate of around 1 word/μs will then be reduced by a factor of 3-4 since there must be at least two store cycles to read the two register contents, send them to the DMA channel, and increment or decrement them. However, this loss in maximum speed is acceptable for many on-line devices, and the arrangement considerably reduces the size and cost of the interface.

A number of small computers include in the central processer a set of general-purpose registers, two of which can be used to store the data address and the word count. Since these registers embody transistors, they are much faster in operation than the main store, and thus the maximum data-transfer rate is greater than in the alternative arrangement using the main core store.

1.10. INTERRUPT HANDLING

The majority of devices connected to the computer need to signal to the computer when they are ready to send or receive data. Such a signal is usually called an "interrupt," and is dealt with when the current instruction cycle has ended. Some method is required to identify which device is causing the interrupt signal; the current program must be halted and the control of the computer transferred to another program (already stored) which will service the device requiring attention. When the service routine is finished, control must be restored to the original program.

Finding the source of the interrupt can be done by program or directly by hardware (the latter method is faster but more expensive). Generally a number of devices are connected to the computer, and more than one device may request service at the same time. It is thus necessary to assign to the devices a degree of priority, and arrange that the highest-priority device always get attention first. Again, this can be done by program or hardware.

All interrupt arrangements depend upon having some information stored in the device interface which can be selectively interrogated by the computer. In earlier computers this was stored in single digit stores, called "flags," which could be tested one at a time by the computer. More recent machines use a complete word, the "device-status word," which can be read at one operation by the computer, each bit representing some state or function of the device. Other bits of the word can be used to control the operation of the device by writing data into the status-word register from the computer. Interrupt techniques are described in more detail in Chapter 4.

The flexible and comprehensive techniques developed for connecting a wide range of on-line devices to a controlling computer, and described in general terms in this chapter, have been applied to other types of computer.

For example, computers used for general commercial data processing require a number of peripheral input and output devices which are "on-line" to the central processor. These devices may be connected to a form of data highway as described in section 1.8 to give rapid and convenient access to the computer. However, to cope with a range of data rates, several different access channels can be provided.

Another concept which originated in on-line computers and is now found in some general-purpose machines is that of a "standard interface." This means that, as far as possible, all devices connected to the computer have a standard set of data, control, and timing lines, all operating at the same logic voltage levels. Such an arrangement is a necessity for on-line computers which have all external devices connected to a common data highway; in general-purpose machines it gives a considerable degree of flexibility and greatly simplifies the task of enhancing the machine's processing power by connecting extra peripheral devices.

1.11. FEATURES OF TYPICAL MINICOMPUTERS

The word size of current minicomputers lies in the range of 12–32 bits. The choice of a 12-bit word was made by the designers of an early machine, the Digital Equipment Corporation's PDP8, as the best compromise between cost and performance. As technology developed, particularly that of integrated circuits, falling hardware costs enabled more complex computers to be built economically. These mostly used a 16-bit word size, with a few designers preferring a 24-bit word size. The demand for additional computing power later led to the development of a few 32-bit machines. Examples of these are the DEC VAX 11/780, the Prime 50 series, and the Perkin-Elmer (formerly Interdata) 3220. The Data General Corporation is reported to have a 32-bit machine in production.

Early machines such as the PDP8 had a store size of only 4K words. Later versions of this machine could be expanded to 64K words, and 16-

bit machines can now be extended to incorporate several megabytes of main storage.

A particular feature of recent families of minicomputers is the very wide range of computing systems which can be based upon them. These range from microprocessor-based single board systems with, typically, 4K of store to large systems with several hundred thousand words of storage, a full range of magnetic tape and disc backing stores, and multiple keyboard and printer terminals.

Both the Digital Equipment Corporation's PDP11 and the Data General Nova series have a single board microprocessor version at the bottom of the range, and include also several powerful and fast machines for critical applications. In both cases the same basic instruction set is used in all members of the families.

The PDP8 is also produced in a number of versions, some microprocessor based, and there is also a single chip microprocessor, the Intersil IM6100, which executes the PDP8 instruction set but is not electrically compatible with its I/O bus.

As the original PDP8 had a simple architecture its design is a useful introduction to the features required in on-line computers.

The first machines in the range had a simple single accumulator architecture with a 1.5 μs store cycle time, and used single-word instructions. This means that store reference instructions use 3 bits for the operation code, 1 bit for indicating an indirect address, and a further bit to indicate whether the address is on the current page or page 0, thus leaving 7 bits for an address. The instruction thus has access directly to a "page" of 128 instructions or operands. The format of a store reference instruction is shown in Fig. 1.4. The early machines had a 4-K main store, all of which could be addressed indirectly by using the full 12 bits of a word for the address. In order to avoid using indirect addressing, which takes two core cycles, for nearly all store accesses a "paging" system was used in which the five most significant bits of an address in the program counter are stored in a "page" register. The lower 7 bits of the address are supplied by the instruction. Thus indirect addressing is needed only when access to a new page is required.

Despite the limitations imposed by a 12-bit word, the PDP8 family of computers has been developed in successive versions to keep pace with computer-hardware technology, and has been produced in greater numbers than any other small computer. The current machines use the same basic order code and input-output philosophy as the early machine but have a few extra instructions, for example, for byte-swapping operations. The interfaces are not compatible but require level-changing circuits, since current machines use medium-scale integrated circuits and positive logic with TTL signal levels, whereas early machines used germanium transistors and negative logic. Programs for the early machines will all run on the later machines, however.

A very wide range of standard peripherals is available, including magnetic disc and tape backing stores, CRT displays with light-pen input, graph plotters, D-A and A-D converters, etc., and current models can have up to 64K words of main storage. Program-controlled transfers can take place through a parallel I/O bus, or through an internal data highway called the "Omnibus." There is also a one-cycle or three-cycle "data-break" facility which bypasses the processor and provides direct memory access. The one-cycle version requires registers in the interface to provide the current address for the store and to keep track of the number of words transferred. This procedure requires only one store cycle, about 1.5μs, per word. The three-cycle data break uses two store locations to hold the current address and the word count, thus simplifying the interface but slowing down the data transfer rate as two further store cycles are needed: one to increment the current address, and the other to decrement the word count in preparation for the next transfer.

1.12. 16-BIT COMPUTERS

A survey of small computers shows a preponderance of 16-bit machines. This word size allows single-length numbers to provide sufficient resolution for many calculations (1 part in 65,536) and two-word floating point numbers to provide at least seven-decimal digit resolution. It also enables the contents of one word to specify up to 64K separate addresses, and so can be the basis for a powerful computing system. By employing extra registers, the main store capacity can be extended to 128K or more for large systems.

The number of internal registers available to the programmer has increased from the single accumulator provided on early machines. The Hewlett-Packard 2000 series used two accumulators, the original Data General Nova had four, the PDP11 has eight; and the Interdata series, based on the IBM 360 family, has 16 general purpose registers.

The Nova range exemplifies the simpler type of architecture; it has four accumulators, AC0–AC3. Accumulators AC2 and AC3 can be used as index registers, as can the program counter. An 8-bit displacement contained in the instruction word can be added to the contents of the index register to compute the actual address of the operand. Thus, any store reference instruction can directly access four groups of 256 words each: those in page 0 (the first 256 locations) and the three groups of 256 words centered on the address contained in the accumulators AC2 and

AC3 and in the program counter. The 8 instruction bits are interpreted as a 2's complement displacement which must lie in the range −128 to +127 decimal.

A "Move Data" instruction of this type must also specify which accumulator is involved, and has the format shown in Fig. 1.4. An additional bit is used for indirect addressing.

The original Nova could be fitted with two types of ferrite core store having cycle times of 1.2μs and 800ns or with semiconductor storage having a cycle time of 300ns, and could also incorporate modules of read-only store.

The smallest version currently available is the MicroNOVA, which uses the mN601 16-bit microprocessor chip. In order to diminish the number of pins on the chip, the conventional parallel I/O bus is replaced by a 16MHz serial data line. At each peripheral interface an I/O controller converts the serial address and data stream into a conventional parallel I/O port. This controller has considerable logical complexity as it performs the tasks of device selection, Busy and Done flags, and interrupt control and interrupt masking, in addition to data transfers. In order to reduce the bus loading special buffer elements are interposed between the I/O bus and the devices attached to it; other packages perform the same function for the store bus. The store is built in 4K modules using 4K × 1 RAM packages. Programmable ROM modules are also available.

The MicroNOVA is program compatible with earlier Nova computers

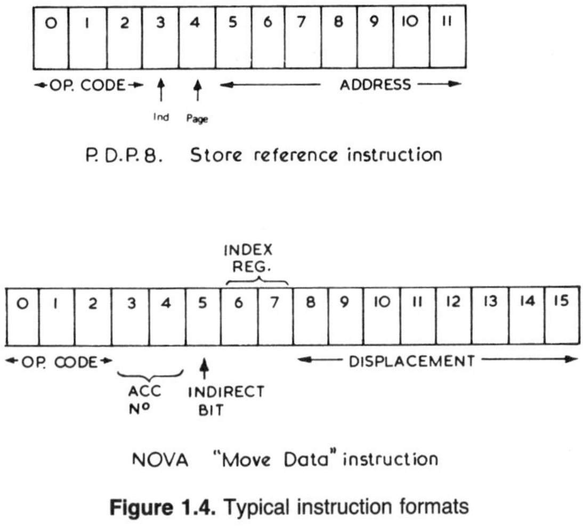

Figure 1.4. Typical instruction formats

but has a few extra instructions. Thus, like the Nova 3, it has a stack for storing return links and processor states during subroutines or interrupt servicing. Multiplication and division are performed by hardware.

Despite using MOS technology the MicroNOVA performs creditably in comparison with conventionally built Nova computers. For example, its execution time for arithmetic operations such as Add, Subtract, Increment, etc., is 2.4μs, three times greater than that of the Nova 2 with an 800ns store, and 2.88μs for Load and Store Accumulator (1.6 times greater than that of the Nova 2).

The first change in architecture from the original Nova occurred in the Nova 3, which added a hardware stack and an asynchronous store bus. This allowed modules of 700ns semiconductor store and 800ns and 1μs core store to be mixed in the same machine. Some overlap in instruction fetching and execution also speeded up the operations, giving an Add/Subtract time of 0.7μs, a Load Accumulator time of 1.2μs, and a Store Accumulator time of 1.5μs. The addition of a Memory Management Unit enables the store size to be extended to 128K words, compared with the normal limit of 32K words.

The current series is the Nova 4, the most powerful member of which is the Nova 4X. With a memory management unit this can have the store size extended to 256K bytes of 400ns MOS storage. This uses 4-way interleaving, so that when extracting data or instructions stored sequentially, 1 word can be read every 100μs. Optional hardware for multiply/divide and for floating-point arithmetic is available.

In order to provide a more powerful computing range the Data General Corporation introduced the "Eclipse" range a few years ago. This is program compatible with the Nova range but has more instructions for performing 32-bit arithmetic and fast interrupt vectoring. It has a fast 200ns cache store to reduce the effective access time, and an optional writeable control store for user–written microprograms. The main store can be extended to 2048K bytes.

Although the Nova range of computers has now an asynchronous store bus, its I/O bus is synchronous, so that a peripheral data transfer has to be effected under the control of the processor clock. This restriction was avoided in another range of machines, the Digital Equipment Corporation's PDP11 series, introduced a short time after the Nova range.

The PDP11 was designed as an asynchronous machine in that no fixed time is specified for the duration of a data transfer. The various stages of the process are controlled by "handshaking" signals which are interchanged between the controller of the transfer (the "bus master") and the other device (the "slave"). Normally, the processor has control of the bus but can relinquish this to a peripheral interface for interrupt handling. Normally, the bus master puts address and data on the line (for a write transfer) followed after a slight delay by the timing signal. The timing signal, when received by the slave, is used to copy the data into its internal storage, and after a further slight delay to originate an acknowledgment signal back to the processor. The processor will wait for this acknowledgment before continuing the process. The same protocol is used for both peripheral interface locations and main storage locations, so that store modules which have different cycle times can easily be plugged into the Unibus and used in the same computer.

A possible defect of this arrangement could appear if an address in the program were coded incorrectly or became corrupted. The address could then specify a nonexistent location and the computer could wait indefinitely for the signal from the slave location. In order to prevent stalling in this manner, the PDP11 has a ''time-out'' feature. A timer is started after each master synchronizing signal is issued and, unless a slave reply signal is received within 5-20μs, an interrupt occurs to a predetermined location at the bottom of the store, location 004. The sequence of operations which occurs during the data transfer is described in greater detail in section 2.14.

The other main innovative feature of the PDP11 is its ''universal address'' scheme. This avoids the use of a separate set of device select lines for addressing peripheral devices by allocating them addresses in the same manner as the main store modules.

The basic PDP11 can use a complete 16-bit word to specify an address; as it can address each 8-bit byte individually, it can deal with 64K bytes or 32K 16-bit words. Of this total address space 28K words are allocated for main storage and 4K words for peripheral interface addresses. This universal addressing feature enables the complete computer to be built around a data highway called the ''Unibus''; this is connected to the processor and all store units, peripheral interfaces, etc., can be plugged into the Unibus in party-line fashion. The full instruction set of the processor can then be used to manipulate data from a peripheral interface in the same manner as data from a main store location, so avoiding the need for special I/O instructions. The equivalent of DMA transfer can be performed by allowing an external device to acquire control of the Unibus and to transfer data directly to or from the store. During this time the processor can continue operations which do not involve the Unibus.

This architecture means that all 16 address lines must be sensed by all peripheral interfaces, instead of by the 6-device select lines needed for a program-controlled transfer on the PDP8 or the Nova. However, there is no need for a separate set of store address and store data lines for DMA transfer, so on balance the Unibus concept reduces the number of lines needed between the processor and an interface.

The "handshake" protocol does, however, involve a more complex set of signals between processor and interface and also a more complicated design of interface than is needed for a program-controlled transfer on the PDP8 or the Nova.

The PDP11 embodies a more complex architecture than that of earlier machines, and has eight processor registers. One of these is used as a program counter, another as the stack pointer. The remaining six registers can be used as accumulators, as the source or destination for data transfer, or to contain the addresses of source or destination. Some double operand (two address) instructions are provided. Consequently, when these instructions refer directly to external locations, three words are needed to hold an instruction; the first for the operation code and the remaining two for the 16-bit addresses of source and destination.

Relative addressing is allowed, and any register can be used as an index register. Furthermore, when any register contains the address of an operand, it can be automatically incremented or decremented during the execution of an instruction. This permits rapid access to a block of data items stored in successive locations.

The stack pointer contains the address of the blank location at the top of the stack, which occupies a reserved portion of the main store. The stack is normally used to hold data during an interrupt or the execution of a subroutine.

Early machines of the PDP11 family used magnetic core stores with cycle times of around 1μs, but later designs incorporated faster semiconductor stores with cycle times of either 300 or 450ns, and the more powerful versions could have a memory management unit fitted, so permitting a maximum storage capacity of 128K words. The PDP11/45 is intended for multiprogramming applications, and so has three operating modes: Kernel, Supervisor, and User. When the machine is in Kernel mode a program has complete control of all machine resources and of the peripherals; in any other mode the processor cannot execute some instructions and it can be denied access to the peripherals. These features allow the executive program to be protected against mutilation by a faulty user program.

In order to increase the speed of handling interrupts and subroutine calls the processor is equipped with a duplicate set of registers, allowing one set to be used for Kernel or Supervisor mode and the second set for a User program. This avoids the time delay involved in storing the contents of working registers before embarking upon an interrupt service routine, and restoring them afterwards. In order to save time three stack pointers are incorporated, one for each working mode.

A further enhancement of the PDP11/45 compared with smaller machines in the range is the provision for hardware multiplication and division and for multiple shifting. A fast floating-point option is available which can handle either 32 or 64-bit numbers.

The PDP11/60 is a more powerful machine with similar arithmetic facilities to the PDP11/45 but with a faster optional floating point processor which can add or subtract 32-bit numbers in 1.0μs and multiply them in 1.5μs. A larger memory management unit enables the main store to be expanded to 248K bytes, and a fast 2K byte cache store effectively increases the speed of the main store.

An additional option is the User Control Store, a writeable store which can hold 1K of 48-bit microinstructions. This can be used to generate additional instructions which can perform functions not provided in the standard instruction set.

1.13. MICROPROCESSORS

As the technology of large-scale integration developed, enabling many thousands of transistors to be fabricated on a single chip of silicon, a milestone was reached when a complete digital processor could be produced in a single package. The design of early microprocessors was greatly constrained by the manufacturing technology, so that their architecture was far from convenient for the user or the programmer.

The first device produced in volume was a 4-bit processor, the Intel 4004, with a limited set of 50 instructions, handling 4-bit data items and 8 or 16-bit instructions. It was soon followed by 8-bit devices with more instructions and more convenient architecture. Some aspects of the design were modelled upon minicomputer practice, particularly the provision for storage and interfaces.

Almost since their inception minicomputers have been designed so that the user could buy the amount of storage needed for his particular application, plugging this in to augment the normal minimum amount provided. In the same way various interfaces could be plugged in to suit the application and added to later as required.

To allow the same design flexibility all early microprocessors were designed to work with external storage and interface packages, their number and capacity being chosen to suit the application.

It was later realized that many small applications could be handled by a program store of 2K bytes or less, 50–100 bytes of data storage and 3 or 4 external ports or 1-byte interfaces. This considerable portion of the market could be satisfied very economically by making a ''single-chip'' microprocessor in which all of these features were incorporated, together with some clock circuits and perhaps a counter/timer. Since many applications require a still greater store and more interfaces, alternative processors are available which can be attached to a much larger store and more interfaces than the single-chip microprocessor provides.

Since the microprocessor is generally used in an environment calling for automatic operation as soon as power is supplied, the program is held in a read-only store, and the arrival of power operates a start-up circuit. This creates a special type of interrupt which directs the processor to the beginning of the program held in the read-only store.

The read-only store is fabricated by its manufacturer for large-volume production. This is done by controlling the final metallization which connects all of the cells, so as to generate the required instructions in each byte (the masked ROM). For smaller production runs the user can buy a blank PROM (programmable read-only memory) which he can load himself. This can be a fusible-link PROM in which a small nichrome strip in series with each data cell can be blown by applying a pulse of current to insert the required data. More expensive but more convenient for development is the EPROM (erasable programmable read-only memory). This is programmed by applying a higher than normal voltage to a cell, so causing migration of charge by electron avalanching. The charge can be removed, so erasing the data, by applying a reverse voltage, or by exposing the chip to ultraviolet light.

As microprocessor technology developed to enable 16K, 32K, and finally 64K bits to be stored on a single chip, it became economically possible to fabricate, on one chip, the tens of thousands of transistors necessary to construct a 16-bit microprocessor. Several of these are available, some being new designs like the Zilog Z8000 and the Motorola 68000, others like the DEC LSI11 and the Data General MicroNOVA being microprocessor versions of existing minicomputers. Although 16-bit systems have advantages of speed and precision of calculation and a large address space, at present the majority of microprocessor applications can be handled by 8-bit processors, and these comprise the largest fraction of the market.

The earliest of these was the Intel 8008, soon followed by the Intel 8080. The 8080 used the almost universal 40 pin dual-in-line package, nominally 2 ins. long and 0.6 ins. wide, with separate address and data lines in place of the 8 multiplexed lines of the 8008. By using 16 address lines a total of 64K storage locations could be accessed. The 8080 has one accumulator, 6 general registers (which can also be used in pairs for 16-bit operations), and a program counter and stack pointer (both 16-bits wide). One pair (H,L) of the general registers is used as a data pointer. A stack is used for temporary storage, usually occupying part of the writeable store.

Later developments of this microprocessor are the Intel 8085 and the Zilog Z80, both program compatible with the 8080 but having a few additional instructions. The 8085 has serial data input and output pins and several more interrupt lines than the 8080. In order to release pins for these extra functions the lower half of the address lines are multiplexed with the data lines. This feature complicates interfacing, since this half of the address information has to be stored while the data is transmitted in the following clock period.

The Z80 has a duplicate set of internal registers for use during subroutine or interrupt service routine execution. These avoid the need for saving and restoring internal registers and so materially speed up interrupt servicing and subroutine calls.

The Intel 8080 has 78 instructions, with a minimum execution time of 2μs, and requires power supplies of +12V, +5V, and −5V.

Another widely used 8-bit microprocessor is the Motorola M6800. This has 72 instructions, 7 addressing modes, and a minimum instruction time of 2 μs. It can also address 64K locations in all, but requires only a single 5V power supply. Both the M6800 and the 8080 have been produced in various single-chip versions.

The reduction in the size of logic circuits which large-scale integration allows means that a complete microcomputer comprising an 8-bit CPU, a start-up circuit, a clock pulse generator, several thousand bytes of storage, and a few I/O ports, (perhaps with A-D and D-A converters), can be assembled on a single board 10 ins. by 6 ins. The power required would be in the range 5–10 watts and the cost around a tenth of that of a conventional minicomputer.

As mentioned above, most microprocessors are used in control applications in which a fixed program is used, so only a few hundred bytes of writeable store are needed for handling the transient data. The increasing use of microprocessors for commercial work in offices has led to a different configuration, one rather closer to that of minicomputers. The need here is for a set of programs for particular functions, such as stock control, payroll, invoicing, etc., to be available on demand. These are usually held on a floppy disc backing store and loaded into the main store as required. In this situation the ROM contains a small monitor and file-handling executive which has facilities for data entry and for calling for information from the backing store and returning it after processing. This capability calls for a writeable store large enough to contain the longest program used together with its data.

The microprocessor systems mentioned above are partitioned functionally into several packages, containing central processor, program store, data store, interface logic, etc.

Another partitioning method has also been used to permit greater flexibility in the final microcomputer. This is the "bit-slice" microprocessor, in which each package contains a 2 or 4-bit "slice" through the microprocessor. By assembling these the user can construct an 8, 10, 12, etc. bit microprocessor. The disadvantage is that the unit so produced must have a separate control store, an advantage is that it can be microprogrammed to produce a variety of instruction sets. Thus the user has much greater flexibility but also a much greater design task. The arrangement is particularly convenient for emulation, that is, the execution of the instruction set of one machine by a different machine.

In view of the design effort required, bit-slice microprocessors are not widely used, but their components have been incorporated in central processors of main-frame computers, generally using bipolar transistor bit-slice elements to obtain maximum operating speed. One feature which distinguishes microprocessor usage from that of minicomputers is the method of using the machine to assist programming. In minicomputers the machine on which the program will finally be run is generally used to write, edit, and prepare the program, using either an assembler or, for high-level languages, a compiler. The microprocessor system which will ultimately form part of a finished product will usually have only a few hundred words of writeable store and no keyboard/printer facilities; thus, it cannot be used for preparing programs.

One solution is to use a special microprocessor development system which has a large writeable store and a terminal for program input and checking, with an editor, debugging program, and assembler available either in read-only store or held on a floppy disc drive. For outputting the final binary program there may be a paper tape punch whose output can be sent to the manufacturer to generate a read-only store. Alternatively, the system may incorporate a PROM programmer which can load the program into a user-programmable read-only store. This latter is suitable only for small-scale production.

A faster and generally more comprehensive system uses a minicomputer to input, edit, and assemble the program. This requires a "cross-assembler," that is, a program which runs on one machine but produces binary code suitable for running on another machine. The advantage of this method is that the minicomputer is larger and faster than the microprocessor, has a larger backing store, and is likely to have a better editor and better diagnostics. Some manufacturers of microprocessors have produced cross-assemblers written in high-level languages such as Fortran, which can be run on almost any minicomputer or on a main-frame machine. Versions are available which allow the programmer to write in a high-level language, such as a subset of PL/1 or Pascal, thus making his task easier.

1.14. CONCLUSION

In this chapter we have introduced the outline features of an on-line computing system and indicated how it differs from a general purpose computer. In succeeding chapters the various topics are considered in greater detail, starting with the logic and storage elements which are required for building an interface and which also comprise the greater part of the central processor.

BIBLIOGRAPHY AND REFERENCES

ASPINALL, D., and DAGLESS, E.L. *Introduction to Microprocessors,* Pitman Publishing Ltd., London, 1977.

BANNISTER, B.R., and WHITEHEAD, D.G. *Fundamentals of Digital Systems,* McGraw-Hill, New York, 1973.

BARTEE, T. *Digital Computer Fundamentals,* 4th ed., McGraw-Hill, New York, 1977.

BOYCE, J.C. *Microprocessor and Microcomputer Basics,* Prentice-Hall, Englewood Cliffs, N.J., 1979.

DIETMAYER, D.L. *Logic Design of Digital Systems,* 2nd ed., Allyn and Bacon, Mass., 1978.

DIGITAL EQUIPMENT CORPORATION. PDP-8/a Miniprocessor Handbook, 1975-76.

HEALEY, M. *Minicomputers and Microprocessors,* Crane, Russak & Co., New York, 1976.

HILL, F.J., and PETERSON, G.R. *Digital Systems: Hardware Organization and Design,* John Wiley, New York, 1973.

JOHNSON, D., et al. *Digital Circuits and Microcomputers,* Prentice-Hall, Englewood Cliffs, N.J., 1979.

KORN, G.A. *Microprocessors and Small Digital Computers for Engineers and Scientists,* 2nd ed., McGraw-Hill, New York, 1977.

LEWIN, D. *Theory and Design of Digital Computers,* 2nd ed., Nelson, London, 1980.

OGDIN, C.A. *Microprocessor Design,* Prentice-Hall, Englewood Cliffs, N.J., 1978.

PEATMAN, J.B. *The Design of Digital Systems,* McGraw-Hill, New York, 1972.

SANDERSON, P.C. *Minicomputers,* Newnes-Butterworth, London, 1976.

Chapter 2

Principles of Interfacing

2.1. INTRODUCTION

The need for an interface to connect external devices to a computer was introduced in Chapter 1. Chapter 2 deals with the elements of logic and storage hardware which comprise the interface, the way in which the interface controls the flow of data, and its logical design. The components required for the interface are essentially similar to the standard logic and storage elements used in the central computer, with some special-purpose driving and receiving units for connecting to data highways or buses. We begin by examining some sections of interface hardware which require only logical elements, without the need for storage.

2.2. ADDRESS SELECTION

Early computers used a radial mode of connection, shown in Fig. 2.1a, in which each device connected to the central processor had its own set of control and data circuits. This involves a large amount of equipment in the processor and a great deal of wiring. A more economical and flexible system is the "daisy-chain" or highway mode of connection in which a single set of circuits is connected into and out of each device,

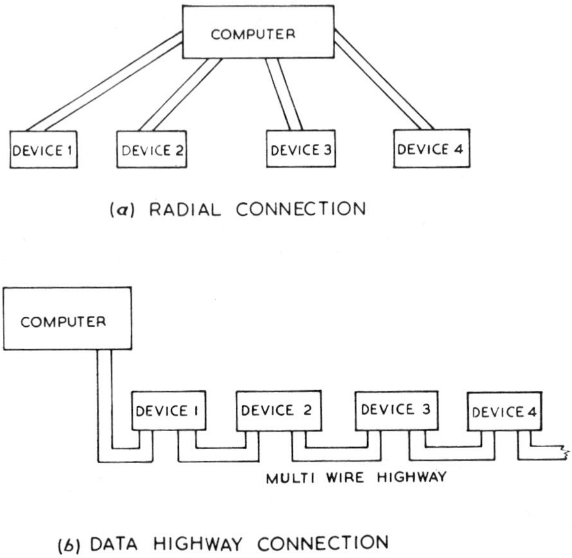

Figure 2.1. Methods of connecting peripheral devices to a computer

as shown in Fig. 2.1b. The output connection of the last device contains components to terminate the highway lines correctly to avoid signal reflection. This mode requires only one set of equipment in the central computer, rather than one set per device. The maximum rate of handling information is the same for either system of connection, since only one device at a time can interchange data with the computer.

An essential part of the equipment in the highway mode of operation is a means whereby the computer can select only one of the many devices connected to it for the interchange of data. This is usually implemented by a set of device selector lines or address lines incorporated in the highway. A unique digital code is fed to these selector lines for each device; suitable AND gates at the device interface ensure that each device responds only to its own code and not to any other. Thus, six selector wires enable $2^6 = 64$ separate devices to be addressed individually.

The simplest selector device is thus a six-input AND gate. However, many devices require more than one command from the central computer, so that it is usually more convenient to allocate say four adjacent numerical codes to a device, thus permitting four different signals to be interchanged between computer and device. The most economical design is then a single four-input AND gate to select the four most significant digits, followed by four three-input gates which combine the output of the first

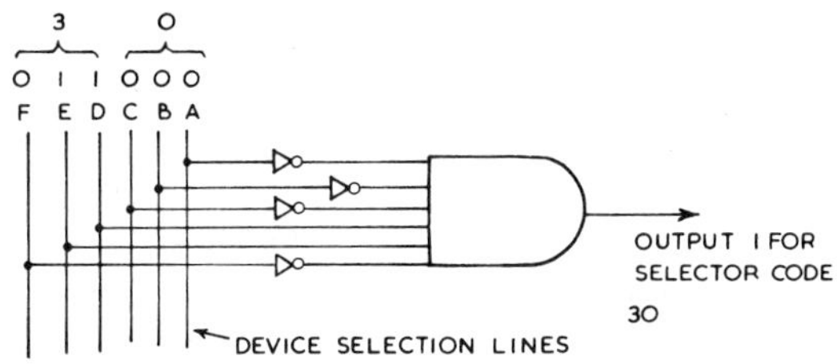

Figure 2.2. Device-selector gate, 1 wire/bit

gate with the four combinations of the two least significant digits and their complements as shown in Fig. 2.3.

For example, if in octal notation the four selector codes were 30, 31, 32, and 33, the binary codes would be as follows.

30	011 000
31	011 001
32	011 010
33	011 011

The single wire per bit scheme of Fig. 2.2 requires an inverter in each gate input which is coded 0. An alternative scheme involves two wires per bit, sending the correct code and its complement for each digit. Thus, for code 30 the first set of wires would carry the code 011 000, and the second set the code 100 111. This method simplifies the interface by

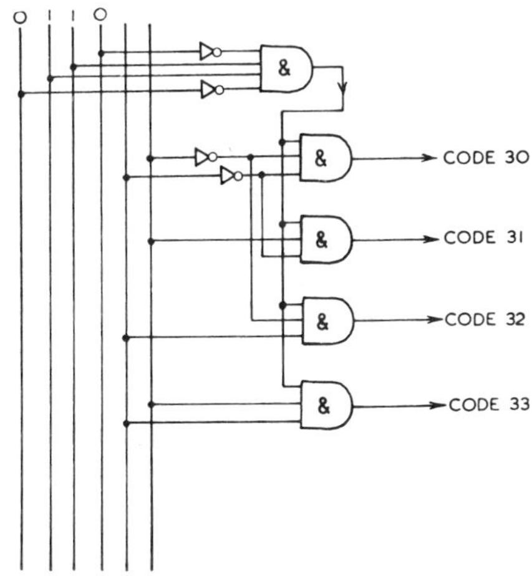

Figure 2.3. Device selector for four output codes using AND gates and inverters

incorporating a single set of inverters at the computer, but requires more cabling. The arrangement for code 30 is shown in Fig. 2.4.

Although the use of device select lines dedicated to I/O operations affords electrically simple interface designs, it has some disadvantages. Since the processor needs a full set of 16–18 address lines to communicate with the main store, these will all require extending outside the processor for direct memory access transfers (see Fig. 1.3).

If device select lines are also added to the I/O bus, the total number of wires involved becomes excessive. In addition, the instruction set must contain special instructions for input and output. These generally permit only data transfers between device and accumulator, and any further testing or modification of the data needs extra instructions.

In order to overcome these disadvantages the designers of later machines, and in particular of the PDP11, provided only one set of address lines which were connected to the main store and to all peripheral interfaces. The interface registers were then selected by allocating to them addresses which would otherwise be used for the main store. For example in the smaller PDP11 models there are 16 active address lines; in all, 64K bytes or 32K words (of 16 bits each) can be individually addressed, using addresses from 000000 to 177777 octal. Instead of incorporating 32K words of main storage, a machine with maximum storage has only 28K words, the remaining 4K addresses from 28K to 32K being allocated to peripherals. Certain of the addresses are reserved for particular devices, for example:

177566	Console teleprinter output data
177562	Console teleprinter keyboard input
177546	Line frequency clock
177510-16	LP 11 line printer
177460-76	RF 11 disc store

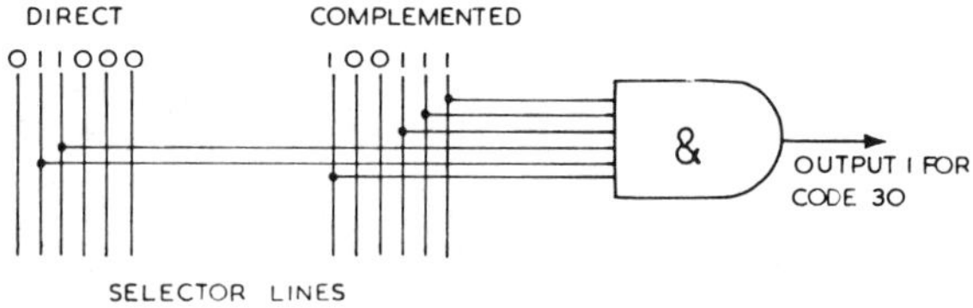

Figure 2.4. Device-selector gate, 2 wire/bit

The complete list extends down to location 167756. User interfaces for other devices can be allocated free addresses in the range 164000 to 167750.

A typical device will have four addresses assigned to it, providing a data register and a control and status register for each direction of data flow. Devices such as paper tape readers or displays which transfer data in one direction need only two addresses. The "control" function relates to signals from the processor to the device to command various operations which it can perform. The "status" function is concerned with signals from the peripheral to the processor which can be read by a program and which indicate the peripheral states such as "busy," "ready," "error condition," "power off," etc.

Early microprocessors used a form of device select coding in which typically 8 of the address lines also acted as device select lines during I/O operations. However, most microprocessor applications involve storage external to the processor. Thus all of the address lines must be accessible outside the processor, and it becomes simpler to regard the peripheral interface registers as a continuation of the main store addresses, as is done in the PDP11 and some other minicomputers. This procedure is called "memory-mapped" I/O addressing. It has the advantage that no special I/O instructions are needed and that all of the normal instructions for moving, testing, and modifying data are applicable equally to data in the main store and in the peripheral device registers. It can, of course, also be used with microprocessors which were not originally designed to use memory-mapped I/O.

Although typical microprocessors have 16 address lines and so could have 64K bytes of store attached to them, few applications require more than a fraction of this amount. It then becomes possible to allocate separate areas of the total address space for various purposes and thus to avoid the need for all the address lines to be decoded.

For example, the bottom of the store, locations 0000 to 01FF (hexadecimal), could be allocated to the writeable data store; locations 8000 to 81FF to peripheral interface registers; and locations C000 to FFFF to read-only program store. This would provide 512 locations for data and for interface registers and for 16K program locations.

The peripheral packages require only a few registers so that there is no need to decode all address lines. For example, if there are 4 packages each containing 4 registers, 16 separate addresses are needed, so that only the least significant 4 address lines, A0-A3, need decoding; it is, however, necessary to connect the "peripherals" output of the A15/A14 decoder to either a "chip-select" or a "chip-enable" pin on each package to ensure that no reference to a store location could also access a peripheral device register. A diagram showing the connections to the address lines of such a system is shown in Fig. 2.5. Each package has four addresses selected by two register select inputs RS0 and RS1, and there are three "chip-enable" inputs which must all be at logical one to select the package. Two of these are used to select one of the four packages; the other is connected to the "Peripherals" line corresponding to the first digit 8 of the address. In the table, X denotes a line which is decoded by the package, and blank spaces correspond to "don't care" address bits which do not need decoding. This arrangement is much simpler than full decoding, since the peripheral packages are connected only to four address

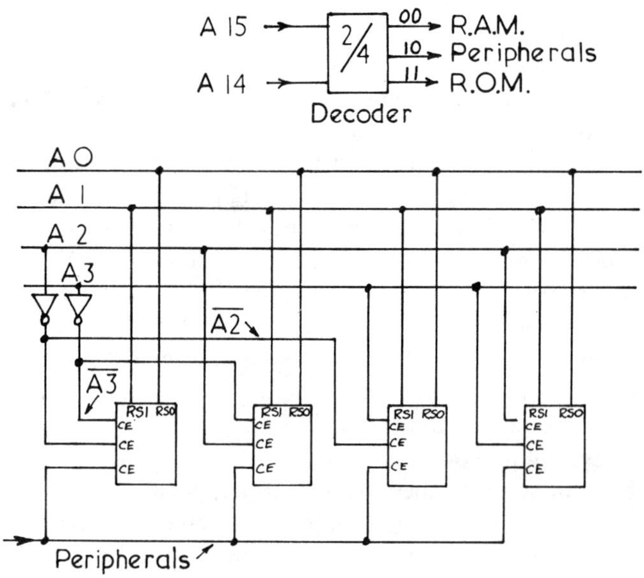

MEMORY MAP

Addresses	A 15	A 14	A 13	A 12	A 11	A 10	A 9	A 8	A 7	A 6	A 5	A 4	A 3	A 2	A 1	A 0
R.A.M. 0000-0IFF	O	O							X	X	X	X	X	X	X	X
Periph. 8000-3	I	O											O	O	X	X
" 8004-7	I	O											O	I	X	X
" 8008-B	I	O											I	O	X	X
" 800C-F	I	O											I	I	X	X
R.O.M. C000-FFFF	I	I	X	X	X	X	X	X	X	X	X	X	X	X	X	X

X = Decoded by package Blank = Don't care

Figure 2.5. PIA addressing and memory map

lines and the "peripheral" line, rather than to all 16 address lines needed for full decoding.

A simple 2-input decoder could then distinguish between the three address fields by decoding the two most significant address lines, that is, A15 and A14.

The three decoder outputs would be:

A15	A14	Field
0	0	Writeable Store (RAM)
1	0	Peripherals
1	1	Read-Only Store (ROM)

The 0 1 line is unused.

In each case the appropriate decoder output is taken to a "chip-enable" or a "chip-select" input on the external device to ensure that the device can respond only when A15 and A14 contain the correct code, regardless of the address on the lower address lines.

2.3 USE OF INTEGRATED CIRCUITS

Most small computers are now assembled from TTL integrated circuits, and the I/O bus and DMA channels are thus operated at TTL signal levels of, say, +3 V and 0 V. It is thus convenient to use similar elements in interfaces so that signal levels in the computer and the interface equipment are compatible. The basic interface components are thus NAND gates and inverters and data stores. Many medium-scale integrated circuits based upon these components are also useful to the interface designer, for example multistage counters, shift registers, four-bit adders and arithmetic units, 16-line data multiplexers, multistage data registers, etc.

The main exception to the use of TTL occurs in microprocessors. These at present use MOS logic, which is slower than TTL but can be made with a higher packing density. The signal levels are different from those of TTL so that level-changing circuits are required to interconnect TTL and MOS devices. Some MOS elements already include TTL-compatible outputs, otherwise level-converting stages are themselves available in integrated form.

2.4. DECODING

A frequent requirement is a device which will examine the state of N independent input signals, and energize one of 2^N output lines for each combination of input signals. This is called a decoder, and is needed for any digital addressing or selection process. For example a two-input decoder has four possible output signals corresponding to inputs 00, 01, 10, and 11, and can be assembled from four two-input AND gates as shown in Fig. 2.6. Where the input comes from a counter, or single-bit storage units, both the direct and complemented signals are generally available, and the inverters are not needed. The arrangement of Fig. 2.6 may be extended for larger arrays, but when $N>4$ it is more economical to decode in two stages. Three-input and four-input decoders are now available in integrated circuit form, incorporating an additional "enable" input to each gate in order to permit a strobe or timing signal to be used, and simplifying the assembly of large decoders from several smaller units.

2.5. DATA MULTIPLEXING

Many on-line computer installations require one of a number of digital inputs to be connected to the computer, selected either sequentially by a fixed routine or on demand from the computer program. This operation is called "multiplexing" and requires AND and OR gates, together with a set of selecting signals. Using NAND logic the direct replacement of AND gates followed by OR gates leaves two redundant inverters in each connection to the output gates. These can be eliminated to give the arrangement of Fig. 2.7. For clarity only the circuits for two digits of the full computer word are shown, the four pairs of input signals being A_1 B_1, A_2 B_2, A_3 B_3, and A_4 B_4. One of these pairs will be transmitted to the two output wires A and B by putting approximate signals on the selection or enable wires E_1, E_2, E_3, and E_4. Three of these must have a 0 signal, and the selected one a 1 signal. Thus if signals 0100 are connected to E_1, E_2, E_3, E_4, input 2 is selected and the output signals are A = A2, B = B2. The logical expression for output A is

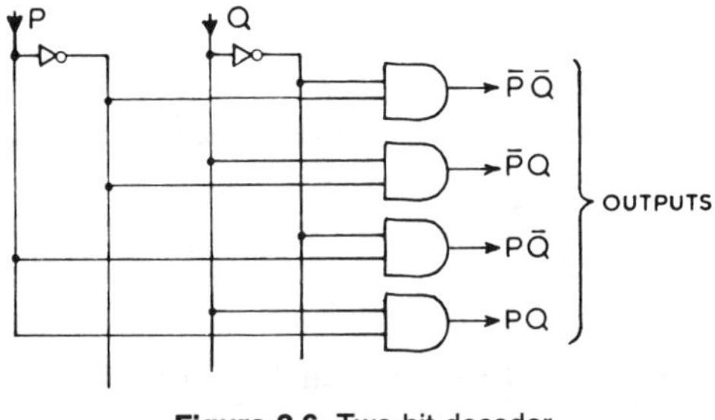

Figure 2.6. Two-bit decoder

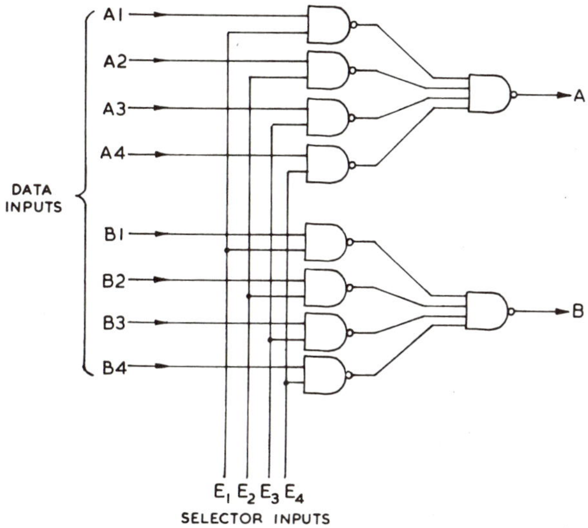

Figure 2.7. Four-way 2-bit multiplexer

$$A = A_1.E_1 + A_2.E_2 + A_3.E_3 + A_4.E_4.$$

The four enable inputs E1 to E4 can conveniently be derived from a decoder such as shown in Fig. 2.6, which ensures that only one of the enable lines can have a 1 signal at any particular time.

The two-digit number PQ then determines which of the four data inputs will be selected. The interconnections required between Figs. 2.6 and 2.7 are then:

$P\bar{Q}$ to E_1, selected by $P = 0, Q = 0$
$\overline{PQ}$ to E_2, selected by $P = 0, Q = 1$
$\overline{PQ}$ to E_3, selected by $P = 1, Q = 0$
$\bar{P}Q$ to E_4, selected by $P = 1, Q = 1$

A multiplexer with decoder, as described above, is now available as an integrated circuit using TTL logic (eight inputs, one output).

2.6. COMPARATORS

A logical unit which is often useful in data transfers is one which detects when two numbers are equal. It is called a comparator. A typical application occurs in any sequential file, such as a magnetic tape unit in which data is divided into blocks, each block being preceded by an identifying number. When searching for a particular block of data, each block number is compared with the required block number, and the tape is stopped when the two are equal. It would be possible to use the arithmetic unit to perform this operation by subtracting the two numbers and signaling when the difference became zero. However, in many rapid-transfer operations it is preferable to avoid using the arithmetic unit within the computer, since this slows down the recognition process considerably as several instructions are required and the previous contents of the accumulator must be preserved in the store and subsequently restored. The comparator is a special-purpose logic unit which detects equality between the numbers fed to it much more rapidly than the central processor could, and which can be incorporated in an interface, thus simplifying the organization of the data transfer.

The principle of operation may be explained by considering only a three-bit comparator which has as inputs the two binary numbers ABC and DEF. If the numbers are equal, each digit pair must be equal. Thus A = D, B = E, and C = F. The two cases involving A and D are A = D = 0 and A = D = 1. The logical expression which gives an output 1 for either of these cases is:

$$X = A.D + \bar{A}.\bar{D}$$

The same conditions must apply to B and E, and to C and F. Thus the logical expression for a comparator which produces a 1 output when, and only when, ABC = DEF is:

$$X = (A.D + \bar{A}.\bar{D})(B.E + \bar{B}.\bar{E})(C.F + \bar{C}.\bar{F})$$

The logical network for this is shown in Fig. 2.8. This provides a single output X when ABC = DEF. For some purposes it may also be useful to have outputs, say Y when ABC < DEF, and Z when ABC > DEF. The above expression for X may easily be extended for numbers involving more than three binary digits; if there are *N* digits X comprises *N* brackets.

A four-bit comparator is now available in integrated form, giving three separate outputs, for >, =, and <.

2.7. BISTABLE STORAGE ELEMENTS

All computer interfaces require some storage for data and also generally for control or status information. These are usually assembled from single-

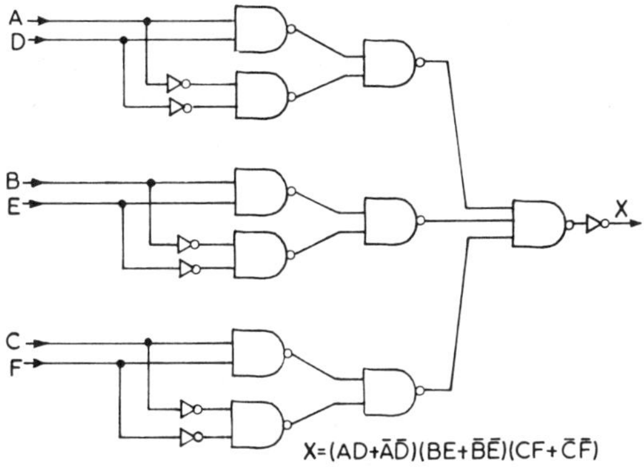

Figure 2.8. Three-digit comparator

digit stores comprising bistable multivibrators and gates. The basic cross-coupled bistable is the essential storage element, but several different gate arrangements are used depending upon the number and function of the input signals.The simplest version is the R-S bistable or flip-flop, but this has the disadvantage that a 1 signal at both R and S input terminals results in an indeterminate output. Thus in integrated form R-S bistables are not usually available. Clearly if only one signal input is provided, say to the S terminal, and an inverter feeds the R terminal, R and S cannot simultaneously be 1. Thus there will be no ambiguity, and this version is a useful unit. It is usually produced in a "clocked" form; that is, the inputs are gated off until the arrival of a 1 at the clock or timing input. The R-S bistable can be constructed from two NOR gates cross-coupled and has the following characteristic.

Inputs	Outputs
R = 0 S = 0	Unchanged
R = 0 S = 1	Q = 1 $\bar{Q}$ = 0
R = 1 S = 0	Q = 0 $\bar{Q}$ = 1
R = 1 S = 1	Not allowed

The logic diagram of a single-input bistable is shown in Fig. 2.9a. The Q output follows the input to the D terminal when the clock signal is a logical 1. As soon as the clock changes to 0, the input is locked out and the Q output is held at the level it had when the clock changed. This

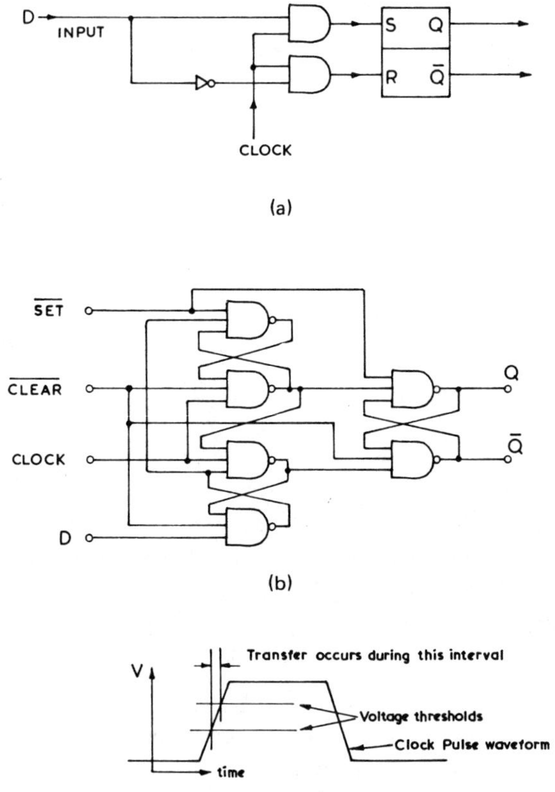

Figure 2.9. (a) bistable latch; (b) D-type bistable; (c) transfer time of D-type bistable

circuit is usually called a "latch," and is available in eight-bit or four-bit versions as dual-in-line integrated circuits.

An alternative version is useful for a data register in interfaces. This was originally used with a differentiated clock signal, so that the two AND gates in the S and R input lines were enabled by short pulses. During these pulses the signal present at the D terminal was transferred to the Q output. With the inevitable distortion which arises when distributing clock pulses round a complex computing system, such triggering methods which rely on the speed of the rising or falling edge of a pulse are unreliable, and current integrated versions of the circuit use level triggering. The circuit is biased so that, as the clock signals rise through a level about halfway between 0 and 1, the input gates are enabled and the signal on the D line is transferred to the Q output. The circuit is usually arranged as a "dual-rank" or "master-slave" bistable, as shown in Fig. 2.9b, and is called a "D-type" bistable. It is available in integrated form as a four-bit package. It is often convenient to have two additional inputs whose action is independent of the clock signal. These are called "set" and "clear," or "preset" and "preclear," and are used to force the bistable to a particular state regardless of the clock or D inputs. These two inputs are mainly used for initializing counters and registers before data transfer begins.

The D-type circuit is convenient for data registers, but less so for counting circuits. These latter are simpler to implement if two input terminals are present. In order to avoid having an indeterminate output when the two inputs are both zero, the J-K type of circuit is used. This has a characteristic similar to that of the R-S bistable, but changes state when J = K = 1. Thus it must be a clocked unit, but differs from the D type in that the output transition occurs on the *falling* edge of the clock waveform, not the rising edge.

The logical relation between outputs and inputs J and K is as follows.

J	K	Q_{n+1}
0	0	Q_n
1	0	1
0	1	0
1	1	$\bar{Q}_n$

By using the J and K terminals separately the circuit operates as an R-S bistable, but without the indeterminate action when J = K = 1. Also, by connecting J and K together as an input, the action of a T-type or counter circuit may be copied. In integrated circuit form it is convenient to use a circuit in which the outputs Q and $\bar{Q}$ may be used to gate the J and K signals without logical conflicts occurring. This can be effected by using a "dual-rank" or master-slave arrangement, as shown in Fig. 2.10. In the normal state between clock pulses, the clock input signal CP is 0, so that the J and K inputs are isolated from the master. Since $\overline{CP}$ is 1, the master state is copied to the slave and thence to the Q and $\bar{Q}$ slave outputs. Thus if, for example, the master is set and Q_M = 1, AND gate C has two 1 inputs and delivers a 1 output to the slave S terminal, thus giving Q = 1 as an output.

When a clock pulse arrives, the d.c. conditions are arranged so that the rising edge of the clock waveform first disables gates C and D, thus

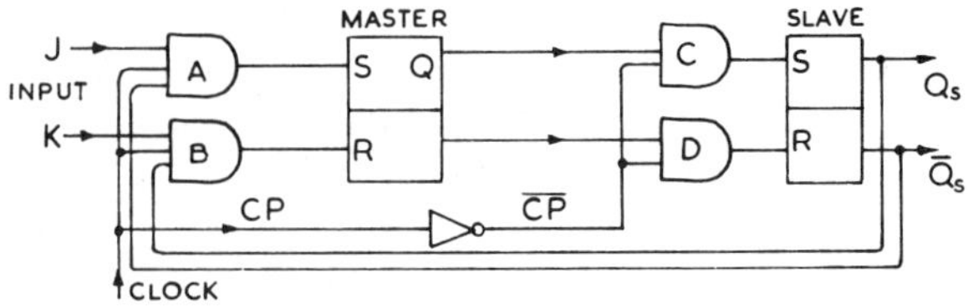

Figure 2.10. J–K master-slave bistable

isolating the slave from the master. A little later gates A and B are enabled, thus allowing the J and K signals to reach the master. On the falling edge of the clock pulse the events occur in the reverse order; gates A and B are first disabled, thus isolating the master from the inputs, and then gates C and D are enabled by $\overline{CP}$, thus propagating the master state to the slave and to the outputs. This arrangement gives a unit which depends for its action only upon the clock-pulse voltage level and not upon its rise time or fall time. It thus produces a more reliable circuit than one which depends upon pulse edges for satisfactory triggering. It also ensures that there is a delay between the acceptance of the J-K inputs to the master and the subsequent change of state (if needed) at the slave output. Consequently, the output signals may be connected to logical networks feeding the J-K inputs and, provided that the delay through the networks is less than the duration of the clock pulse, no logical hazard will occur. Such a logical feedback may cause unreliable operation of a single-rank J-K multivibrator, since an input signal may be cut off as soon as it starts to cause a change in output.

In practice, D-type and J-K bistables in integrated circuit form also have additional asynchronous input pins. The inputs mentioned previously are called ''Synchronous'' or clocked, since their effect on the bistable output appears only after the arrival of a clock pulse. The TTL bistables are usually provided with a negated preclear $\bar{P}_c$ and, when pins are available, a preset $\bar{P}_s$ also. These are asynchronous since they produce an immediate effect irrespective of the clock pulse. Thus the $\bar{P}_c$ is normally high for clocked operation, but when taken low it immediately sets Q to 0 and $\bar{Q}$ to 1 regardless of the signals, the clock and synchronous input pins. By using both synchronous and asynchronous inputs a single bistable can perform operations of some logical complexity without any extra gates.

The CMOS bistables generally used with microprocessors have similar asynchronous and synchronous inputs but, confusingly, the asynchronous inputs are held low for normal clocked operation and taken high to set or clear the outputs.

2.8. DATA REGISTERS

An essential component of any computer interface is a register to store data being transmitted to or from the computer. This is required to act as a temporary or buffer store, so that information can be interchanged efficiently between a computer and a device which may have different rates of information flow. Without this provision the faster of the two (almost invariably the computer) would spend a large proportion of its time waiting for the slower.

The amount of information stored may be only a character (say, six bits), a byte (usually eight bits), a complete word, or a number of words. The largest amount is probably that incorporated in some visual display units. Because the picture must be "refreshed," or re-presented on the tube 10-20 times each second, the entire body of information presented on the screen must be read out at the same rate. In order to avoid monopolizing the computer to which they are attached, some display units incorporate a store holding several thousand bits which contains the display information. A typical arrangement for holding data output from a computer is shown in Fig. 2.11.

The computer control unit sets up the selection code allocated to the device on the device selector lines, and a "device-select" signal is emitted by the device-selection gate. This is used, together with a timing pulse from the computer, to gate the data from the data lines into the register. The timing of this operation is determined by the computer. Subsequently

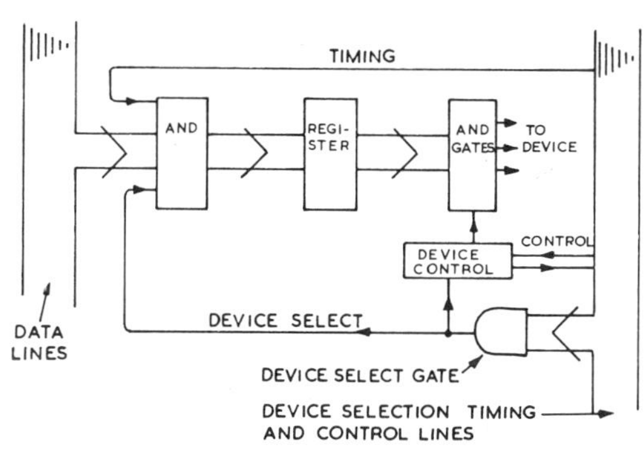

Figure 2.11. Block diagram of single output interface

the device may transfer the data elsewhere, at a time dependent upon its own cycle of operations.

The detailed flow of information for one bit of the output is shown in Fig. 2.12. This requires two AND operations and a D-type bistable. The signal on the data line is gated to the bistable D input when the device select pulse appears, and the exact moment at which the data is valid is signaled by the timing pulse. In order to ensure correct operation of the bistable, the signal at the D terminal should be present a short time before the clock pulse arrives. This is the "set-up" time; the minimum figure for satisfactory triggering is given by the manufacturers of the bistable. In consequence, the last pulse involved in the data transfer should determine the timing of the clock pulse. This is most conveniently arranged, as in Fig. 2.12, by using the timing pulse itself to clock the data into the bistables.

Figure 2.13 shows the same operation carried out by an R-S bistable. Two timing pulses from the computer are required in this case, the first to reset the output to 0 and the second to gate data into the S input.

For some purposes, where the data in the device register is not transferred elsewhere, no further control signals beyond those shown in Figs. 2.12 and 2.13 are required. Typical examples are lamp displays, in which a lamp is energized when the corresponding bit in the device register is set to 1, or outputs to an oscilloscope or meter via a digital-to-analog converter.

However, where the data in the device register is used for some other action in the device, it is necessary to prevent the computer from trans-

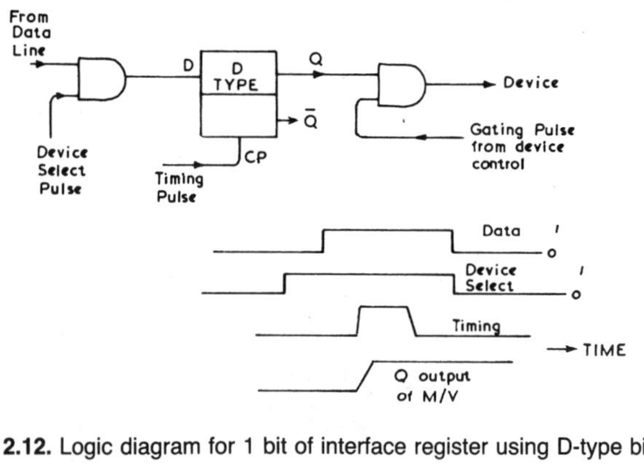

Figure 2.12. Logic diagram for 1 bit of interface register using D-type bistable

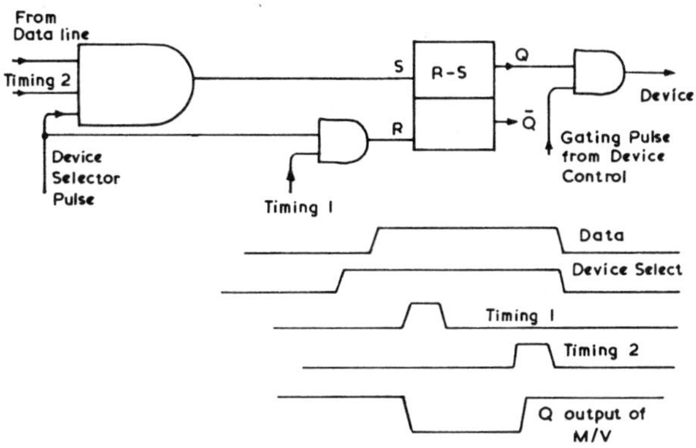

Figure 2.13. Logic diagram for 1 bit of interface register using R-S-type bistable

ferring more information to the register until the device has finished using the current data. The usual mechanism for this is a single-bit store or "flag" which is set when the device has finished with the current data and is ready to accept a further transfer. The computer can test the state of the flag by program and wait in a loop until the device is ready. Each time a new data word is loaded into the device the flag is cleared. The computer may be organized to test each flag independently and signal back along a common "skip" line, or may read a word at a time from the device status register and then select the flag bit required.

2.9. PARALLEL-SERIAL CONVERSION

The data interchanges we have previously considered have been concerned with parallel transfer of data, requiring one wire or one pair of wires per bit. This is the data mode used in nearly all computers, and is the simplest method of transmission over short distances (up to a few hundred feet). Beyond this the number of separate circuits required, typically 16, involves a disproportionate expenditure on transmission lines. This becomes an unjustifiable charge when the data must be carried by a public telephone system.

The solution to the transmission problem is to change the data mode from parallel to serial, thus requiring only one circuit. The disadvantage is that for the same transmission speed (bits per second) the information takes longer to transmit, 16 times longer for a 16-bit word machine. Thus at each end of the transmission path we require a device which converts from parallel mode to serial mode and the reverse. The simplest arrangement comprises a set of bistables, one for each bit in the word, arranged as a "shifting register."

For transmission the stages of the register are loaded in parallel from the computer data lines, and are unloaded onto the line in serial mode one bit at a time. When shifting the data out some delay is needed between the stages, since each stage must, between clock pulses, shift out its current state to the succeeding stage and change its stage to that of its preceding neighbor. Thus R-S bistables and pulse-delay units could be used, but a simpler solution is to use the delay which is an essential feature of the dual-rank J-K bistable. In this case the master can assume the state of the previous stage, while the slave continues to emit the previous output state. This phase lasts while the clock pulse is at 1.

The general arrangement of a part of such a register is shown in Fig. 2.14. Data is loaded parallel from the D_n lines when the parallel load line goes to 1. Thereafter 16 pulses on the clock line will emit the 16 data bits sequentially on the "serial output" line.

Although many devices connected to computers are designed to accept parallel data, the exception is the teleprinter, which is frequently used to allow the operator to input programs, data, and commands, and to print out data and messages. This device was designed and its operating code was internationally standardized long before computers were developed. It was intended for use over two-wire telegraph circuits and consequently used serial-mode transmission. Since it is widely used and mass produced for the telecommunications market, it forms a cheap and convenient input-output device for small computers, but requires a small

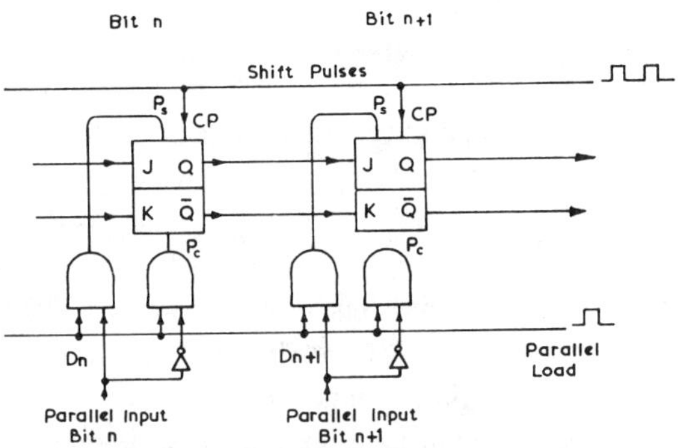

Figure 2.14. Logic diagram of part of shift register

interface unit which converts from serial to parallel mode at input, and the reverse at output. Such an interface unit is used so widely that it is now available as a small integrated circuit package.

2.10. COUNTERS

A frequent requirement in interface design is a register with interstage connections arranged so that an external pulse can increase or decrease the register contents by one. Such a register is called a counter, and it is conveniently assembled from a set of J-K bistables. Integrated circuits are now available which include four or more stages, together with interstage gating, for a counter which can count up or down according to the signals fed to one of the input leads.

A typical application for a counter is the interface for a block data transfer, where it may be used to check the progress of the transfer. The counter is initially loaded with the number of words to be transferred by a parallel data input. It is then arranged so that a pulse is fed to it for each word transferred, thus decreasing the contents by one. The operation is completed when the number stored in the counter has fallen to zero. This situation is detected by a multiway AND gate connected to each stage of the counter. The counter here functions as a "down-counter." An alternative arrangement, but less convenient for the user, would be to use an "up-counter," initially loaded with the complement of the number of words and arranged to count upwards.

The connections for two stages of an up-counter are shown in Fig. 2.15. This uses a form of J-K bistable produced by several manufacturers, in which the preclear and preset inputs are negated. Thus the normal state is that for which P_S and P_C are positive (at logical 1), the state of Q and $\bar{Q}$ being then determined by inputs J, K, and the clock pulse CP. If P_S is changed to logical 0 the output Q is changed to 1 regardless of the J, K, or CP signals. Similarly changing P_C to 0 resets Q to 0. A short positive-going pulse on the load data line PL will gate any information present on the data in lines into the counter, and subsequently each pulse on the INC line will increase the contents of the counter by 1. The end of the data transfer is detected by an AND gate connected to all the $\bar{Q}$ outputs, which detects the condition 1 1 1 . . . for $\bar{Q}_1$, $\bar{Q}_2$, $\bar{Q}_3$, etc. This implies that Q_1 Q_2 Q_3 . . . is 000 . . .; that is, the counter is empty.

2.11. SIMPLE COMPUTER INTERFACES

Having examined the elements used in assembling computer interfaces, we now proceed to consider the simpler ways in which these elements

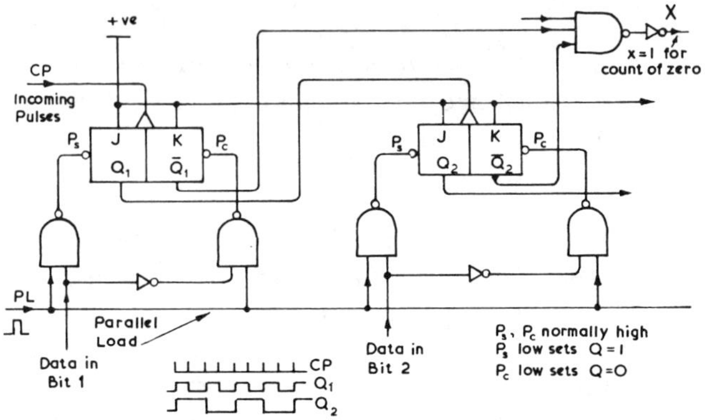

Figure 2.15. Logic diagram of first two stages of parallel-loaded counter

may be united. Probably the simplest arrangement is a single digital output which will switch some device on or off. This consists of a single-digit store which can be set or cleared by program. The scheme of Fig. 2.16 shows an R-S bistable used for the store to switch some display indicator on or off. Since it is usually a matter of chance how a bistable settles when the power is first switched on, a computer usually has facilities for setting all such circuits, internal and external, to a standard condition before starting computation. Here we assume that no display is the initial condition required, so that the 1 pulse on the initial clear line is mixed with the OFF signal in an OR operation which provides the reset input to an R-S multivibrator.

The control signals have come from two address codes set up on the device select lines, for example code 20 for ON, 21 for OFF (octal notation). The five most significant digits, 01000, are detected by the

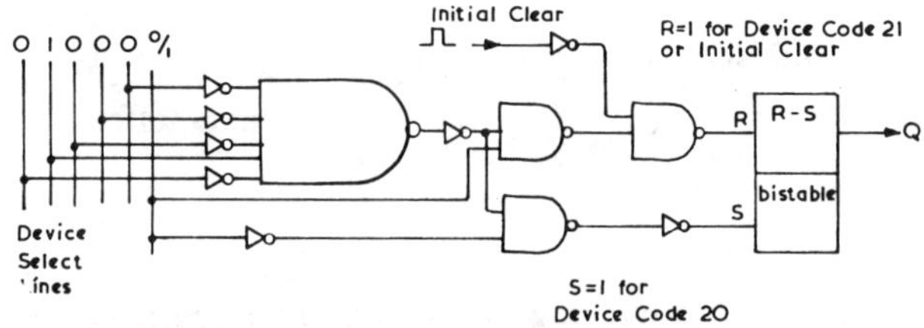

Figure 2.16. Simple switch interface

five-input NAND gate, and two further gates detect the two codes 20 (010 000) and 21 (010 001). If a large number of other devices are connected to the computer, it may be necessary to use only one device-select code for the two operations, and to select the ON or OFF condition by signals on the subdevice-select lines. For some purposes only a transitory output indication may be needed; the bistable circuit can then be replaced by a monostable circuit with a single input terminal. This will generate an output for a prescribed interval each time the corresponding device-select code is transmitted from the computer.

2.12. D-A CONVERTER INTERFACE

A slightly more complex interface is used for a digital-to-analog converter, which could for example move a spot on a cathode-ray tube, control a pen recorder, or produce an output on an indicating voltmeter. In its simplest form this arrangement produces an analog output each time a digital number is sent to it, each output remaining until it is displaced by new information.

For this interface we need to gate data from the data lines into an interface register under program control. The register holds one number until the next number overwrites it, and is permanently connected to the D-A converter. The arrangement is shown in Fig. 2.17; it produces the

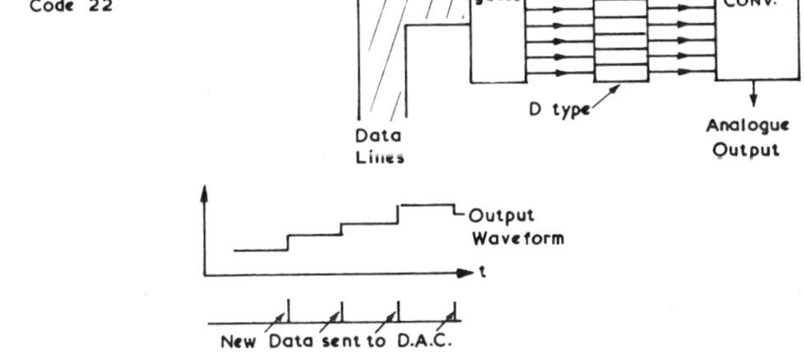

Figure 2.17. Simple D-A converter interface

"box-car" output waveform shown. If several analog outputs are required, a multiplexer may be connected to the output of the converter to enable it to energize several different circuits. These would then require some form of analog storage.

2.13. A-D CONVERTER INTERFACE

The D-A converter interface described above is an output device which accepts data transmitted from the computer to the device. We frequently require the reverse process; that is, we require to sample an analog voltage occurring outside the computer, convert its value to a digital representation, and store this value for subsequent computer processing.

Essentally the interface can be similar to that of Fig. 2.17 but with the digital data flow reversed. However, some care is required when using such an arrangement. Unless a very expensive converter is used, the time taken to undertake a conversion with an accuracy of 10-12 binary digits may be many machine cycles, say 30-50 μs. Thus having once started the process of conversion it is essential to wait for an appropriate time before trying to transfer the contents of the converter buffer register into the accumulator.

It would be possible to write the control program to generate an appropriate delay by including a simple counting loop between the "start conversion" instruction and the "read converter buffer" instruction. This would provide a fixed delay which may not always be convenient.

Some A-D converters can be switched to provide a range of different output word sizes, the smaller sizes giving a less accurate but quicker conversion. It is thus possible to select manually the most suitable combination of speed and accuracy for each particular application. In such cases no advantage is obtained unless the program delay is automatically adjusted to be just in excess of the conversion time. This can be ensured if there is some means whereby the computer can detect when the conversion process has finished and immediately read the contents of the converter buffer register into the accumulator. One simple method of achieving this is the use of a single-digit store or "flag" to signal the end of the conversion process. This flag may, for example, be cleared to zero when the conversion process is started and set to 1 when the conversion has finished.

The method of communication back to the central computer is via a common "skip line" linking all peripheral devices. This is normally energized, and to send a skip condition back to the computer a saturated transistor is connected between earth and the skip line. In order to differentiate between the devices connected to it, each device is allowed to return a skip condition only when its selection code is set up on the device-select lines. Thus, although all devices can set their flags simultaneously, these flags may be sensed individually by setting up the appropriate device-select code. A more detailed description of the operation of the skip line is given in Chapter 3. The action it produces in the computer is that, when energized, the next instruction in sequence is skipped; otherwise, if the flag is not set and the skip line potential is not changed, the next instruction is executed.

The program required to activate the A-D converter and read its output into the accumulator would be as follows.

(1) Start conversion process.
(2) Test converter flag and skip if set.
(3) Jump back to previous instruction.
(4) Read converter buffer onto data lines and so transfer to accumulator.

The precise numerical code corresponding to these instructions of course depends upon the computer used and the device-select code assigned to each operation.

The computer action is as follows.

(1) An out-transfer instruction energizes the device-select lines with the particular code assigned to the device function: ''Start A-D converter and clear flag.'' This is octal code 24 in Fig. 2.18.

(2) The next instruction is again an output-transfer instruction which sets up the code 25 on the device-select lines. This, together with the A-D converter flag output and a timing pulse is taken to a NAND gate and inverter. If the flag is set to output 1, the inverter output changes to 1 for a microsecond or so, depending upon the duration of the timing pulse. During this interval, the transistor T_1 is saturated, thus reducing the potential of the SKIP line to near zero. This is detected in the computer-control unit, and causes the contents of the program counter to be incremented by 1. Since it has already been incremented by 1 immediately after instruction (2) was fetched from the store, the subsequent instruction which will be executed is number (4). If, however, the converter flag is cleared, no skip will occur and instruction (3) will be executed. This causes the computer to fetch and executive instruction (2) again, and the computer will stay in this loop until the conversion process is completed and the flag is set. The final operation is reading the data.

(4) This instruction issues code 26 on the device-select lines and also primes the computer for a read in from the data lines to the accumulator.

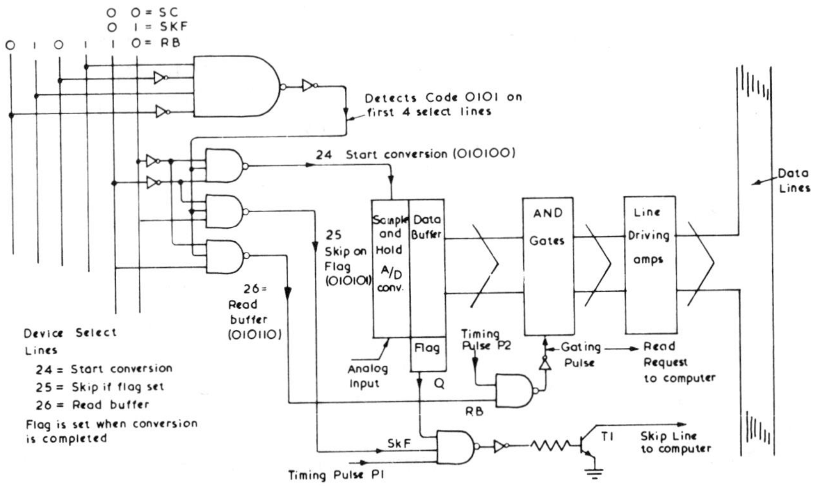

Figure 2.18. A-D converter interface

The output from the gate which responds to device-select code 26, together with a timing pulse, is taken to a further gate which controls the transfer of data from the converter buffer register via line-driving circuits to the data lines. The timing pulse P2 which controls this operation is generally a little later than P1 which controls the SKIP operation, since time is required to clear the accumulator before loading new data in, and further time must be allowed to permit any transients on the data lines to die away before the data-line information is gated into the accumulator. Since this instruction is an inward transfer, some computers require a "read request" signal to be generated also in order to set up the appropriate conditions in the computer. The two paths followed by the computer through this segment of program are shown below.

Path during conversion.	**Instruction**	**Path when conversion has finished.**
1,2,3,2,3 etc.	1. Start conversion	2,4, rest of program
	2. Test flag and skip if set	
	3. Jump back one instruction	
	4. Read buffer into accumulator	

In this example we have assumed that the A-D converter has a sample-and-hold circuit associated with it, and that the flag bistable is connected to the converter control circuits so that the flag is cleared by a "start conversion" signal and set by a "conversion finished" signal from the converter. More details of sample-and-hold circuits and converters are given in Chapter 6.

For completeness a final method of organizing the converter interface using "interrupt" facilities should be mentioned. In the above example the computer is not kept waiting very long for the converter to finish its cycle of operations, and the method of interfacing is generally acceptable. However, if the waiting time were longer, it would be wasteful of computer time to keep it waiting in a loop until the device became ready again. In such cases an interrupt system enables the computer to issue a "start conversion" instruction and carry on with other tasks for a time. When the converter has finished its cycle, it energizes the interrupt line and as soon as possible the computer leaves its current task, jumps to a small subroutine which reads the converter buffer and does any necessary data reduction and storage, and then jumps back to continue the main program where it left off. When several devices are connected to the computer this interrupt procedure gives much increased efficiency. More details of the process are given in Chapter 4.

The use of flags for signalling back from the device to the computer, and separate facilities for sending control signals in the reverse direction, were typical of early minicomputers such as the PDP8 and the Nova. Later machines and most microprocessors have a more systematic approach in which all of the control and status flags and signals are collected together into a single control and status register. This is normally 1 word in size, the control bits being under the control of the CPU and the status bits being under the control of the peripheral device. In order to test the status bits or flags the program must read the control and status word, mask off all but the flag bit, and then branch depending upon the state of the flag bit.

The easiest bit to test is the most significant, as no masking is needed; a test for a negative value will determine whether the bit is set to 1. For other bits masking is necessary using a mask word which has a 1 in the position to be tested, and zeros elsewhere.

For example in a microprocessor control register at address 8005, the following program could be used to wait in a loop until bit 6 (the flag bit) is set.

	INSTRUCTION	COMMENT
Loop:	→ LDA A 8005	Load accumulator A with control word at location 8005
	AND A #40	And with mask word 40 to isolate bit 6
	← BEQ LOOP	Branch back to LOOP if the result is zero

The numbers in the program are in hexadecimal notation, so that the mask in binary is 0100 000. This will leave bit 6 unaltered after the AND operation, but will clear all other bits to zero.

2.14. ASYNCHRONOUS OPERATION

The examples of simple interfaces given above are concerned with synchronous operation, that is with systems in which all operations are governed by the constant-frequency pulses from a master clock supply. Although this technique leads to simple arrangements, it allows only a small limited time for the computer to transmit signals and for the interface to recognize these, act upon them, and return other signals to the computer. This in effect limits the maximum length of input-output bus which can be connected to the computer. Depending upon operating speed and organization this maximum length may vary from about 10 to 50 ft. Clearly some additional flexibility would be allowed in system configuration if this length limit could be relaxed. The usual way of doing so is to abandon fixed-system timing and use synchronizing signals sent from each unit concerned in the data transfer.

Thus, if we take as example a transfer of data from the computer to a device buffer register, the timing signal for gating the data into the register is transmitted along the bus-control lines together with the data, but say 200 ns later. Whatever the line delay along the bus, the timing signal will still arrive 200 ns later than the data, thus allowing time for the voltages on the data lines to settle before gating them into the buffer register. A simplified logic diagram of the interface is shown in Fig. 2.19, the source being the computer and the acceptor the interface. The source transmits the "source sync" signal to indicate to the acceptor when to gate the data in. The gating signal is returned to the source as an "acceptor sync" signal to indicate that the data has been accepted. Upon receiving the acceptor sync the computer waits for a fraction of a microsecond and then removes the data, control, and address information from the bus. When the acceptor senses the removal of source sync it also removes the acceptor sync signal. When this removal is detected at the source, the data transfer is concluded.

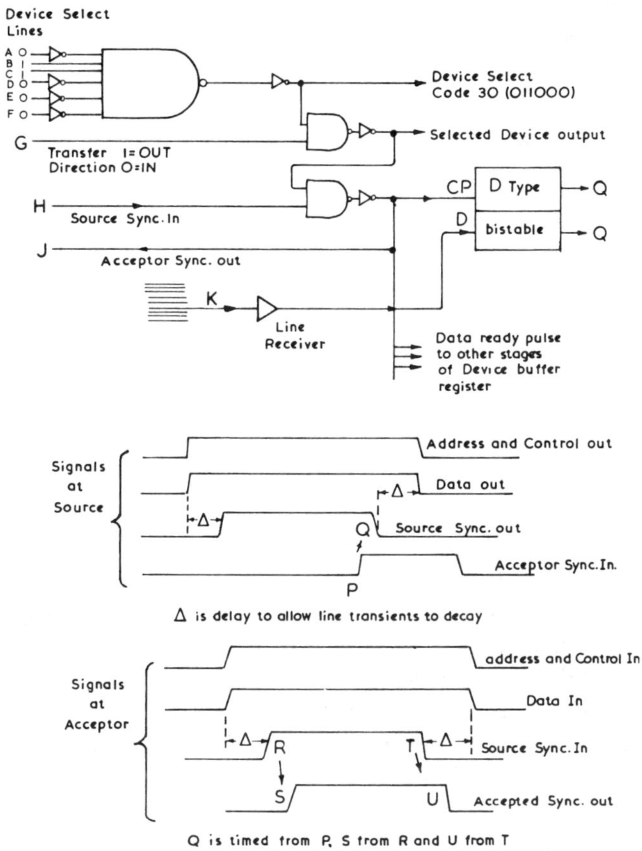

Figure 2.19. Diagram of simple output asynchronous interface showing one stage of buffer register

The arrangement shown is a simple one in which there is no check that the acceptor has finished using the previous information. It would be suitable for a D-A converter output. If, however, it were necessary to transfer the data from the device buffer to some other part of the interface, it would be necessary to check that the buffer had been cleared and the information removed from it before attempting to reload. This could be done by using a skip line as described in section 2.13, or by using additional control lines to check that the receiving device is free to accept data before energizing the data lines. The flow of information is then as follows.

Signal	Source → Acceptor
(1) Request transfer	→
(2) Available for transfer	←
(3) Data present on lines	→
(4) Data accepted	←
(5) Transfer ended	→
(6) End of transfer acknowledged	←

Only signals (3)-(6) are transmitted by the circuit of Fig. 2.19; they correspond to the leading and trailing edges of the source sync and the acceptor sync signals. An additional line is shown in the figure, labeled G. This indicates to the interface whether the data transfer is to be inwards or outwards, and is sent from the computer.

The diagram shows a simple device-selection arrangement, using six lines, arranged to respond to octal code 30. The "data ready" pulse is used to load all stages of the data register simultaneously from the data lines; for clarity only one line, labeled K, and one stage of the register, are shown.

The relative timing of the operation is shown also in Fig. 2.19. The fixed delay Δ built into the computer bus-driving circuits allows time for the line voltages to settle, and the edges connected by an arrow are also timed with a fixed delay. Thus the receipt of the leading edge of acceptor sync at the source is used to terminate the source sync signal, and the edges of source sync at the acceptor are used to time the edges of the outgoing acceptor sync. This arrangement allows all operations to occur as rapidly as possible, limited only by the transmission delay along the bus lines.

2.15. CONCLUSION

In this chapter we have examined the elements of computer interfaces and ways in which simple peripheral devices can be connected to a computer. In the next chapter some of these topics, such as the design of data buses and their associated circuits, and the facilities needed in the computer itself, are discussed in greater detail.

BIBLIOGRAPHY AND REFERENCES

BOYCE, J.C. *Microprocessor and Microcomputer Basics,* Prentice-Hall, Englewood Cliffs, N.J. 1979.

DATA GENERAL CORPORATION. *How to use the NOVA Computers,* 1973.

DIGITAL EQUIPMENT CORPORATION. *PDP11 Processor Handbook,* 1975.

INTEL CORPORATION. *Intel 8080 Microcomputer User's Manual,* 1975.
INTEL CORPORATION. *Intel 8085 Microcomputer User's Manual,* 1977.
KNOBLOCK, D.E., et al. *Insight into Interfacing*. IEEE Spectrum, Vol. 11, No. 5, May 1975, p. 50.
MOSTEK INC. *Z80 Microcomputer Family Hardware Manual,* 1975.
MOTOROLA SEMICONDUCTOR PRODUCTS INC. *M6800 Microcomputer System Design Data,* 1978.
ZILOG INC. *Z80 CPU Technical Manual,* 1977.

Chapter 3

On-Line Computer Architecture

3.1. PROGRAM-CONTROLLED TRANSFERS

An introductory account of various methods of transferring data to and from a small computer was given in Chapter 1. In simple computers program-controlled transfer via the accumulator is the standard provision, and faster methods such as direct memory access (DMA) are optional extras. We consequently begin a more detailed examination of input-output arrangements by considering the flow of data and control signals during a program-controlled transfer.

The data usually moves via the accumulator and the process can be initiated by the program. The only intervention which the external device can make is to delay the transfer until it is ready. For this purpose the external device has a single-bit store called a flag which is usually cleared when the device is busy and set when it is ready for a data transfer. The simplest program technique is to hold the computer in a waiting loop until the device is ready, and then make the transfer. For an outgoing transfer, from computer to device, the sequence of operations is as follows.

(1) Load accumulator with data.
(2) Test device flag, and skip if set.
(3) Jump back to previous instruction and try again.
(4) Device ready; transfer data from accumulator via I/O bus to device.

Thus, if the device is busy, with the flag cleared, the computer will stay in the two instruction loops (2) and (3). As soon as the flag is set, the skip instruction (2) is executed and the new data is transferred. For the transfer of a block of data from the computer store to an external device, the program would also include an instruction to increment the address of the first "load accumulator" instruction, and also to increment a location used to keep account of the number of data words transferred. If, for example, there are 20 words in the block, the count location is initially loaded with −20. After each data transfer the count location is incremented, and when the count reaches zero the data transfer is concluded.

The program can be organized as a loop, and most computers simplify the increment and test operation by having an instruction with a typical mnemonic code ISZ (increment and skip if zero).

3.2. PROGRAM-CONTROLLED TRANSFER ON PDP 8

Considering the operation in greater detail for a PDP 8 computer, the IOT instruction (input-output transfer) consists of 12 bits which can conveniently be grouped as four octal digits. The first digit denotes the op code, which for an IOT instruction is 6. The next two digits denote the device-select code, which has to be transferred across to the device-select lines on the I/O bus (bits 3-8). The connections between the central processor and the I/O bus are shown in Fig. 3.1, and the instruction format in Fig. 3.2. The IOT operation starts with a fetch cycle from the main store. When the first digit of the instructions (bits 0-2) is recognized as 6, the normal clock generator is inhibited and the computer starts an extended cycle. In earlier machines which had only an external I/O bus, the IOT cycle took 3.75 μs. Current versions of the machine (PDP 8/E) have a common data and control bus called Omnibus. This connects the

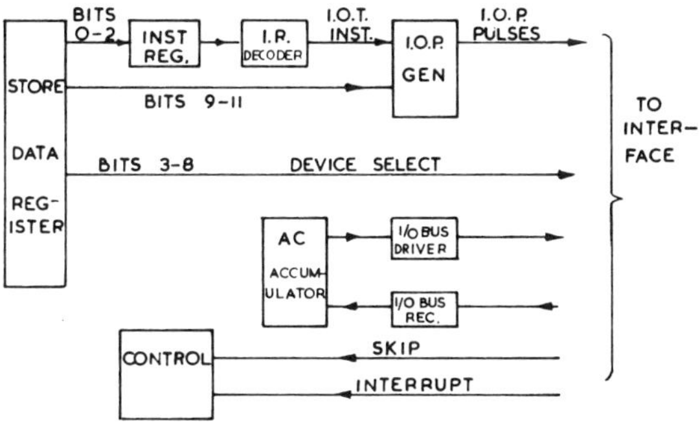

Figure 3.1. PDP8 I/O bus circuits

central processor, the main store, and interfaces for standard peripherals such as a teleprinter and tape and disc backing stores. It can also be used for external peripherals, but as it is used synchronously with a fixed store cycle time its length is restricted to a few feet, otherwise signal delay times become excessive. The normal cycle time for an I/O transfer by means of the Omnibus is 1.2 μs.

Since many users have equipment, which has interfaces designed for the I/O bus of earlier versions of PDP8, a positive I/O bus interface which has output lines electrically identical to the I/O bus lines on earlier machines can be plugged into the Omnibus. This allows all devices from earlier machines to be used on current machines without alteration, but since the data has to traverse an additional interface, the transfer may be rather slower. The maximum possible time is 4.6 μs if all IOP pulses are required, but if only one IOP pulse is used this can be reduced to 2.6 μs.

In order to control the relative timing of several operations during the cycle, the last digit of the instruction controls the output of three timing pulses, each having its own line in the I/O bus. These pulses are called IOP1, IOP2, and IOP4, and they are controlled individually by the three bits 9, 10, 11. Thus IOP1 is emitted if bit 11 is 1, IOP2 is emitted if bit 10 is 1, and IOP4 if bit 9 is 1. Any combination of these bits may also

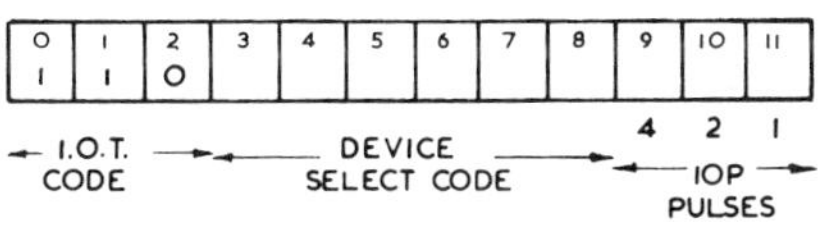

Figure 3.2. PDP8 IOT instruction format

be microprogrammed. Thus, if the last digit of the IOT instruction is 5 (101), IOP pulses 1 and 4 will be transmitted.

The IOP pulses can be used, together with the device-select code, to control three different activities of the interface. They may, however, be required to control operations which must be carried out in the correct sequence. For example, IOP1 may be used to clear the device buffer ready to accept data from the computer, IOP2 to gate the data from the I/O bus into the buffer, and IOP4 to start some operation in the device which will use the data. The usual function of the IOP pulses is as follows:

IOP1 Test flags, skip
IOP2 Clearing flags, clearing AC
IOP4 Reading, loading, clearing buffer registers

It is at first glance surprising that with this arrangement there is no need for a control line from the device interface which would indicate to the computer which way the data is being transferred. There are two sets of data lines, 12 input and 12 output. The output lines are permanently connected via isolating buffer amplifiers to the accumulator outputs. Thus any information in the accumulator is always available on the output I/O bus and can be gated into any device selected by an IOT instruction without further action by the central processor. In the reverse direction, the IOT instruction gates any data on the I/O bus data-input lines into the accumulator.

The logical operation is an OR between the previous contents of the accumulator and the data on the input bus. Thus the operation of loading data from the I/O bus into the accumulator requires a "clear accumulator" instruction to precede the IOT instruction on earlier machines, or a pulse on the AC CLEAR line at load time on current machines.

For a specific example of an inward data transfer which requires a waiting loop, we consider an A-D converter interface. This requires three commands: sample the analog voltage, start conversion, and clear the flag; test the flag and skip if set; read the digitized value from the converter buffer register into the accumulator. These three commands can all be provided with a single device code by associating a separate IOP pulse with each command. The device code allocated for the standard A-D converter is 53, and the first octal digit of the instruction must be 6 for an input-output transfer. Thus the octal codes for the three commands are as follows.

ADSF	= 6531	(IOP1)	Skip if flag set
ADCV	= 6532	(IOP2)	Start conversion, clear flag, set flag when finished
ADRB	= 6534	(IOP4)	Read buffer into accumulator, clear flag

The binary versions of these commands are given in Fig. 3.3.

The program for taking a single sample of an analog voltage, converting it, and transferring it to the accumulator is as follows.

```
(1) CLA        /clear accumulator
(2) ADCV       /start conversion, clear flag
(3) ADSF       /test flag, skip if set
(4) JMP.—1     /jump back to previous instruction
(5) ADRB       /read buffer
```

The instruction JMP.—1 in this code means "jump back one place from the current instruction," the waiting loop in this case consisting of the two instructions (3) and (4).

The interface for the A-D converter is show in Fig. 3.4. The three commands are distinguished by using the device-select pulse (which appears for all three) AND gated with the three different IOP pulses, each of which occurs on a separate I/O bus line. The "start conversion" signal must begin the A-D converter cycle and also clear the flag. A subsequent pulse from the converter indicates the end of the conversion process and is used to set the flag. The "read buffer" instruction gates information from the buffer via the data input lines to the accumulator, and also clears the flag. The "test flag" instruction gates a 1 to the skip line, causing the program to skip an instruction if the flag is set (Q = 1).

Several versions of the I/O bus have been designed. The earliest with negative logic (OV and −3V), used three I/O pulses (IOP) emitted on three separate lines and staggered in time. These were designated IOP 1, IOP 2, and IOP 4 and were controlled by bits 9, 10, and 11 of the IOT instruction. Thus, if the last digit of the instruction were 5 (101), IOP 1 and IOP 4, would be transmitted. The time sequence was convenient when R-S bistables were used in device registers, since these were loaded

1	1	0	1	0	1	0	1	1	0	0	1	ADSF	6531
1	1	0	1	0	1	0	1	1	0	1	0	ADCV	6532
1	1	0	1	0	1	0	1	1	1	0	0	ADRB	6534
	6			5			3						

Figure 3.3. Binary form of A-D converter commands

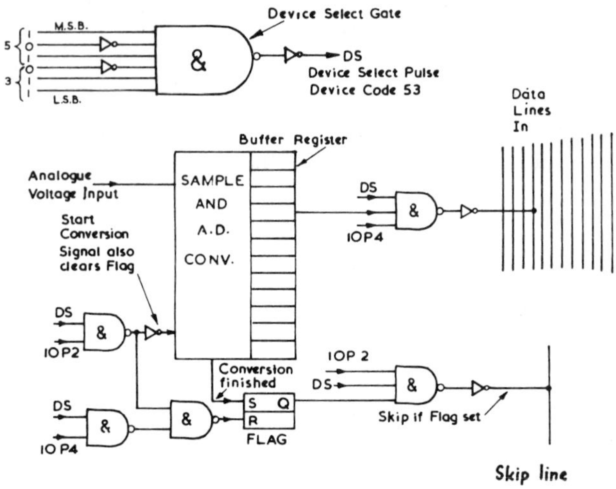

Figure 3.4. Interface for A-D converter

by first clearing all stages and then setting those necessary. When integrated D-type bistables became available, a single event, the clock pulse, could load either 1 or 0 into the register. There was thus less need for a sequence of pulses, and the positive I/O bus was modified so that bits 9, 10, and 11 of the IOT instruction controlled directly the levels of three function lines. This enabled a total of 8 different function codes to be set up and so control 8 different activities in the peripheral device. In general, the simplest method of using the function lines is to connect them directly to the inputs of an 8-way decoder. One of the 8 output lines will be energized for each function code emitted and, when gated with the device select pulse and an I/O SYNC timing pulse, can be used to control various activities in the peripheral device.

In early machines, separate data input and data output lines were used. These, however, are not logically necessary since data can be transferred in only one direction at a time. Consequently, later models used a conventional set of 12 bidirectional data lines connected in party-line fashion to all interfaces, as discussed in section 3-15.

The final state of the accumulator is still decided by an OR operation between the incoming data and the previous contents. Thus, to read the contents of any peripheral register correctly, the accumulator must be cleared before executing the input IOT instruction. This required a separate instruction on early machines, but it can be performed electrically on current machines by pulsing the AC CLEAR line at load time.

3.3. ANALOG MULTIPLEXERS

The A-D converter and its associated sample-and-hold circuits require a number of high-precision resistors and a stable and accurate voltage reference, and are thus relatively expensive. Consequently if more than one voltage needs measuring, it becomes too expensive to provide each with its own A-D converter, and a multiplexer in the form of an analog switch is generally used to allow many voltage inputs to be connected in turn to the A-D converter. It is convenient to place this under computer control by providing a further multiplexer buffer which can be loaded or incremented by a program-controlled transfer. Thus, to sample input 12, for example, the binary equivalent (1100) is loaded into the accumulator and transferred to the multiplexer buffer. This is decoded and connects input 12 to the A-D converter. Subsequent sampling and conversion of the analog voltage proceeds as described above. The maximum number of multiplexer channels is usually in the range 64-256.

The multiplexer may be operated in several different modes. As described above, each channel sampled is selected by a separate IOT instruction before the A-D converter is activated. An alternative mode of operation, which is particularly convenient if the computer is scanning round a set of points and is merely searching for any reading which is out of the desired range, is to use the incrementing mode. In this the multiplexer is incremented to the next channel before each reading, and when a channel is found which needs attention it can be identified by reading into the accumulator the current contents of the multiplexer buffer, thus giving the channel number.

3.4. PROGRAM-CONTROLLED TRANSFER ON NOVA COMPUTER

The Nova range of computers have a 16-bit word, and thus the instruction can encode more information than is possible with a 12-bit word size. The IOT instruction format is shown in Fig. 3.5. The operation code for an IOT is 011, contained in the first three bits. There are four 16 bit accumulators, and the data can be transmitted between any one of them and the external device by setting up the appropiate code in bits 3 and 4. Each device may contain up to three registers, and the register concerned in the transfer together with the direction of the data flow is indicated by bits 5, 6, and 7. The codes used are as follows.

Bits 5	6	7	Direction	Device register	Bus line
0	0	1	In	A	DATIA
0	1	0	Out	A	DATOA
0	1	1	In	B	DATIB
1	0	0	Out	B	DATOB
1	0	1	In	C	DATIC
1	1	0	Out	C	DATOC

Each of the six different transfers is signalled to the external device by energizing one of six bus lines. The device interface must detect which line is energized and set up the appropriate data paths.

Each interface needs a number of single-bit flags to control its operation and signal its current state back to the processor. Two of these, the Busy and Done flags, are controlled by bits 8 and 9, and their state is signaled back to the processor during each IOT instruction along I/O bus lines labelled SELB and SELD. This allows the processor to respond to various skip instructions which depend upon the states of the Busy and Done flags. The final six bits in positions 10-15 contain the device-select code, thus allowing 64 different code combinations. The first (00) is not used and the last (77_8) is reserved for special functions, so only 62 devices can be connected.

The I/O bus of the Nova comprises 50 lines, 16 bidirectional data lines, six device-select lines transmitting from processor to devices, and 28 other control lines carrying unidirectional signals. Signal levels are nominally 0 V and +2.7 V.

Bits 5	6	7	Direction	Device register	Bus line
0	0	1	In	A	DATIA
0	1	0	Out	A	DATOA
0	1	1	In	B	DATIB
1	0	0	Out	B	DATOB
1	0	1	In	C	DATIC
1	1	0	Out	C	DATOC

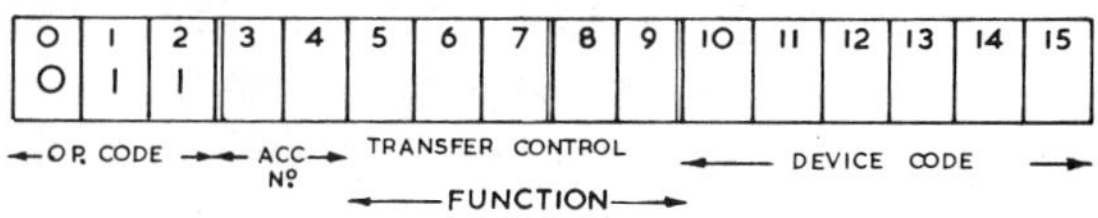

Figure 3.5. Nova instruction format for IOT

Some simple output interfaces, for example to a D-A converter, do not require flags, since the converter is always ready to accept new information and has no "busy" interval when it cannot have new data fed to it. A similar situation exists for input from, say, a position encoder. This always indicates the current position and can be read as often as required by the program. It again has no "busy" time, as does an A-D converter, during which it is computing the digital output and cannot be read.

Fig. 3.6 shows an output and an input interface for a D-A converter and a position encoder, both using device-select code 34. A NAND gate, with some inverters, connected to the six device-select lines, responds to this code. The Nova has no sequential timing pulses which can be selectively transmitted, but has instead six data-control lines on the I/O bus which are energized one at a time to indicate the data direction and device register to be used. In this case the buffer register which drives the D-A converter is designated as the A register, so that the instruction code to load it is DATOA. This instruction energizes the DATOA bus line which is used at the interface to gate the data from the I/O bus data lines into the converter buffer. In a similar manner the position-encoder outputs are regarded as the B register, and data from them is gated onto the data lines by the DATIB signal. In this particular interface it is impossible to write into the position-encoder data lines, and no useful

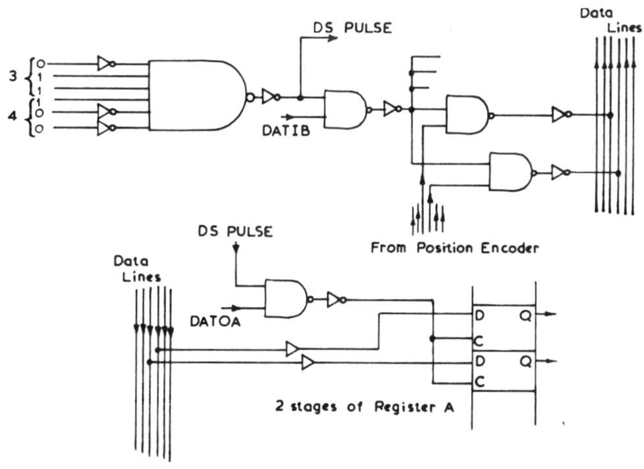

Figure 3.6. Simple interface for Nova computer

purpose is served by reading from the converter buffer. Thus the DATIA and DATOB commands are available for other purposes on the interface.

The instruction to output a word from the processor to the interface register A must specify the accumulator from which the word is read (say AC2) and the device code (here 34 in octal notation). The mnemonic for data output to register A is DOA, so that in assembly language the instruction is:

```
DOA    2    34
```

This is compiled to the binary form:

```
011    10    010    00    011100
```

The five groups of binary digits signify respectively:

011	Op code for IO Transfer
10	Code for AC2
010	Code for output to device register A
00	Control code—no change in flag status as flags are not used
011100	Device-select code 34

Similarly the data input to the processor from the shaft encoder is an input from register B and the assembly language instruction is:

```
DIB    3    34
```

Here we assume that the data has to be loaded into accumulator 3.

The binary version will be:

```
011    11    011    00    011100
```

3.5. TEST AND SKIP FACILITY

The facilities for testing the status of a peripheral device and issuing commands to it are based upon the use of two flags, one signifying "done" and the other "ready." These can be controlled both by the interface logic and by the processor using bits 8 and 9 of the IOT instruction. The action of these two bits is as follows.

Bus line energized	Bit number 8	9	Operation	Mnemonic
NONE	0	0	None	
START	0	1	Start device by clearing DONE and setting BUSY	S
CLEAR	1	0	Clear DONE and BUSY, device idle	C
IO PULSE	1	1	Pulse I/O Bus control line	P

The code 11 causes a pulse to be issued by the processor on a separate line of the I/O bus so that some additional operation in the device may be controlled without changing the state of the Done and Busy flags.

Instruction bits 8 and 9 are decoded in the processor and the three codes produce signals on the three I/O bus lines as shown. The Nova standard interface uses D-type bistables for the flags, with complemented "set" and "reset" inputs which are independent of the clock signal. By using both clocked and unclocked inputs maximum use can be made of the bistable logic, and a minimum of external logic is needed for combining the various triggering signals.

The connections between the bus control lines and the flag bistables are shown in Fig. 3.7. This diagram does not include the interrupt circuits,

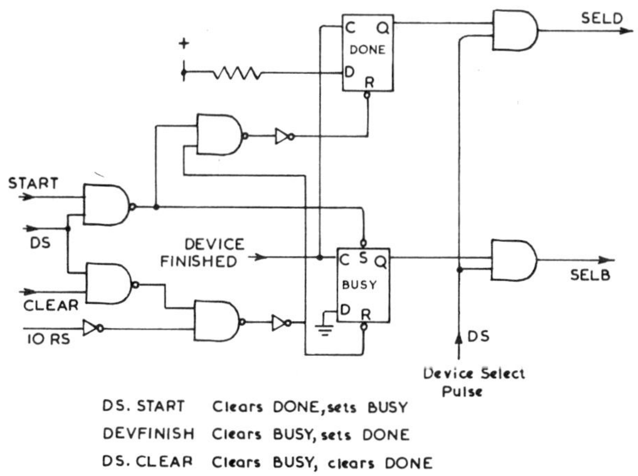

Figure 3.7. Busy and Done flags on Nova interface

which are considered later. For clarity the device-select gate is omitted. The start and clear pulses are common to all devices on the I/O bus, so that they are gated with the device-select pulse DS to ensure that they are used only when the correct device code is issued for this particular interface. The start pulse clears the Done flag and sets the Busy flag. This combination is used by the device logic to start its operating cycle. At the end of the cycle the device sends a "finished" signal to the clock terminal of both flags. Since the Busy flag data input is logical 0 and the Done flag data input is logical 1, the finished signal clears the Busy flag and sets the Done flag. This change of status can be tested by the computer as the condition of the two flags is signaled back by each IOT instruction along the SELB and SELD bus lines. The clear pulse resets both flags to 0 and this combination is used to return the device to the idling condition.

In order to ensure that the two flags are cleared to the idling state when the machine is first switched on, the IORST pulse is sent along the I/O bus which is used at each interface to clear the two flags. In Fig. 3.7 it is introduced at the reset input of the flag bistables.

3.6. PROGRAM INTERRUPTS

Where a device has a considerable period in the Busy state it is wasteful of computer time to keep the processor waiting in an unproductive loop until the device is ready again. A better way of organizing the program would be to issue a start command to the device and continue computation until it notified the computer that it had finished and was ready again. This procedure avoids continually testing the device flag but requires some method of allowing an externally applied signal to interrupt the computer's normal sequential execution of programs.

A simple way of meeting the requirement is to arrange that the interrupt signal always causes a jump to a fixed store location. Since the computer must be able to return to its previous program as soon as the interrupting device has received attention, it is necessary to store the position reached in the current program before executing the jump. This can be done by disregarding the interrupt signal until the current instruction has been completed. The computer then stores away the contents of the program counter and link, or carrying bit, usually in store location 0, and takes the next instruction to be executed from the following location.

In the unusual situation that there is only one device connected to the machine, location 1 can contain a jump instruction which takes the computer to a service routine which will deal with the interrupting device. Since the first few store locations are generally reserved for particular functions it is not convenient to have the service program itself stored in locations following location 1.

Generally there are a number of devices connected to the I/O bus and any number of them may send an interrupt signal along the interrupt bus line. Thus the first action of the computer in this situation must be to disable the interrupt facility, then determine which device has caused the interrupt. If more than one device has signalled an interrupt there must be a predetermined priority order so that the computer will first service the device with the highest priority.

The cheapest solution, but also the slowest, is to use a software procedure for determining which device to service. This procedure is usually in the form of a skip chain, in which each device flag is tested in sequence. Any device which signals an interrupt also sets its device flag and the program tests each flag in turn.

The complete set of operations is as follows.

Main program.
Interrupt occurs.

—

Store program counter in location 0 and jump to skip chain, turn off interrupt.

—

Skip chain determines which device to service.

—

Jump to service routine for device.

—

Return to main program via link stored in location 0, restore interrupt facility.

In order to avoid another interrupt interfering with servicing the current interrupt, the processor normally turns off the interrupt circuits as soon as an interrupt is acknowledged. The program restores the facility at the end of the service routine.

The skip chain program comprises three instructions per device. The priority is decided by the position in the chain, since the program always starts at the top and tests each device in turn, servicing the first device which has its flag set. The sequence is as follows.

IOT to test device 1 flag and skip if set
Skip (if flag is not set)

Jump to device 1 service routine
IOT to test device 2 flag and skip if set
Skip (if flag is not set)
Jump to device 2 service routine
etc.

The service routine will generally require use of the accumulator, so that its contents must first be stored away before making a data transfer. The required IOT instruction can then be issued and the incoming data stored away (assuming an inward transfer). When the data transfer and any word or character counting has been finished, the contents of the accumulator can be restored and the interrupt circuits turned on again. It is customary to delay restoring the interrupt circuit for one instruction time so that the indirect jump back to the main program can be executed before the interrupt is again on. This prevents any other device from interrupting the service routine and ensures that control has returned to the main program before any subsequent interrupt is allowed. The return to the main program uses an indirect jump to location 000. The address of the next instruction to be obeyed in the main program was loaded by the interrupt hardware into this location when the interrupt request was first acknowledged by the computer.

This procedure, although requiring a minimum of hardware, is rather slow and not acceptable in some circumstances, since once a service routine has been entered no other interrupt can be operated, however high its priority. Thus if one service routine is rather lengthy it can prevent a device needing fast access from getting quick service, and some data may be lost. Instead of trying to modify the interrupt procedure, the best solution is usually to use a DMA channel for fast devices. Where this facility is not available, some improvement can be made by using the above procedure for fast devices, but including an "interrupt on" instruction in the service routines for slow devices, after first clearing the device flag. These routines can then be interrupted by higher priority devices.

In order that this arrangement can work, it is necessary to form a "stack" or push-down store of the contents of the accumulator, link, program counter, and other active registers for each program interrupted at the start of the skip chain. If this is not done, the second interrupt will overwrite the previous return address stored in location 000, and it will not be possible to return to the first program.

As an example of interrupt handling with a simple machine architecture, we next examine the interface and program for a PDP8 computer.

3.7. PROGRAM INTERRUPT ON PDP8

Generally there are several devices connected to the I/O bus, so that the program must first identify the source of the interrupt, then jump to the corresponding service routine. The interface connections are shown in Fig. 3.8. Each flag is connected through an inverting line driver to the interrupt bus. This bus is operated, like the other lines on the bus, with negative logic. Logical 0 corresponds to a positive voltage provided by a resistor or potential divider connected to the +5 V supply. A logical 1 corresponds ideally to 0 V, in practice to less than 0.5 V, and is signalled by turning on to saturation a transistor connected between the line and earth. Some of the electrical characteristics of data highways are discussed in more detail in section 3.15.

With the arrangement shown in Fig. 3.8 any device flag which is set immediately signals an interrupt. This is normally granted at the end of the current instruction and causes the current contents of the program counter to be stored in location 000, and the next instruction to be fetched

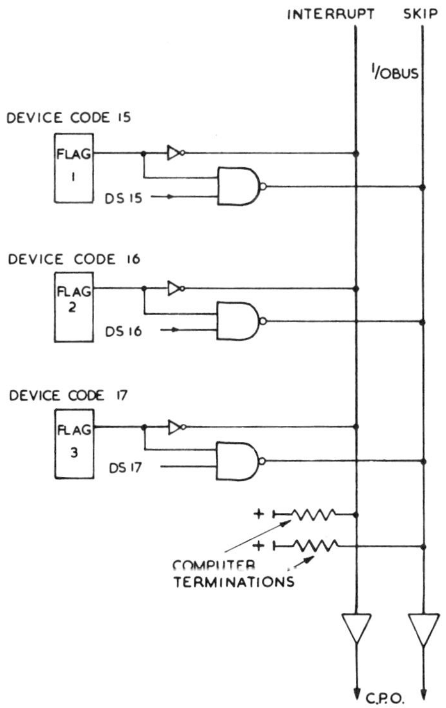

Figure 3.8. Connections to interrupt and skip lines in PDP8 I/O bus

from location 001, as described in the previous section. The interrupt circuits are also disabled automatically by the processor. The program required can be divided into three segments, the interrupt handling routine, the flag-testing, register saving, and restoring routine, and the individual device service modules.

The first segment needs only two instructions and is loaded into the second and third store locations, 0001 and 0002. The first location 0000 is left vacant to hold the return address. The second location contains an indirect jump to the flag-checking routine. The location containing the actual address can be the next location. This method allows the computer to jump out from page 0 to the page containing the flag-checking routine. The first three storage locations thus contain the following.

```
Address Contents
  0000     0000
  0001    JMP I  2
  0002    FLGTST
```

Any device handler will usually need to use the accumulator, and perhaps the link or overflow bit. Thus the contents of these and, if used, other arithmetic registers must be saved before jumping to the service routine, and also restored before jumping back to the main program. In order to avoid doing this in every device service routine the sequence is incorporated into the flag-checking program. This is in the form of a skip chain as described in section 3.6, and for two external devices will be as follows.

```
FLGTST  DCA      ACSAVE   / Save AC and clear
        RAL               / Shifts link contents to AC
        DCA      LNKSAV   / Save link and clear
        DEV1 SF           / Check device 1 flag
        SKP
        JMP      SERV1    / Jump to service routine 1
        DEV2 SF           / Check device 2 flag
        SKP
        JMP      SERV2    / Jump to service routine 2
END     CLA      CLL      / Exit routine-clear AC and
                            link
        TAD      LNKSAV   / Load original contents of
                            link
        RAR               / Shift into link
```

```
TAD      ACSAV       / Load original contents of AC
ION                  / Turn on interrupt
JMP I    0000        / Jump to return address in
                       location 0000
```

Three instruction routines to test other devices and skip if needed can be added just before the statement labelled END. This program will go down the skip chain and then return to the main program without any external action if the interrupt is caused by some other device. In order to trap this condition a halt instruction may be added at the end of the skip chain, just above the END label. Then any unexpected interrupt will halt the computer.

The final routine required is that to service a particular device. For an output device this must load the accumulator with the data, perform the appropriate IOT instruction and then jump to the END routine to restore the contents of accumulator and link. Thus the simplest version is as follows.

```
CLA                    / Clear AC
TAD      DATA          / Load data
IOT      DEVICE K      / Transfer to device buffer
JMP      END           / Jump to restore routine
```

This deals only with an isolated word of data. If a block of data is to be output, it is necessary to have a counter, loaded beforehand by the program, which keeps track of the number of words transmitted. This is usually loaded with a number $-N$, to transmit N words, and incremented upwards each time a word is output. In order to read a block of data from the store, it is convenient to use an auto-index register to hold the address of the data, so that the same instruction can be used for each transfer. The hardware will then increment the address each time before it is used in an indirect addressing instruction. If we allocate location 12 for this purpose, and the first item of data is stored in the location labelled BLOCK, the contents of location 12 must initially be set to BLOCK -1. We assume that a further location COUNT has been loaded with $-N$, if there are N words to transmit.

The device service routine could then be as follows.

```
CLA                    / Clear AC
TAD      I 12          / Load data from location in 12
IOT      DEVICE K      / Transfer to device buffer
ISZ      COUNT         / Increment counter, skip if finished
```

```
JMP    END       / Return to main program, more data to
                   be transferred
JMP    FINISH    / Jump to program segment which denotes
                   the end of the block, and after necessary
                   action jump to END to restore PC, L,
                   and AC and return to main program
```

The segment labelled FINISH will generally send some control signals to the device to signify the end of the block. The device interface must clear the device flag, and thus the device interrupt also, as soon as the data has been transferred. The flag remains clear until the device has finished with the data. Then the flag can once again be set, thus causing an interrupt if one is not already being serviced.

The interrupt handling can be made more flexible by using an additional flag in the interface to denote "interrupt enabled." Only when this flag is set will a device interrupt be passed to the control processor. This "interrupt enable" flag can be set and cleared by program, so that the user can decide which devices he allows to cause an interrupt at each stage of the program.

3.8. PROGRAM INTERRUPT ON NOVA COMPUTER

Since it has a 16-bit word, the Nova range of machines can make provision for a greater range of interrupt instructions than a machine with a smaller instruction format.

The interface control circuits require four D-type bistables, signifying DONE, BUSY, INTERRUPT REQUEST, and INTERRUPT DISABLE. The device can signal an interrupt only if the device DONE bistable is set and the INTERRUPT DISABLE is cleared. If these conditions are satisfied, the next REQUEST ENABLE pulse (RQENB) sent from the processor will clock the request into the INTERRUPT REQUEST bistable and signal an interrupt in the I/O bus interrupt line. The RQENB pulse is generated at every processor cycle in order to synchronize the interrupt signals.

The essential connections are shown in Fig. 3.9 (which omits the $\overline{\text{SELB}}$ and $\overline{\text{SELD}}$ lines). The IO reset pulse clears all four bistables, but subsequently the INT DISABLE bistable is controlled by the mask output signal MSKO. In order that the program shall have complete control over which devices are permitted to interrupt the processor, the MSKO instruction allows the processor to set or clear all device INT DISABLE bistables simultaneously. This is done by connecting each device INT DISABLE bistable to one of the data lines. The MSKO instruction then

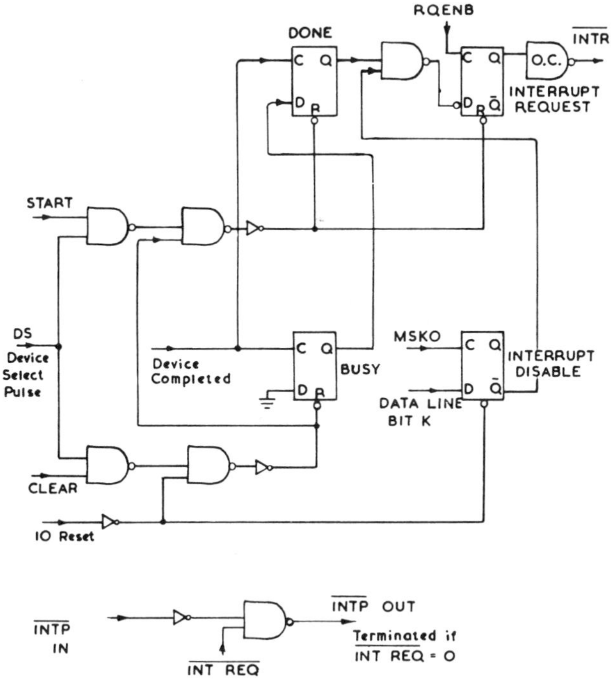

Figure 3.9. Device Interrupt control circuits for Nova computer I-O bus

connects one accumulator to the data lines and issues an MSKO pulse along the I/O bus. Then the bit pattern previously loaded into the accumulator sets or clears all INT DISABLE bistables when the MSKO pulse appears. The control circuits of Fig. 3.9 shows a connection to data line K. If K = 8, say, and the mask output instruction is

MSKO 0

a 1 bit previously loaded into bit 8 of accumulator 0 will set the INT DISABLE bistable, drive the $\bar{Q}$ output to 0, thus causing a 0 input to the D terminal of the INT REQ bistable and preventing the device from signalling an interrupt. If bit 8 of the accumulator contains a 0 the interrupt will be permitted.

In addition to the skip-chain method of identifying a calling device, the Nova computer also has provision for assigning priority by hardware and speeding up the transfer of control to a device-service program. The priority is obtained by sending out a signal from the processor called "interrupt priority." This is transmitted through the interface control logic for each device in turn, and sent on to the next device in the chain if the device INT REQ bistable is clear. If the INT REQ bistable is set, however, the INTP signal is terminated in the device logic and is not sent any further. Thus the first device in the chain which has its INT REQ set terminates the INTP signal. If the program then issues an "interrupt acknowledge" instruction, the device which terminated the INTP signal will transmit its device-select code on data lines 10-15 of the I/O bus and they will be routed to the accumulator specified in the instruction. The device-select code can then be used as a pointer to the starting address of a routine to service the device. This procedure requires rather more equipment at the interface than the skip-chain method of identifying the calling device, but it is much quicker. The priority of each device is here fixed by its position on the I/O bus; the device nearest to the processor has the highest priority, the device furthest away the lowest.

3.9. INTERRUPT VECTORING

The method of using hardware to transfer control to the required device-service routine is called "vectoring" and may take several forms.

One possible method is to arrange for the interrupt to store the current contents of the program counter and then execute the instruction in location N, where N is the device code. Location N contains a jump instruction which transfers control to the first instruction of the service routine. Taking three devices only, teleprinter input, teleprinter output, and paper tape reader, with device codes 10, 11, and 12, the map of the lower end of the store would be as shown in Fig. 3.10.

Location 000 could here be used to store the current contents of the program counter at the moment of interruption and provide a link back to the main program. However, if there are fast devices on the I/O bus which need to interrupt the service routines of slower devices, a separate location must be used by each service routine which can be interrupted to store the return link. This can be provided by allocating two storage locations per device, one to store the program counter and the second to store the pointer to the service routine.

At the expense of additional hardware in the processor the transfer of control to a service routine can be speeded up by arranging that the device code or address provided by the device which has priority is sent to the store address register. The store then performs a read operation from the location specified and routes the resulting word to the program counter. The processor then reverts to the fetch mode and extracts the next instruction from the address given by the program counter. This will

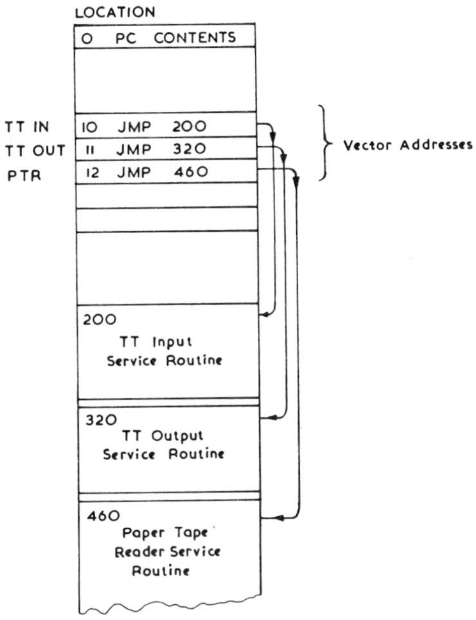

Figure 3.10. Map of store, interrupt vector, addresses, and service routines

be the first instruction of the service routine. This procedure eliminates the execution of one jump instruction. Hardware may also be used to deposit automatically the contents of the processor registers, but this requires one store cycle per register. If there are many registers this process can slow down the transfer of control. One way of avoiding the multiple store accesses is to incorporate a duplicate set of registers, one for the main program and a second set for the interrupting program. This permits a very fast transfer of control for the first interrupt, but if any subsequent interrupt occurs before the first has been serviced extra time is needed to store register contents before starting the second service routine.

3.10. DMA TRANSFERS

The fastest input to an on-line computer is obtained by avoiding the arithmetic unit and sending information directly to the main store. This involves additional bus lines, since the device interface must send an

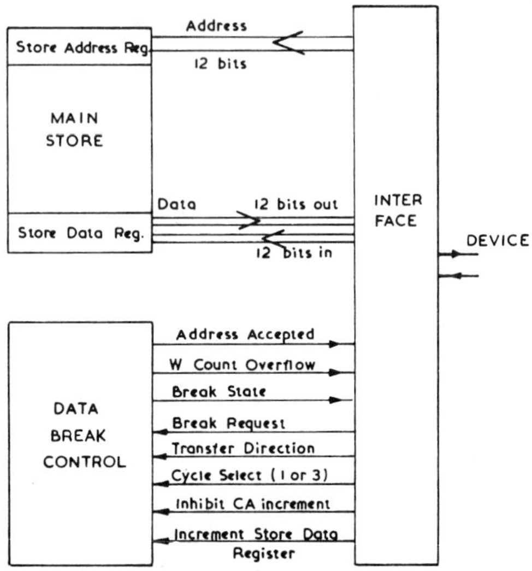

Figure 3.11. Interface connections for data-break transfer on PDP8 computer

address directly to the store address register and data directly to the store data register.

The simplest version of this process occupies a single store cycle in which computation is halted, no processor registers are altered, and the external device writes a single word into the store. This is often called "cycle stealing." The interface for this is more complex than that required for a program-controlled transfer, since at least two registers are required, one to contain the data, the other the address into which it is loaded. If a number of words are to be transferred, a further register, the "word count" register, is needed to keep track of progress and terminate the transfer when the required number of words has been stored. Similar facilities are required if the transfer direction is from the store rather than into it. During the cycle-stealing operation the processor is halted, usually by stopping its timing generator.

In the PDP8 three versions of the DMA facility are available, single-cycle, three-cycle, and increment store. The connections between the processor and the interface are shown in Fig. 3.11.

The single-cycle data break is used to put data into the store, to output data from the store, or to increment a particular location. The address of the data must be supplied by the interface and, for a block transfer, incremented each time before use. There must also be a word count register, loaded with the 2's complement of the number of words in the block. This is also incremented each time before use, and when it reaches zero further transfers are stopped. Both the address register and the word count register are loaded by program-controlled transfers before the DMA transfer is started. The time for a single-cycle break is 1.5 μs.

By accepting a slower data rate the number of registers required in the interface can be reduced from three to one. This is the reason for the three-cycle data break for which the word count and current address are held in the main store. The time required is about 4.5 μs, rather more than three store cycle times, since the word count and current address must first be incremented before the third cycle can be used for data transfer.

Each device using the facility is assigned a different pair of store locations for the word count and current address. The first location, for the word count, is sent to the processor from the DMA interface and is normally wired permanently to the appropriate logic levels, since the address is assigned when the interface is installed and should not need subsequent alteration. After incrementing the word count the program counter is incremented and the current address, stored in the adjacent location, is fetched, incremented, and returned to the store. The final phase is the actual data transfer to or from the location just calculated. In the PDP8 data-break facility one line to the computer calls for either a one-cycle or a three-cycle break and another indicates whether the transfer is incoming or outgoing. In order to indicate to the interface that a block of data has been finished, a word count overflow pulse is transmitted from the processor when the word count register contents reach zero. The interface can then terminate the transfers and if necessary interrupt the computer program to allow the data just received to be processed before starting another block.

In order that the interface may synchronize its activities with the processor, an "address accepted" pulse is generated which can be used to reset the Break Request bistable (if the next cycle is not to be a break) and increment the address and word count registers. In the three-cycle break the address-accepted pulse occurs in the first cycle; the last cycle, during which data is transferred, is signaled by a BREAK pulse.

The relative timing of the various signals is given in Fig. 3.12 for a single-cycle input transfer. The Break Request signal is connected to a bistable in the CPU which is timed by the T1 clock pulse. This occurs halfway through the computer cycle and, if the Break Request signal is present at this time T1, the bistable is set; the next processor cycle, starting at time T2, is the break cycle. The processor generates an "address accepted" pulse when the current address from the interface has been loaded into the store address register. This can be used, as shown

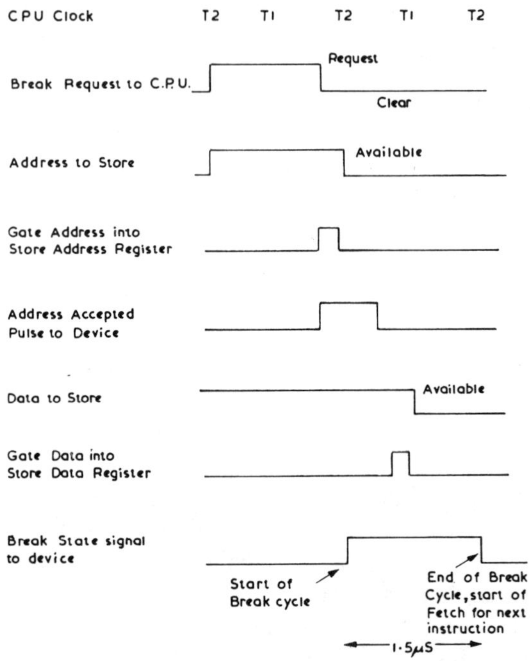

Figure 3.12. Single-cycle data break (input) timing diagram for PDP8

in Fig. 3.13, to increment the contents of the current address register ready for the next cycle. If there is only one Data Break device, its current address register can be permanently connected to the Data Break address lines, but for more than one each address register must be connected to the address lines only when active. The address register must also be connected to the I/O bus since it must be initially loaded by a program-controlled transfer which stipulates the first address of the block of data.

The word count register must have similar facilities for loading by program from the I/O bus, but its output feeds only the multiway AND gate which recognizes when the contents reach zero. The data register is loaded by the device and feeds the Data Break data lines. It can be reloaded immediately after the T1 pulse which occurs halfway through the Break cycle. The Data Break output transfer is generally similar, but requires a timing signal at the interface which gates the data output into the inferior register and signals the device that the data is available for use.

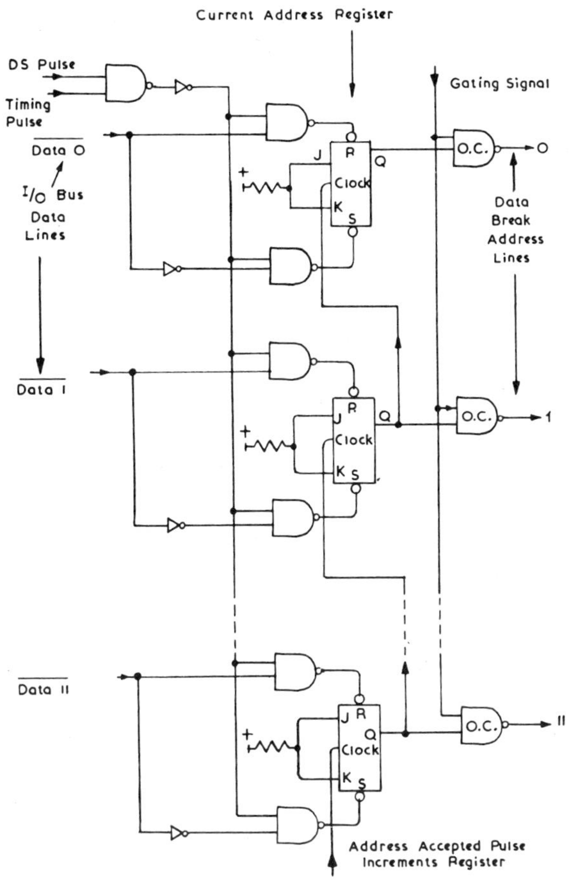

Figure 3.13. Loading and incrementing the data-break current-address register

3.11. MEMORY INCREMENT BREAK

The third type of single-cycle break is used to increment the contents of a particular store location specified by address lines. This address is often derived by combining the lower-order bits from the device with the higher-order bits loaded by program.

The main application for this facility was originally the sorting of data from nuclear experiments which produced variable-height pulses. It was required to count the number of pulses occurring in each of a number of "windows." Each window comprised a small increment of pulse height. The technique used was to hold and convert to digital form the height of each pulse. This digital quantity was then used as an address, and the corresponding store location had its contents increased by 1. Thus if the system used an eight-bit A-D converter, there would be 256 different height windows (400 in octal notation). If these are allocated positions in the store from 2000_8 upwards, the device would supply eight bits of the current address for a single-cycle memory increment break, and the initializing program would supply the most significant four bits.

3.12. DMA TRANSFERS ON NOVA COMPUTER

The DMA transfers on the Nova computer are called data-channel transfers. Two lines of the I/O bus (DCHM0 and DCHM1) are used for the device to signal to the processor the kind of operation required. The four options are Data Out, Increment Store, Data In, and Add to Store. The last facility enables a number from a device register to be added to the previous contents of a designated store location. It has application for signal averaging, in which samples of a waveform taken on successive cycles at the same point in the cycle are added together.

In order to reduce the number of lines in the external highway, there are no separate address lines for the data channel and the store address is sent over the data lines. The data lines thus handle successively the address information and the data. The address is sent when the processor emits the data channel accept signal (DCHA), and the data when an input (DCHI) or output (DCHO) timing pulse is sent to the interface. In order to allow maximum settling time on the data lines the CPU gates the address into the store at the end of the DCHA pulse and the data in at the end of the DCHI pulse. This arrangement diminishes the number of lines needed for the I/O bus but requires some extra gating in the processor.

Several data-channel interfaces can be installed, the priority being decided by their physical location on the bus. In order to establish which of the calling devices has the highest priority the processor sends out a data-channel priority signal DCHP. This is taken through logic in each data-channel interface, and the calling device nearest to the processor intercepts the signal and inverts it to produce a device data-channel priority signal DEV DCHP. Other device interfaces in which the DEV DCH REQ flag is clear will not intercept the DCHP signal and will pass it on to the next interface.

All data channel requests on the Nova must be synchronized to the CPU, so three flags are required, Device Data Channel Sync, Device

Data Channel Request, and Device Data Channel Select, as shown in Fig. 3.14. The procedure begins with all flags cleared. This condition occurs at the end of a transfer or initially when the IORST pulse is generated as the power is applied to the processor. The data-input terminal of the first bistable is connected to a positive supply for logical 1, so the Device Ready signal sets it to 1, giving a DEV DCH SYNC output of 1. The positive edge of the next RQ ENB (request enable) pulse then sets the second bistable DEV DCH REQ, thus sending a Data Channel Request signal (DCHR) to the processor to ask for a DMA cycle. As soon as this has been granted a Data Channel Acknowledge signal (DCHA) is sent from the processor. The interface then gates the store address onto the data lines and removes it at the end of the DCHA pulse. The arrangement of Fig. 3.14 is for an inward data-channel transfer, so the signals required on the data-mode lines are DCHMO = 1, DCHM1 = 0. Since the bus lines are normally held at logical 0 (about +3V), a driver is required only for the line DCHMO which needs to signal a logical 1. Thus there is only one bus driver needed in this instance, for mode line 0 (DCHMO). This signal is sent to the processor when DCHA arrives at the interface.

When the address has been loaded into the store address register, the Data Channel Input (DCHI) pulse is sent from the processor and used at the interface to gate the data onto the data lines. The priority input signal DCHP IN is normally available at the beginning of the processor cycle, and the first RQENB pulse sets DEV DCH REQ and thus prevents the DCHP signal being passed on. When the device has been granted a data-

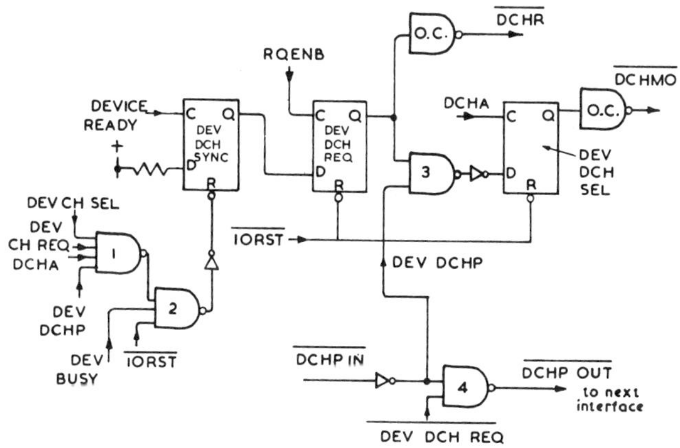

Figure 3.14. Control circuits for Nova data channel (data input transfer)

channel cycle, DEV DCHP = 1, DEV CH REQ = 1, and DEV DCH SEL = 1.

When next the DCHA signal changes to 1 there will be four 1 inputs to gate 1, thus giving, via gate 2 and the following inverter, a reset signal to clear the DEV SYNC bistable. The next RQENB pulse will clear the DEV DCH REQ bistable, thus giving a 0 to the data terminal of the DEV DCH SEL bistable. Finally the next DCHA pulse, which is allowing some other device to gain access to the data channel and setting its DCH SEL bistable, will simultaneously clear the DEV DCH SEL bistable of this device.

The same arrangement as shown in Fig. 3.14 may be used for control of the other types of transfer (Data Out, Increment Store, and Add to Store) with minor changes to produce the correct code for the DCHM0 and DCHM1 lines. These are as follows.

	DCHM0	**DCHM1**
Data Out	0	0
Increment Store	0	1
Data In	1	0
Add to Store	1	1

Thus a data output transfer needs no driving circuits, data input and increment store need one, and add to store needs two.

In addition to the standard data-channel facility provided on all Nova computers, the 800 series and the Supernova have an additional high-speed data-channel option. Interfaces for these must be plugged into the processor main frame and use high-speed logic. The control signals used for the higher-speed operation have a shorter duration than for the standard data channel, and the interface must respond more quickly.

As an indication of the maximum transfer rates, the 1200 series (store cycle time 1.2 μs) has data-input and data-output rates of 833 K and 555 K words/s respectively. The faster 800 series (store cycle time 0.8 μs) have corresponding transfer rates of 1250 K and 1000 K words/s for high-speed data-channel transfers.

The DMA transfers described above generally require three interface registers, for data, current address, and the word count. This is the customary arrangement, but an alternative used in current Interdata computers is to store the data starting and finishing addresses. With this system the starting address is incremented after each transfer. When it becomes equal to the finishing address the next transfer must be the last in the block.

3.13. ASYNCHRONOUS OPERATION

Data transfers between peripheral devices and the processor described earlier are all synchronous, the timing for the complete cycle of operations being provided by the processor. The device interface must respond within a prescribed interval, otherwise the transfer cannot take place. This has the practical consequences of limiting the permissible distance between processor and interface and introducing some complications when transferring data between devices such as a processor and a disc store which are not running in synchronism.

Greater flexibility is possible if the interface need not operate synchronously but can use a timing signal sent with the data from the processor, and in the reverse direction can supply its timing signal along with the data it returns to the processor. Such an arrangement is usually organized as a master-slave operation with a protocol called "handshaking." Every signal transmission from the master is acknowledged by a return signal from the slave. Not until the return signal has been received does the next phase of the transfer start. This interchange procedure avoids the need for a fixed time cycle. As a practical measure, in order to avoid the processor coming to a halt it is customary to fix a maximum time interval during which the slave must respond, say 20 μs. If no response has occurred during this interval it is assumed that a fault has developed and the processor is diverted into an error routine. The master-slave procedure involves somewhat more logic and signal interchange than a synchronous data transfer but allows greater flexibility in the flow of information and substantially removes the previous limitation on the distance between processor and interface.

One fairly widely used computer which is organized for asynchronous operation is the Digital Equipment Corporation PDP11. This includes several different 16-bit processors with an upwards-compatible instruction set. The main feature of the machine architecture is that all the major units of the system, the processor, the store modules, the standard peripherals, and the external devices are connected to a single data and control highway called the Unibus (Fig. 3.15).

The device data registers used in the interfaces are allocated addresses above the highest address in the main store. Thus a single set of address lines can be used to select a word from the main store or any device register. This arrangement reduces the number of address lines on the highway but requires a little more logic at the interface since there are 18 address lines to be decoded.

The standard DEC address-selector module provides four output signals, corresponding to four adjacent addresses. Three of these may be

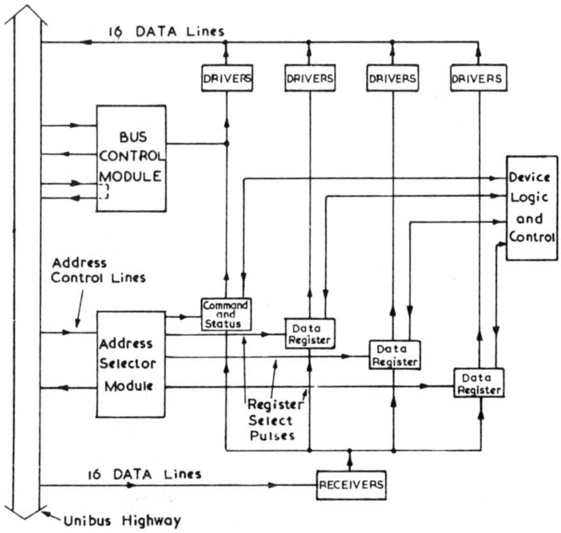

Figure 3.15. Block diagram of basic PDP11 device interface

used to select data registers, and one to select the command status register (CSR). The CSR allows up to 16 control bits to be used, read, or loaded in one instruction and takes the place of the separate flags used in earlier machines. Generally few devices will need all 16 bits for their control, but some complex peripherals such as disc drives may need two status registers.

There are no specific IOT instructions since the normal instruction code allows the program to transfer information to and from device registers in the same manner as it addresses main store locations. Thus to the programmer there is no essential difference between a device register and a store location. For example, the MOV instruction can specify two storage locations which are respectively source and destination. The instruction

```
MOV      TEMP    R0
```

will transfer one word from the main store location TEMP to the CPU register R0. Similarly the instruction

```
MOVB     TKB     R1
```

will move an 8-bit byte (one character) from the teleprinter keyboard buffer into the CPU register R1. The teleprinter keyboard buffer TKB is allocated the address 777562 and this will be substituted for the symbolic address TKB by the compiler. However, a nonstandard peripheral device will use an unallocated address which is not known to the compiler. Thus, if a symbol such as DEVBUF is used to denote a device buffer, its actual address must be included in the program, otherwise the compiler cannot complete its symbol table.

3.14. ASYNCHRONOUS TRANSFERS

There are six different operations which can occur between a device interface and other units on the Unibus, four for data transfer, one to transfer control of the bus, and one to cause a program interrupt. The four data-transfer operations (two output and two input) are identified by signals sent on two control lines C0 and C1.

The general arrangement for the interface is shown in Fig. 3.16. This allows for the full range of interface activity, including the four data transfers and facilities for program interrruption, for requesting control of the bus, and for directing bus operations. Many device interfaces do not need all four registers, and it may not be necessary both to load and read the device buffers from the highway.

For example, the teleprinter keyboard interface needs only one data register, 8 bits wide, which is loaded from the teleprinter but need only be read by the highway circuits, and its status register need only store 4 bits. Such an interface will transfer one byte of data at a time, under program control, and can be set into operation and tested to find whether a new byte is ready by program.

On the other hand an interface which must transfer blocks of data at high speed will need to gain mastership of the bus, and must have a register to supply the current address for the highway and a further register for word counting. This mode of operation is similar to the DMA operation in a synchronous computer and requires a similar quantity of logic and storage.

The provision for operating 8-bit bytes or 16-bit words requires a little extra logic at the interface. The input operation is arranged to handle a full 16-bit word, and the device may transfer any required number of bits to the processor. A data-output operation, on the other hand, may consist of a complete word or a single byte; these cases are distinguished by signals on the C0, C1 highway lines. Thus the interface, if using byte

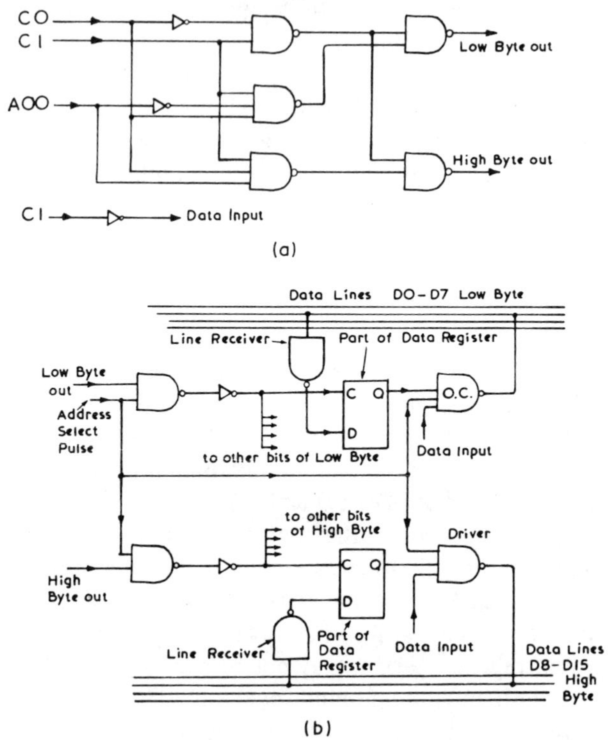

Figure 3.16. Word and byte data transfers in PDP11 interface: (a) data-transfer decoding; (b) data flow for 2 bits of data register

transfers, needs the output gating from the highway to the interface register split into two halves, upper and lower byte. The signals for this are supplied by decoding the C0, C1 signals (01 for word output, 11 for byte output). The byte is specified by the least significant bit of the address lines, 0 for the low byte and 1 for the high byte. For a word output both byte lines are energized.

The two data-input transfers (Data Input, and Data Input-Pause) require the same action from the interface register, namely to gate the contents on to the data lines. For both transfers C1 = 0. Thus the input transfer must occur when C1 = 0 and the register-select pulse is emitted by the address-selector module. The logic equations for the data transfers are:

$$\begin{aligned} \text{low-byte output} &= \overline{C0}.C1 + C0.C1.\overline{A00} \\ \text{high-byte output} &= \overline{C0}.C1 + C0.C1.A00 \\ \text{word input} &= \overline{C1} \end{aligned}$$

The signals required to read and load a device data register consist of these three, each being gated also with the register-select pulse.

The device interface may also gain control over the bus in order to make a data transfer if, when it energizes the Bus Request line, no other device (or the processor) which also requires the bus has a higher priority.

The address decoding logic is a standard item which has provision for inserting links to select any group of addresses in the top 4K store locations. For specific interfaces dedicated to particular devices, this degree of flexibility is not essential and less logic is required. For example, Fig. 3.17 shows an address selector for the addresses 16777X, where X can be 0, 2, 4 or 6. Four separate outputs are provided, labelled SEL0, SEL2, SEL4, and SEL6. The logic units connected to the bus are special high-impedance receivers, described in section 3.15, which have the logic function of 2-input AND gates with negated inputs. Since the address lines operate with negative logic, a gate connected to address lines which should both carry logic 1 will produce a 1 output in positive logic only when the two input lines are fed correctly. The logic function of the receivers is shown in the following table:

INPUTS		**OUTPUT**
A	**B**	
L	L	H
L	H	L
H	L	L
H	H	L

Here H denotes a high voltage (1 in positive logic) and L a low voltage (0 in positive logic).

Thus those address lines which should be low (logic 1 in negative logic) can be connected in pairs to the receiving gates, and only in the presence of both low inputs will the output be high. These outputs can be combined in an 8-way NAND gate to produce the ADDR pulse, signifying an address 16777X, where X can have any value. Address lines which should be high (in this case only A12) must be connected individually to a receiving gate and followed by an inverter.

The ADDR pulse is connected through a CR delay circuit to an open collector line driver which generates the $\overline{\text{SSYN}}$ to return to the processor, signifying the end of the data transfer. The $\overline{\text{MSYN}}$ signal is also gated

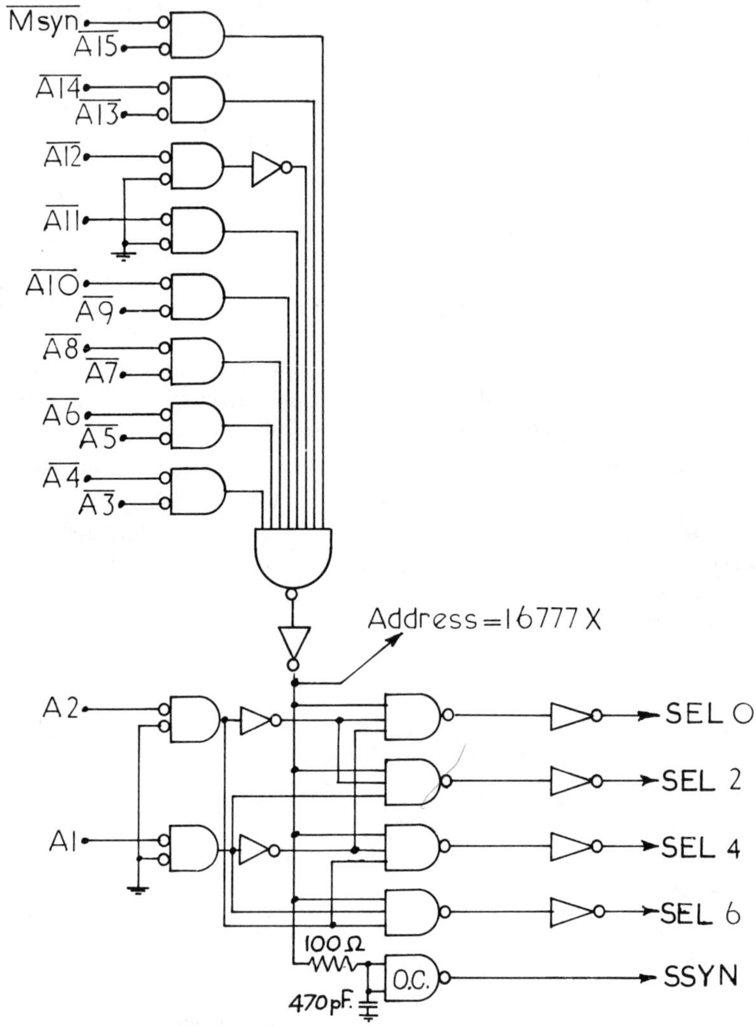

Figure 3.17. Address decoding on PDP11

with the address lines to establish the correct timing for the transfer. The signal is sent out from the processor at least 75 μs after the address and data to allow any initial transients and ringing to die away. The $\overline{\text{SSYN}}$ signal is delayed about 50 μs in the CR circuit to allow plenty of time for signals to propagate through the logic and effect the data transfer.

In Fig. 3.17 and the foregoing description, the address lines, $\overline{\text{MSYN}}$ and $\overline{\text{SSYN}}$, are shown as negated signals to indicate that they use negative logic. The address used in Fig. 3.17 is chosen to provide economical decoding logic, but a more complex arrangement is required for addressing any peripheral location. The standard general-purpose address decoder for the PDP11 connects each of the 10 address lines A3—A12 to its own line receiver, which is followed by an exclusive −OR gate. The second input to the gate can be strapped to earth or taken via a resistor to +5V; this causes the gate to act as a buffer (no change in logic level) if earthed, or as an inverter if taken to +5V. Thus any address may be selected between 16000X and 17777X by connecting or disconnecting the straps. The final AND operation involves more inputs than the 8-way gate shown in Fig. 3.17, and is performed by using open-collector exclusive −NOR gates which are connected in parallel to a 1kΩ load. The circuit for two of the address lines is shown in Fig. 3.18.

3.15. DATA HIGHWAY DESIGN

In order to economize on the number of lines used in data highways, many of these, particularly the data lines, are bidirectional. They may

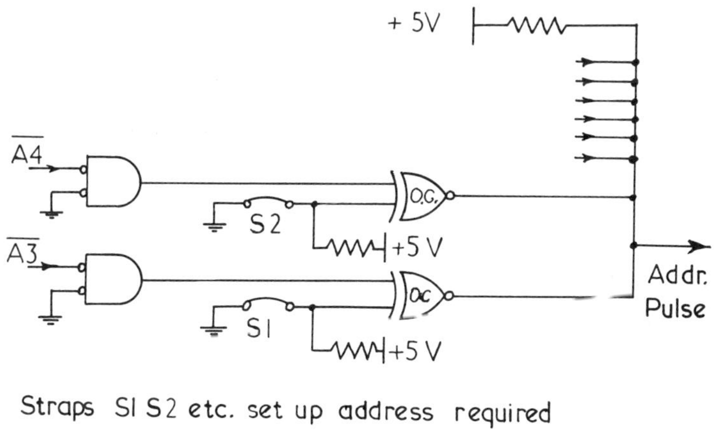

Figure 3.18. General purpose address decoder for PDP11

then be used to effect data transfers outwards from the computer or into it, by using what is effectively a wired-OR arrangement. The bus line is normally held at a positive potential of around 3 V when no transfers are taking place, and all communication with it is through special line-driver and line-receiver circuits. The line-driver circuits are similar to standard TTL gates, but the output stage comprises a single open-collector transistor connected between line and earth. The load resistor is connected at one or both ends of the data line, and thus no load resistors are required at the interface.

The line receivers may be normal TTL gates, but only a limited number of these can be connected to the highway as they may draw nearly 2 mA each and the highway current is limited. Where a considerable number of devices are connected to the bus, special line receivers can be used which are generally similar to TTL gates but have an emitter-follower input stage. These require an input current of only around 150 μA and are generally arranged to have rather greater noise immunity than normal TTL.

A typical bus arrangement is that shown in Fig. 3.19, the resistor values being those recommended for the PDP11 data highway. The effective resistance terminating the line at each end is normally 180 Ω in parallel with 390 Ω, or 123 Ω. This is a very close match to the flexible printed wiring used to extend the highway outside the computer chassis, which has a characteristic impedance of 120 Ω. In order to minimize cross-talk the conductors are alternately signal and earth.

The line receiver shown is a special integrated circuit (Digital Equipment Corporation No. DEC 380A). The line driver can be any open collector circuit which can sink 50 mA with a collector-emitter voltage of less than 0.8V. The maximum number of interfaces which can be connected depends upon the leakage current of the nonselected driver transistors and the current drawn by all of the line receivers. Both of these currents mainly affect the high-voltage state of the bus line and reduce the bus potential. If the potential is reduced too much, the bus receivers have little noise immunity and errors in transmission may occur. Generally the high-voltage state is taken as logical 0, and the low-voltage state as logical 1. The drivers are then equivalent to wired-OR circuits.

As the specified resistor tolerance is ±5%, the actual values of R1 and R2 in Fig. 3.19 may vary between 171 Ω and 189 Ω (180 Ω nominal) and 370.5 Ω and 409.5 Ω (390 Ω nominal). Thus the nominal open-circuit voltage on the line may vary between +3.31 V and +3.53 V (+3.4 V nominal).

The maximum transistor current occurs when the open-circuit line voltage is greatest (R1 low, R2 high) and the driver transistor is trans-

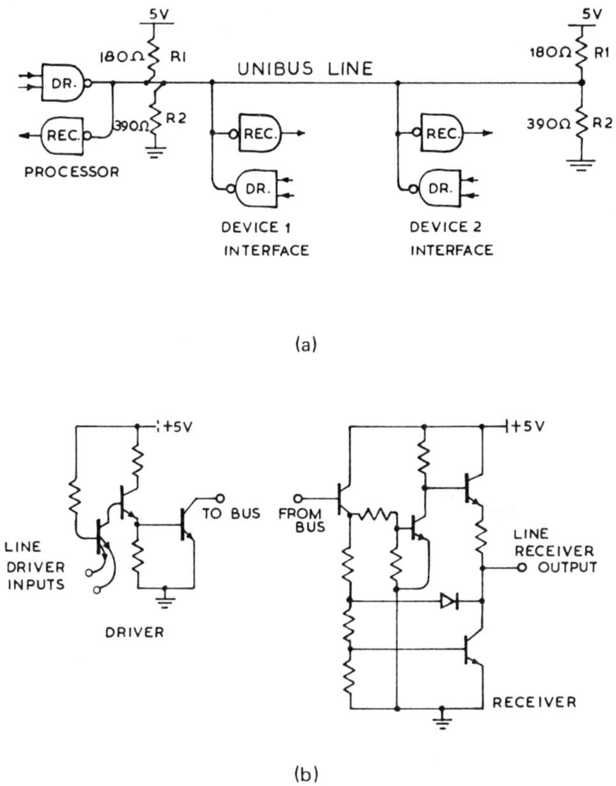

Figure 3.19. Diagram of bidirectional unibus circuit of PDP11 computer: (a) connections to Unibus; (b) typical line driver and receiver circuits

mitting a logical 1 with a bus potential of, say, 0.4V. The current in R1 is then:

$$I_1 = \frac{5 - 0.4}{0.171} = 26.9 \text{ mA}$$

The current in R2 is:

$$I_2 = \frac{0.4}{0.4095} = 0.98 \text{ mA}$$

Thus the collector current is, per termination:

$$I_1 - I_2 = 25.9 \text{ mA}$$

If both terminations have worst-case resistor values, the total collector current is thus:

$$I_c = 2\times (I_1 - I_2) = 51.8 \text{ mA}$$

The driver circuits are rated at 50 mA, and will thus only need to handle this current under worst-case conditions. If both terminations have R1 high, R2 low the corresponding driver current for logical 1 is 46.5 mA. These collector currents occur only when there is no other interface connected. Each interface takes a small current from the line and so reduces slightly the pull-down current that the transistor has to carry.

With a high-input-impedance line receiver, the current drain per interface is typically:

$$I = 160 \ \mu\text{A (receiver)} + 25 \ \mu\text{A (driver leakage)} = 185 \ \mu\text{A}$$

Thus for 20 interfaces the current drain for a logical 0 is:

$$20 \times 0.185 = 3.7 \text{ mA}$$

The minimum open-circuit voltage is 3.31V, so that the minimum loaded voltage is:

$$3.31 - 0.5 \times 3.7 \times 0.125 = 3.08\text{V}$$

Here the source resistance of the termination is 0.125 kΩ, and the factor 0.5 is required because there are two terminations in parallel. Since the threshold voltage of the logic is about +2 V, there is an adequate noise margin, but the manufacturers do not recommend that more than 20 interfaces should be connected to a single bus line.

A similar arrangement is used in the Nova computer bidirectional bus lines, with R1 having a value of 330 Ω nominal in place of 180 Ω. This provides a line-terminating impedance of 179 Ω. If it is assumed that the resistors have 5% tolerance, the limits of the bus open-circuit voltage are 2.58-2.83 V (nominal value 2.7 V). The worst-case collector current for an open-circuit bus is 27.4 mA. The manufacturers recommend that not more than 10 standard 7400 series gate inputs should be connected to the bus. The worst-case driver current will then be the bus termination current plus the worst-case input current (10 × 1.6 mA), that is:

$$I_c = 27.4 + (10 \times 1.6) = 43.4 \text{ mA}$$

The line driver for this bus arrangement is rated at 45 mA.

In selecting suitable operating conditions for a data highway the designer is faced with conflicting requirements. In order to minimize cross-talk the line impedance should be low, but flexible printed wiring or twisted pairs usually have an impedance in the region of 120-150 Ω and little can be done to reduce this. For adequate noise immunity a signal swing of several volts is desirable, and, since the load on any driver is half the characteristic impedance of the line, a substantial driving current is required. For example, with 120-Ω lines properly terminated the driver load is 60 Ω and a 3-V signal swing signal requires a current of 50 mA. If the current level is increased much beyond this, it is difficult to provide adequate drive from an integrated circuit and the output transistor may severely limit the switching speed.

A highway which uses a rather high current level is that of the PDP 15 computer. This has a 68-Ω termination at each end, one going to the +5-V supply and the other to earth. Taking the same conditions as before, namely a logical 1 potential of 0.4V and a 5% resistor tolerance, gives a worst-case driver current of about 66 mA.

3.16. POSITIVE LOGIC BUS CIRCUITS

The bus circuits described in the previous section employ negative logic, since a logical 1 is more negative than a logical 0. The internal logic in both processor and interface is usually TTL which is categorized on the basis of a positive logic convention. Thus to the logic circuits which drive and receive data on the bus all of the bus signals are negated, and generally require inversion.

It is possible to use a similar "party-line" wired-OR arrangement for line drivers with positive-going logic, if the driver output stage is changed from an open-collector transistor to an emitter-follower. Only two emitter-load resistors are required; these are the terminating resistors at each end of the line. Integrated circuits which can interconnect with both TTL and ECL gates are available to drive bus lines in this manner. Many of these are designed to drive 50-Ω or 75-Ω coaxial cable as well as twisted-pair circuits, and so have rather greater current-handling capacity than open-collector circuits, typically 75 mA.

A major hazard with any bus system is that of an accidental short-circuit to earth during testing or commissioning. An open-collector system will suffer no damage from such a fault, since the condition corresponds to a logical 1.

An emitter-follower normally has a low output impedance and consequently when a logical 1 output is short-circuited to earth a high current may flow which is sufficient to damage the transistor. In order to avoid this risk the integrated circuits developed for this application have a current-limiting facility built in. This makes the circuits effectively short-circuit proof by restricting the output current to about 30 mA for any output voltage below 1.5 V. The maximum rated current for a logical 1 output is typically 75 mA at 2.4V.

3.17. MICROPROCESSOR BUS CIRCUITS

Microprocessors require data, address, and control busses which operate in a similar manner to the busses of minicomputers. However, the electrical conditions are different as a result of the constraints imposed by microelectronic technology. In order to fabricate many thousands of transistors on a small chip of silicon it is necessary to restrict individual transistors to the minimum practicable area and also to use a process with the fewest diffusions and thus the highest yield.

Consequently, nearly all microprocessors use MOST transistors of minimum size and of limited current-handling capacity. These are quite unable to sink the 50 mA or 80 mA of drive current which would be required if conventional terminated bus lines, as described in section 3.15, were used. Fortunately, microprocessor bus lines are generally very short, often confined to a single printed circuit board, and they are connected to MOST logic which is considerably slower than the TTL circuits generally used with minicomputers. There is thus no need to terminate the bus lines with their characteristic impedance, and much larger pull-up resistors can be used with open-drain line drivers. The resistors are taken to the positive supply line and usually have values in the range 3.3 kΩ to 10 kΩ.

Since the MOST line receivers require negligible quiescent gate current, the limit on the number of packages which can be connected to the bus is their capacitance, not their current loading. If, for example, the total load is 50 pF, say 20 pF for wiring and 30 pF (typically 6 inputs) for the packages, a 3.3 kΩ "pull-up" resistor will give a bus time constant for a rising voltage of $50 \times 10^{12} \times 3.3 \times 10^{3} = 0.17 \times 10^{6} = 0.17$ μs. Thus, 95% of the positive-going edge of the bus signal will have been completed in 0.34 μs. The negative-going edge is quicker, since the driving transistor can generally handle more than the peak current of 1.5 mA flowing initially in the pull-up resistor.

Although this party-line wired-OR arrangement is adequate for some signals, it is not entirely satisfactory for lines such as the data lines to which virtually every external package, including peripheral and store units, is connected. Here, in order to obtain fast enough signal transitions, it is preferable to have a push-pull circuit similar to that used for normal TTL output stages. This replaces the pull-up resistor by a transistor which will have a much lower "on" resistance. However, in order to allow bidirectional bus operation, all drivers except that currently energizing the bus must be turned off. Consequently they must be capable of three operating conditions:

a) logical 1 output
b) logical 0 output
c) high impedance, both transistors off

Such drives are called "tri-state" and are normally used to energize the data lines from the microprocessor. The circuit of a typical tri-state driver is shown in Fig. 3.20. Where DMA operation is required the processor address line drivers must also be tri-state, and many microprocessors have an input labelled TSC (tri-state control). When energized this turns the data and address drivers into the high impedance state. If the clock supply to the microprocessor is also disabled, a DMA transfer can be effected.

Since tri-state drivers have a fairly small "on" resistance, the transition time for bus signals is generally smaller than that calculated above; the limiting factor is generally the current which the transistor can handle. One microprocessor system allows a maximum capacitance loading on the bus of 130 pF. If more load is required, buffer amplifiers must be

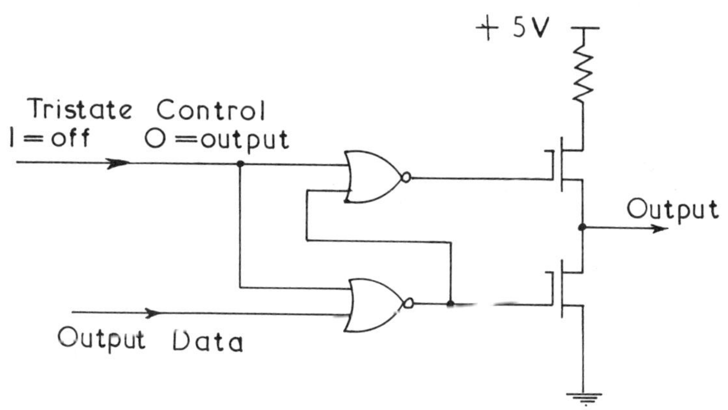

Figure 3.20. Tri-state driver using F.E.T.s.

inserted in the lines so that no one section of the bus has more than the permitted capacitance load.

The buffer amplifiers are gated and connected to each line in pairs, one for each direction of transmission. They are controlled by the read-write line, so that only one amplifier of a pair can be operating at any one time. This prevents the oscillation or locking up that would occur if both amplifiers of the pair could amplify simultaneously. When DMA operation is required the store and peripheral package are usually connected to the bus section next to the processor. Then, if the read-write line is pulled to write when the processor is switched to the offstate, the buffer amplifier will present a high impedance to the bus and will not disturb DMA transfers.

Since tri-state logic is operated with only one driver active at a time the bus lines can be arranged to handle signals with a positive logic convention, and this is the normal procedure. It creates less confusion when tracing signals through the system than the negative bus logic convention usually adopted for minicomputer busses. The confusion may, however, be transferred to the development engineer, who needs to recall what system he is working on to decide whether a low bus voltage denotes logic 1 or logic 0.

3.18. MICROPROCESSOR PARALLEL INPUT-OUTPUT TRANSFERS

Most of the data input and data output in microprocessor systems, as with minicomputers, takes place in parallel operations, when a number of bits are transferred simultaneously. This is such a general requirement that a standard package has been designed for the purpose. In order to exploit fully the benefits of large-scale integrated circuits, only one design, produced in large numbers, should be offered. In order to make this applicable to the widest possible range of devices its functions can, to a limited extent, be programmed by the user. This gives it properties somewhat different from those of a typical minicomputer interface, which is ready for use immediately after power is applied.

A microprocessor I/O package, by contrast, cannot be used until the appropriate internal registers have been loaded. A typical I/O package is the M6820, part of the Motorola M6800 microprocessor set. This provides two I/O 8-bit ports PA and PB which connect to external devices, each port having two control lines (CA1, CA2, CB1, CB2). Lines CA1 and CB1 are always input lines, but CA2 and CB2 can be programmed to act either as inputs or outputs.

Each port has three registers, those for port A being:

(a) Data Direction Register DDRA. Each bit of this controls the direction in which the corresponding data line of port A operates (1 for input, 0 for output).

(b) Control Register CRA. This contains two flag bits CRA7 (controlled by CA1) and CRA6 (controlled by CA2), 3 bits which control CA2, two bits which control CA1, and a switch bit CRA2.

(c) Data Register PA. This holds data being transferred to or from the processor.

To minimize the number of pins needed each port has only two addresses allocated to it, one for the control register (here CRA) and the other shared by the Data Direction Register and the Data Port. The switch bit CRA2 in the Control Register must be set to 0 to select the Data Direction Register and to 1 to select the Data Port, as shown in Fig. 3.21.

Thus, initially the Control Register bit CRA2 must be set to zero, usually by clearing the entire register. Then a data transfer to the other address will set the appropriate bit pattern into the Data Direction Register (0 for input, 1 for output), and a further transfer to the Control Register can set up the operation of CA1 and CA2. It will also provide access to the Data Port PA if bit CRA2 is set. The direction in which each line of the Data Port operates can be changed by the program part way through a task, but this requires a more complicated external circuit. However, a push-button and a lamp which indicates that a call has been received and stored can be connected very simply to the same line.

The individual bits of the Control Register CRA operates as follows:

BIT	CONTROLS	FUNCTION IF 0	FUNCTION IF 1
CRA0	CA1	Interrupt disabled	Interrupt enabled
CRA1	CA1	CA1 active on falling edge	CA1 active on rising edge
CRA2	DDRA/PA Switch	Access to DDRA	Access to PA
CRA3	CA2	Interrupt disabled	Interrupt enabled
CRA4	CA2	CA2 active on falling edge	CA2 active on rising edge
CRA5	CA2	CA2 is input	CA2 is output
CRA6	Flag for CA2	Creates interrupt when set if CRA3 = 1	
CRA7	Flag for CA1	Creates interrupt when set if CRA0 = 1	

The above table indicates the action of the control lines CA1 and CA2 when they are both acting as inputs. These lines set the two flag bits CRA6 and CRA7 when the signal voltage rises (0 to 1 transition) or when it falls (1 to 0 transition), depending upon the value loaded into bits CRA4 and CRA2. The flags will create an interrupt if bits CRA3 and CRA0 are set to 1, but not if they are set to 0.

A minor complication is that the flags cannot be cleared by writing to the control register address, but require a read operation from the data register PA.

In order to use CA2 as an output CRA5 is set to 1. If CRA4 is 0, a pulse is obtained starting when the flag CRA7 is set and ending when the processor reads from the data port PA. The polarity of the pulse is set by CRA3. When CRA4 is 1, CA2 copies the state of CRA2. All of the bits of the control register can be read by the processor, but CRA6 and CRA7 cannot be altered by a write operation.

The second port, comprising CRB, DDRB, and PB, behaves in the same manner as the first port, but there are minor differences in the actions of CA2 and CB2 as outputs.

Although any bit of either data port can be programmed as input or output, port A is more convenient as an input from switches, as its lines have a pull-up resistor. Port B is more effective as an output port as it has tri-state drivers, but as an input from switches it requires external pull-up resistors, typically 10 kΩ connected to the +5V line. The arrangement of the tri-state output circuit is shown in Fig. 3.20.

As an example of the setting up of a PIA, the following program sets up port A and the lower half of port B as inputs, reading 3 decimal digits encoded in BCD format from 3 thumb-wheel switches. The upper half of port B is programmed as outputs, feeding a 4-bit D.A. converter.

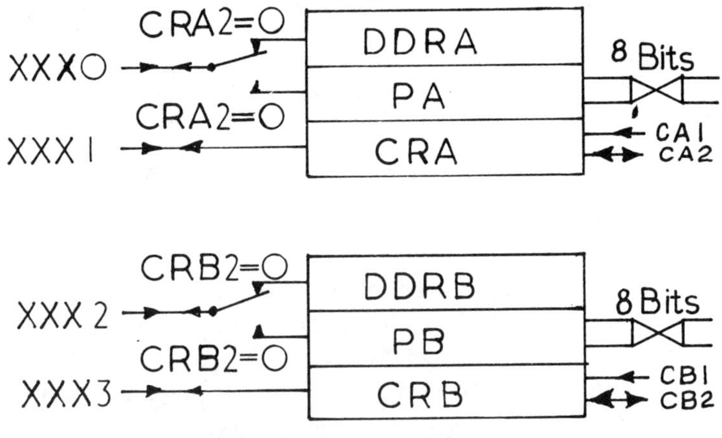

Figure 3.21. Register complement of P.I.A.

Control line CA2, connected to an optical sensor, is used as a flag, and CA1 as input creates an interrupt, fed from a zero-crossing detector supplied by a 50 Hz mains waveform. The program is executed immediately after a restart signal so that all registers are initially cleared. Thus DDRA is already set as an input, and only DDRB needs loading. To set all bits for output the simplest operation is to complement the location, so changing all 8 zeroes to ones.

In this case we need only the upper half to be outputs, so we load the bit pattern 1111 0000 into accumulator A (FO in hexadecimal notation) using immediate addressing. This is then transferred to the data direction register DDRB. The control word for Port A is 07, which programs CA1 as active on the rising edge of the signal, so creating an interrupt which also sets the flag bit 7. Setting bit CRA2 also ensures that further transfers to the DDRA/PA address will be directed to the data port PA. The zeroes in CRA 3-5 provide that CA2 is an input which does not create an interrupt and is active on the falling-edge of the signal. Only one bit is set in the control register for port B, CRB2; this ensures that future transfers will reach the data port PB, not the data direction register. The addresses used are:

8004	**PA/DDRA**
8005	**CRA**
8006	**PB/DDRB**
8007	**CRB**

A slightly different way of performing the same basic parallel input-output task is provided by the Intel 8255 Programmable Peripheral Interface (PPI) intended for use with the 8080 and 8085 family of 8-bit microprocessors. This has 24 I/O pins, divided into three ports A, B, and C. For some operations the ports are split into two groups; group A comprises Port A and the upper half of Port C (PC4-PC7); group B comprises Port B and the lower half of Port C (PC0-PC3).

Each PPI has four addresses, selected by input lines A0 and A1, which are connected to the two lowest address lines A0 and A1 from the processor. The four addresses select registers as follows:

A1	A0	Register
0	0	Port A
0	1	Port B
1	0	Port C
1	1	Control

The processor can write to or read from all three ports but can only write to the control register.

In this interface package the port lines cannot be individually programmed as inputs or outputs, only as groups of four lines.

The port lines can be organized in three different operating modes as follows:

Mode 0 Each group of 12 pins can be programmed in sets of four lines as inputs or outputs. There are 24 data lines and no separate control/status lines.

Program for setting up PIA

INSTRUCTION	CODE	COMMENT
LDA A FO	86 FO	Set up bit pattern 1111 0000 in accumulator A
STA A 8006	B7 80 06	Transfer to data direction register B
LDA A 07	86 07	Set up bit pattern 0000 0111 in accumulator A
STA A 8005	B7 80 05	Transfer to control register A
LDA A 04	86 04	Set up bit pattern 0000 0100 in accumulator A
STA A 8007	B7 80 07	Transfer to control register B

Mode 1 Each of the two groups can be programmed to have 8 input or 8 output lines, three of the remaining pins being used for handshaking and interrupt control signals.

Mode 2 8 lines from Port A are available which form a bidirectional data bus and 5 lines from Port C are available for handshaking. The remaining Port B can be programmed as in the other modes for either input or output.

Examples of control register contents (hexadecimal notation) and the configuration of ports they produce are, for Mode 0:

Control Register Word	Port A PA0-7	Port C Upper PC4-7	Port B PB0-7	Port C Lower PC0-3
80	output	output	output	output
82	output	output	input	output
89	output	input	output	input
98	input	input	output	output
9B	input	input	input	input

There are 16 different configurations in all.

In Mode 1 the two data ports PA and PB can be either all inputs or all outputs and two control lines can be programmed as either inputs or outputs. When set up for input, the ports have latches into which transient data can be entered by driving one of the Port C lines low. On output, the same lines are used as outgoing "strobes" to indicate that the processor has passed data to the peripheral.

The variety of arrangements which can be used with this package enable it to be used with a wide range of peripherals.

The circuit configurations possible with the earlier Intel and Motorola peripheral packages described above are typical of the facilities provided for parallel I/O. Later designs provided faster interrupt handling and other features.

A frequent requirement in microprocessor applications is the generation of time delays or the measurement of time intervals. These can be undertaken by program, but it is difficult to perform any other task at the same time. A greater difficulty arises if interrupts are used, since the counting will be suspended during the execution of the interrupt service routine.

In order to cope with these problems special counter-timer packages have been introduced. The Motorola version of this, the MC6840, has three 16-bit counters which may be driven either by the system clock or by an external pulse generator. The counters can be loaded by program and then enabled to count. Normally, they count down to zero and then emit a pulse which can be used either to create an interrupt or to drive some external device. Alternatively, the counter can be set to emit a logical 1 for half of the count and a logical 0 for the remainder, and then to re-load the starting number. Continuing this cycle generates a square wave whose frequency can be controlled by the program.

As microprocessors developed and their prices fell it became economical to use them for simple applications. Users demanded systems which required a minimum number of packages. Products to satisfy this need had to combine the functions of ROM, RAM, I/O Ports, Timers, CPU., etc., in various ways.

One set designed by Intel comprised the 8085 CPU with clock generator circuits and serial input and serial output lines: the 8155 I/O package, which contains 256 bytes of writeable store, a 14-bit counter timer, and three I/O ports; and the 8355 ROM with I/O, which contains 2K bytes of read-only program store and two I/O ports.

A two-chip system, available from Motorola, comprises the MC6802 processor, which incorporates 128 bytes of writeable store, and the MC6846 peripheral chip, which contains 2K bytes of read-only store, 10 I/O lines, and 3 timer lines.

The final stage of this development is the single-chip microprocessor, which incorporates a microprocessor, program and data storage, some I/O facilities and, generally, a timer. A number of these are available in two versions — with programmable store for development work, and with masked ROM for the final production version.

At the same time as single-chip microprocessors were being developed for small-scale applications, semiconductor manufacturers were extending the scope of their products upwards into the areas previously serviced by minicomputers. In order to make this possible, special-purpose peripheral packages were introduced to provide extra facilities. Examples of this include floppy disc controllers — DMA controllers which allow fast access to the main store, thus bypassing the processor — and Interrupt Priority Packages. The increasing use of the IEEE 488 data bus format by instrument manufacturers led to the design of special interface packages which would allow any instrument with a data port to this standard to be connected directly to the microprocessor bus. This is particularly convenient for 8-bit microprocessors, as the IEEE 488 bus provides for 8-bit parallel data transfers. The operational features of this bus are discussed in greater detail in Chapter 7.

Other more complex packages provide interface logic for connecting CRT raster scanned displays to a microprocessor, and for handling high-level communications protocols. Probably the most adaptable interface package is that which contains a basic microprocessor together with 1K bytes of program store, 64 bytes of data store together with two data ports, a counter timer, and clock circuits. Such an interface can remove many subsidiary tasks, such as code conversion, keyboard scanning, and printer control from the central microprocessor and thus increase the time available for more important tasks.

Many applications require the transmission of data to a visual display unit or a printer, and the input of data from a keyboard. In order to reduce the cost of the data link this is usually designed to use only one pair of wires, and the 7 or 8 bits which represent a character are transmitted serially.

The method of synchronizing receiving and transmitting teleprinters was originally chosen to allow operation even though the rotational speeds of the driving shafts of the terminals (regulated only by centrifugal governors) were slightly different. By preceding each group of bits by a start bit and adding two stop bits at the end, synchronism was established by each start bit and needed to last only during the decoding of each character. This mode of transmission is called asynchronous, and is used at data rates of 110, 150, 300, 600, and 1200 bits/sec.

At speeds above 110 bits/sec, mechanical decoding of characters is impractical, and these data rates are used for sending blocks of characters to VDU's, line printers, or other computers. Since mechanical decoding is not used there is no need for asynchronous operation, and a continuous stream of bits can be transmitted, without stop or start bits. The recognition of the character boundaries is made by always sending a special SYNC character, generally twice, before transmitting data.

The receiving unit can be programmed to enter the "Hunt" mode, during which it will examine every adjacent group of 8 bits being received until it finds a SYNC character. It immediately signals this fact to the microprocessor and thereafter it will regard every group of 8 bits received as a character.

In order to synchronize the detection process with the transmitted data the receiver usually derives its clock from the signal transitions of the incoming bit stream. Clearly, once the transmission has begun sending data it must send a continuous stream of bits, so that if it is temporarily short of data SYNC or IDLE characters must be inserted.

The action of a peripheral package for this type of data transmission almost invariably involves shift registers for serial to parallel and parallel to serial conversion, but the additional logic differs for synchronous and asynchronous operation. Thus, many microprocessor manufacturers offer separate interface packages for the two modes of transmission, for example the Motorola MC6850 for asynchronous operation and the MC6852 for synchronous operation. Intel, on the other hand, offers a single universal serial interface-type 8251 which can be programmed for either mode of working.

Where data has to be sent over a telephone circuit a modulation–demodulation process is required, as explained in Chapter 5. Much of the hardware for this can now be made in integrated form but it is generally necessary to add linear components such as filters and amplifiers to form the complete unit. The inclusion of all digital circuits on one chip does, however, simplify the design of the "modem" required at each end of the telephone line. Most microprocessor families now include such a package.

3.19. THE USE OF BALANCED CIRCUITS

Data highways are generally fairly short and for economy they are operated as unbalanced circuits, one line carrying the signal and the other an earth return. If the lines are operated outside the processor cabinet in an electrically noisy environment they may suffer from common-mode interference in which both signal line and earth may have noise voltages induced in them. Under these conditions a differential receiver designed for balanced lines may give more reliable operation, as a typical receiver can tolerate ±3 V of common-mode noise while operating reliably with a 100-mV differential signal. If the received signal is large, attenuators may be fitted between line and receiver to reduce both common-mode interference and signal. Provided that the signal is not reduced below, say, 200 mV the system will function satisfactorily. However, this procedure can only be adopted for a receiver at the end of a highway where the attenuator can be incorporated in the line termination. Elsewhere on the line the use of an attenuator at each receiver would produce unacceptable loading and mismatching of the line.

Fully balanced lines using differential drivers and receivers have distinct advantages over unbalanced lines in noisy situations, but they are usually necessary only for lines which are considerably longer than the normal data highway.

3.20. CONCLUSION

In this chapter the organization of program-controlled and DMA data transfers has been covered in some detail. In the next chapter the mechanism of priority assessment and interrupt handling is examined.

BIBLIOGRAPHY AND REFERENCES

MINICOMPUTER ARCHITECTURE AND DESIGN

BANNISTER, B.R., and WHITEHEAD, D.G. *Fundamentals of Digital Systems,* McGraw-Hill, New York, 1973.

BARTEE. *Digital Computer Fundamentals,* 4th ed., McGraw-Hill, New York, 1977.

CHRISTY, P. Minicomputer Architecture Links Past and Future Generations, *Electronics,* Vol. 51, No. 13, July 6, 1978, p. 98.

DATA GENERAL CORPORATION. *How to use the NOVA Computers,* 1973.

DAVIDOW, W. The Coming Merger of Hardware and Software Design, *Electronics.* Vol. 48, No. 11, May 29, 1975, p. 91.

DIETMAYER, D.L. *Logic Design of Digital Systems,* 2nd ed., Allyn & Bacon, Boston, Mass., 1978.

DIGITAL EQUIPMENT CORPORATION. PDP8/a *Miniprocessor Handbook,* 1975-6.

DIGITAL EQUIPMENT CORPORATION. *PDP11 Processor Handbook,* 1975.

ECKHOUSE, R.H. *Minicomputer Systems Organization and Programming (PDP11),* Prentice-Hall, Englewood Cliffs, N.J., 1975.

FOSTER, C.C. *Computer Architecture,* 2nd ed., Van Nostrand-Reinhold, New York, 1976.

HARRISON, T.J. (Ed.), *Handbook of Industrial Control Computers,* Wiley — Interscience, New York, 1972.

HEALEY, M. *Minicomputers and Microprocessors,* Crane, Russak & Co., New York, 1976.

HEWLETT-PACKARD COMPANY. *A Pocket Guide to Hewlett-Packard Computers,* no date.

HILL, F.J., & PETERSON, G.R. *Digital Systems: Hardware Organization and Design,* Wiley, New York, 1973.

IEEE Special Issue on Minicomputers, Proc. I.E.E.E., Vol. 61, 1973, p. 1524. McGraw-Hill, New York, 1977.

KORN, G.A. *Microprocessors and Small Digital Computers for Engineers & Scientists,* 2nd ed., McGraw-Hill, New York, 1977.

KRAFT, G.D., & TOY, W.N. *Mini/Microcomputer Hardware Design,* Prentice-Hall, Englewood Cliffs, N.J., 1979.

LEWIN, D. *Theory and Design of Digital Computer Systems,* Nelson, London, 1980.

LIPPIATT, A.G. *Architecture of Small Computer Systems,* Prentice-Hall, Englewood Cliffs, N.J., 1978.

PEATMAN, J.B. *The Design of Digital Systems,* McGraw-Hill, New York, 1972.

SANDERSON, P.C. *Minicomputers,* Newnes-Butterworth, London, 1976.

STONE, H.S. (Ed.). *Introduction to Computer Architecture,* S.R.A. Inc., Chicago, Palo Alto, 1975.

SUGARMAN, R. Computers: Our Microuniverse Expands, IEEE *Spectrum,* Vol. 16, No. 1, Jan. 1979, p. 32.

TANENBAUM, A.S. *Structured Computer Organization,* Prentice-Hall, Englewood Cliffs, N.J., 1976.

TOWNSEND, R. *Digital Computer Structure and Design,* Newnes-Butterworth, London, 1975.

MICROPROCESSOR ARCHITECTURE AND SYSTEMS

ALTMAN, L. Microcomputer Families Expand, Part 1: The New Chips, *Electronics,* Vol. 50, No. 25, Dec. 8, 1977, p 89.

ASPINALL, D., & DAGLESS, E.L. *Introduction to Microprocessors,* Pitman Publishing Ltd., London, 197?.

ASPINALL, D. (Ed.). *The Microprocessor and its Application,* Cambridge University Press, Cambridge, 1978.

BOYCE, J.C. *Microprocessor and Microcomputer Basics,* Prentice-Hall, Englewood Cliffs, N.J., 1979.

CIARCIA, S. *The Intel 8086,* BYTE, Nov. 1979, p. 14.

GARLAND, H. *Introduction to Microprocessor System Design,* McGraw-Hill, New York, 1979.

GREENFIELD, S.E. *Architecture of Microcomputers,* Prentice-Hall, Englewood Cliffs, N.J., 1979.

INTEL CORPORATION. *Intel 8080 Microcomputer,* User's Manual, 1975.

INTEL CORPORATION. *Intel 8085 Microcomputer,* User's Manual, 1977.

INTEL CORPORATION. *Intel MCS-48 Single Chip Family of Microcomputers,* 1978.

INTEL CORPORATION. *MCS-86,* User's Manual, 1979.

INTERSIL CORPORATION. *1M6100 12-Bit Microprocessor Handbook,* 1976.

JOHNSON et al. *Digital Circuits and Microcomputers,* Prentice-Hall, Englewood Cliffs, N.J. 1979.

KLINGMANDE, E. *Microprocessor Systems Design,* Prentice-Hall, Englewood, Cliffs, N.J., 1977.

LEAHY, W.F. *Microprocessor Architecture and Programming,* Wiley—Interscience, New York, 1977.

LENK, J.D. *Handbook of Microprocessors, Microcomputers and Minicomputers,* Prentice-Hall, Englewood Cliffs, N.J., 1979.

LEVENTHAL, L.A. *Introduction to Microprocessors,* Prentice-Hall, Englewood Cliffs, N.J., 1978.

LIN, W.C. (Ed.). *Microprocessor Fundamentals and Applications*. IEEE Press, N.Y., 1977.

MOS TECHNOLOGY INC. *Microcomputer Family Hardware Manual,* 1975.

MOSTEK INC. *Z80 Microcomputer Devices Technical Manual,* 1977.

MOTOROLA SEMICONDUCTOR PRODUCTS INC. *M6800 Microcomputer System Design Data,* 1978.

MUSTON, J. Trends in 16-bit architecture, *Microprocessors and Microsystems,* Vol. 3. No. 3, April 1979, p. 129.

OSBOURNE, A. *An Introduction to Microcomputers,* Vols. 1-3, Osbourne and Associates, Berkeley, Calif., 1977.

OGDIN, C.A. *Microprocessor Design,* Prentice-Hall, Englewood Cliffs, N.J., 1978.

PEATMAN, J.B. *Microcomputer-based Design,* McGraw-Hill, New York, 1977.

POSA, J.G. Microprocessors and Microcomputers, *Electronics,* Vol. 25, No. 22, Oct. 25, 1979, p. 144.

SHIMA, M. Two Versions of 16-bit Chip Span Microprocessor, Minicomputer Needs (Z 8000), *Electronics,* Vol. 51, No. 26, Dec. 21, 1978, p. 81.

SHORT, K.L. *Microprocessors and Microprogrammed Logic: An Introduction,* Prentice-Hall, Englewood Cliffs, N.J., 1977.

SOHN, D.W., & VOLK, A. Third-generation Microcomputer Set packs it all into 3 Chips (Intel 8085), *Electronics,* Vol. 50, No. 10, May 12, 1977, p. 109.

SMITH, D.W. Microcomputer can Stand Alone or Join Forces with Other Chips, (Motorola M6801), *Electronics,* Vol. 52, No. 25, Dec. 6, 1979, p. 143.

SOUCEK. *Microprocessors and Microcomputers,* John Wiley & Sons, New York, 1976.

STRITTERE & GUNTERT. A microprocessor Architecture for a Changing World: the Motorola 68000, *IEEE COMPUTER,* Vol. 12, No. 2, Feb. 1979, p. 43.

VERONIS, A.M. *Microprocessor Design and Applications,* Prentice-Hall, Englewood, Cliffs, N.J., 1978.

WEITZMAN. *Distributed Minicomputer and Microcomputer Systems,* Prentice-Hall, Englewood Cliffs, N.J., 1980.

WHITWORTH, I. Review of Microprocessor Architecture, *Microprocessors and Microsystems,* Vol. 3, No. 1, Jan./Feb., 1979, p. 21.

ZILOG INC. *Z80 CPU Technical Manual,* 1977.

ZILOG INC. *Z80000 Technical Manual,* 1979.

Chapter 4

Interrupt Handling

4.1. HARDWARE INTERRUPT RECOGNITION

The procedure for identifying which device is requesting an interrupt was discussed briefly in the previous chapter. The simplest procedure uses a skip chain to test all device flags in turn, with the provision that any device requesting an interrupt will simultaneously set a flag. This process is too slow for some devices, and faster recognition methods have been developed which rely more on hardware and less on software.

A simple example is the interrupt system on the Nova range of computers. The standard interface for these machines has a flag INT REQ (Interrupt Request) which can be set when the device Done flag is set to denote the end of the current operation. If Done is set and the Interrupt Disable flag is clear, the next Request Enable pulse from the processor sets INT REQ which simultaneously sends an Interrupt Request (INTR) pulse back to the processor. When the processor receives INTR it sends out an Interrupt Priority signal INTP which is connected through all of the interfaces which use interrupt facilities. This is a different arrangement from that used on the other data, address, and control lines, which are operated on a "party-line" basis.

The circuit is shown in Fig. 4.1 which illustrates two interfaces connected in cascade in the Interrupt Priority line INTP. The voltage levels are labelled H and L, where L denotes a low potential, less than 0.4 V, and H a high potential, greater than 2.2 V. Within the CPU and interface, L denotes logical 0 and H logical 1, but the converse holds on most of the I/O bus data and control lines in order to obtain a wired-OR arrangement.

When neither device is requesting an interrupt both INT REQ $\bar{Q}$ lines are high, as both bistables are cleared ($Q = 0, \bar{Q} = 1$). The $\overline{\text{INTP}}$ signal from the I/O bus is then transmitted through the network to appear at the same level at the output. If, however, the first device is requesting an interrupt, the low output of the first NAND gate changes to high, so changing DEV2 ACK to low, and the $\overline{\text{INTP}}$ output to high. Thus neither device 2 interface nor any other interface connected to $\overline{\text{INTP}}$ out will receive DEV ACK. This goes to device 1 alone, which thus has priority over all other devices by virtue of its position on the INTP line. In a similar manner, if device 1 is not requesting an interrupt the device doing so which is nearest to the processor will receive DEV ACK and prevent it propagating further.

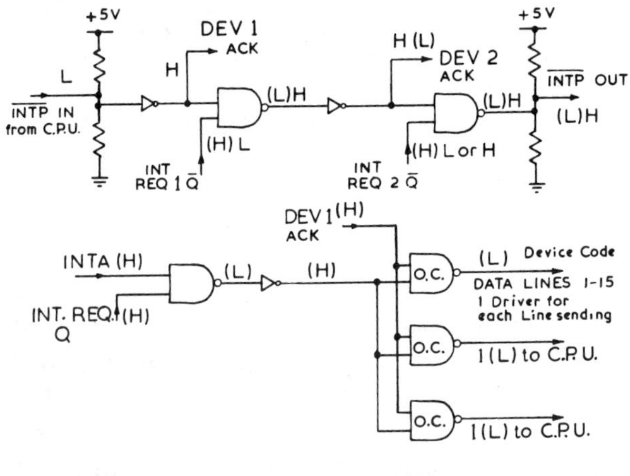

Figure 4.1. Logic for INTP line and for identifying device by INTA instruction: Nova series

When an interrupt occurs the user may identify the calling device by a conventional skip chain, or, more rapidly, by using the instruction INTA N. This causes the device which is receiving the DEV ACK signal to send its device code along data lines 10-15 to be loaded by the processor into accumulator N. The program must then use this unique code to branch to the appropriate device-handling routine. This normally requires an indirectly addressed jump since the first page of the store is much too small to accommodate all of the device-handling routines.

One method is to use the same basic jump instruction for all devices, say, JMP@500 (on this machine @ denotes indirect addressing). The program, after the INTA instruction, then adds the device code to the address in the jump instruction and executes the modified instruction. This can be done by using an indirect indexed jump instruction in which the device code is loaded into the accumulator used for indexing.

Thus if the Interrupt Acknowledge instruction was INTA 2, using AC2, the indexed indirect jump would be of the form JMP @ 200, 2. This uses location 200 + N for the effective address, where N is the device code. Thus the store above location 200 must contain a list of starting addresses for the various device-handling routines; in our example location 200 + N must contain the starting address of the routine to service the device with device code N.

This procedure requires some programming, but it is much quicker than even a short skip chain, and furthermore the time needed to reach the first instruction of the handling routine is independent of the number of devices connected to the I/O bus. This is a major disadvantage of the skip-chain method; the delay in attending to the devices at the bottom of the chain increases as the number of devices increases.

4.2. ENABLING AND DISABLING INTERRUPTS

In the Nova range of computers DMA access via the data channels is the usual arrangement for the fast data rates, and such transfers take precedence over I/O bus interrupts. Apart from this the priority of device interfaces is set by their order in the skip chain or on the INTP line.

A further control over interrupts is, however, available because each interface has an ''Interrupt Disable'' flag. When this is set the device cannot energize the interrupt line and thus cannot cause an interrupt. The program can set or clear the Interrupt Disable flags of all interfaces by using the ''Mask Output'' instruction MSKO.

Each Interrupt Disable flag is connected via a gate to one of the data lines. When the MSKO instruction is executed a word in one of the accumulators is sent to the data lines, and the I/O line MSKO is energized.

This is used to gate a bit from one of the data lines to each Interrupt Disable flag. The restriction here is that only 16 different groups of interfaces may be independently controlled, but this is sufficient for nearly all installations. By this means a single program instruction can cause any required combination of devices to be enabled or disabled as regards interrupts. Thus each device-handling routine can specify which devices can interrupt it and which cannot.

As is usual, the start of any interrupt recognition by the processor automatically disables all interrupts. The program can then enable all, some, or none of the device interrupts during the service routine or wait until control has been returned to the main program before restoring interrupts.

4.3. HARDWARE SCANNING OF INTERRUPTS

One method of speeding the search for the highest priority device requiring an interrupt is to replace some of the software of the skip chain by hardware. It is not convenient to change to a complete hardware system, but the time-consuming search progress can be greatly expedited if each device requiring an interrupt has a separate interrupt line which leads to the processor. A high-speed counter connected to a decoder provides a series of signals in sequence, each of which gates one of the interrupt lines to an interrupt request bistable via a multiway OR gate. The first interrupt line encountered which is energized sets the bistable which stops the counter. The processor can then interrogate the counter to determine which device called for the interrupt, and use its identification code as a pointer to the service routine. When the processor has finished the routine it can return to the previous program, clear the counter, reset the request bistable, and enable the interrupt recognition logic again.

The next scan starts again with device 1 so that some measure of priority can be provided by the order in which interrupt lines are connected to the search hardware. However, once a service routine has started, no higher-priority device can cause a further interrupt until the current service routine has finished. This method requires considerably more hardware than the skip-chain method, but the counter can search down the interrupt lines 50-100 times faster than the several microseconds per device needed to execute the test-flag and skip instructions in a skip chain.

4.4. MULTILEVEL PRIORITY CONTROL

A more responsive system is obtained if only a limited number of priority-request lines are used and hardware is used to identify the highest-priority line which is requesting attention. This automatically inhibits all requests of lower priority and only the highest-priority request is passed to the processor. Two logical networks for determining priority are shown in Fig. 4.2. In both arrangements the occurrence of a 1 on any line inhibits a 1 on any line of lower priority.

The first circuit is faster in operation since the logic delay from input to output is only that of an inverter followed by an AND gate. However, if there are N lines, the lowest-priority line needs an N-way gate. When $N > 6$ or 8, it is necessary to use more than one gate, thus increasing the delay.

The second circuit, on the other hand, is simpler to implement since only two input gates are needed, but the lowest-priority line must wait for $(N - 1)$ AND-gate delays plus an inverter delay if the top-priority line returns to zero and no other intermediate line is energized. Priority

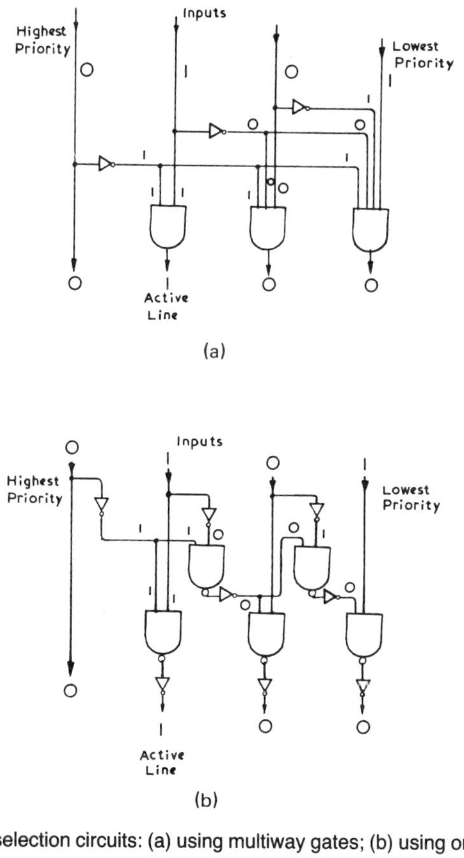

Figure 4.2. Priority selection circuits: (a) using multiway gates; (b) using only two input gates

schemes are so widely used in modern computers than an eight-line priority-selection network is now available in integrated-circuit form.

The networks shown are all that are required for many systems, but some mechanism is required for storing the interrupts of lower priority than that which is being handled so that they may be serviced in due course. With the simple circuits of Fig. 4.2 this storage must be built into the device interface. Alternative priority-assessment schemes are used in which a flag is set for each interrupt line to denote a waiting request. This minimizes storage needs somewhat, since a single flag serves for all interfaces connected to any one line, in place of a flag in each interface.

Many computers with provision for a number of interrupt lines also allow several devices to be connected to each line, with a request-granted signal being transmitted through each in turn. The requesting device which is nearest to the processor will then see the granted signal first and prevent any more remote device from using it. The general arrangement is similar to that shown for the Nova computer series in Fig. 4.1. Any device on the line which is not requesting an interrupt transmits the Interrupt Accepted pulse on to the next interface, but the first device requesting an interrupt traps the signal and prevents it going further.

An important practical matter arises with such circuits. All other I/O bus lines are operated on a ''party-line'' basis, with the interfaces teed to whichever lines are required. Thus for maintenance or fault finding no difficulty should arise if all interfaces are disconnected from the bus except the one under investigation. The Interrupt Accepted line, however, is taken in and out of all interfaces, so that if these are unplugged a connection must be made between the Interrupt Accepted input and output on the computer bus. If this connection is omitted no interface beyond that which is disconnected will be able to accept an interrupt.

4.5. DEVICE IDENTIFICATION

The processing of an interrupt in an on-line system with many devices connected to it can be divided into several stages. The first of these is the storage of the current state of the background program being executed when the interrupt occurs. This is often confined to the storage in some location of the program-counter contents. Generally the device-handling or service routine will use the accumulator and perhaps other processor registers, and the contents of these will also need saving. The most economical procedure is to allow the program to save only those registers whose contents are disturbed by the routine. However, in order to simplify the programmers' task some computers provide automatic storage of all registers by hardware before handing over control to the service routine. A single instruction suffices to restore the registers at the end of the routine.

Having saved at least the contents of the program counter, the next task is to assess priority so that an interrupt will be granted to only one device. This can be arranged by program, by the physical position of the device on a single priority line, or by the logic circuits discussed in the previous section for a multiple-level interrupt system. The skip-chain method automatically identifies the highest-priority device by testing each flag in turn, but the other two methods merely ensure that only the highest-priority device is granted an interrupt. This resolves any conflict arising from multiple requests for an interrupt, but some additional mechanism is required to allow the processor to identify to which device the interrupt has been granted. This normally involves the device sending a pre-wired code unique to the particular interface along the bus.

In some systems the device code assigned to the device interface for program-controlled transfers is used as an identifier. For example, in the Nova range of machines the device-selection code is returned to the processor along data lines 10-15 and is then loaded into one of the accumulators specified by the program. In some other machines a separate set of address lines is used for transmitting the identification. When the device-select code has been received by the processor, it can be used to transfer control to a device-service routine. This usually involves an indirect jump to allow the service routine to be loaded beyond the first page of the store. Also, unless some extra arithmetic operation is performed on the device code, a number of devices will have adjacent select codes, and there is thus room for only one instruction per device. This instruction is either a jump to the start of the service routine which is further down the store, or the address of the first instruction of the service routine, to permit an indirectly addressed jump to reach this starting instruction. These techniques need only 6-8 bits in the device code to reach the word in the first store page which points to the service routine. If 14-16 bits can be used to specify an address, the process can be shortened a little, since for example 14 bits allow the interrupt to specify any one of 16 K locations. In this case the interface is not restricted to a location in page 0, and the address sent by the device interface can be gated directly into the store address register. The processor can then be put into the fetch mode in which it executes the instruction found in the location specified. This can be the first instruction of the service routine. This arrangement needs more logic at both processor and interface, but it shortens the process of transferring to the service routine by one indirect jump.

4.6. MULTIPLE INTERRUPTS

The procedure previously described suffices to select the highest-priority interrupt, to identify it rapidly, and to hand control over to the service routine. All interrupts are automatically inhibited as soon as an interrupt is granted and cannot be restored until the service routine has been completed and control has been returned to the original program. This is an unsatisfactory situation since a fast device of high priority may be locked out and unable to gain service while a slow device of lower priority is being serviced. Ideally any request from a high-priority device should be granted if the device currently being serviced has lower priority.

The procedure described cannot satisfy this requirement directly since any second interrupt granted while a first interrupt is being serviced will overwrite the return address planted in location 0000 and the first interrupt will be unable to return to the original program. In order to avoid this difficulty it is necessary to store each return address in a separate location known to the service program, so that no other device routine can destroy the return link.

One method of combining this with the hardware switch of control to a service routine is to allocate two store locations to each device interface. Thus, for example, if the first 20 locations in the store are reserved for other information, device code N could be allocated locations $2N + 20$ and $2N + 21$. The first location could be used to store the contents of the program counter to provide a return link, and the second location to store a pointer to the first instruction of the service routine.

Another method of storing return addresses and the contents of other active registers is to use what is called a "stack" or last-in-first-out store. This is a type of store in which data can be entered and removed only via the top of the stack. Thus it is essentially a zero-address store in which the only two instructions are "Push," or load another item on the top of the store, and "Pop," or remove an item from the top of the store. This ordered loading and unloading is exactly what is required for return addresses and register contents when programs are interrupted.

This facility is available on the PDP11 computer, in which the current state of the processor is stored in a status register. The servicing of an interrupt starts with the storage of the program-counter contents and the current status word on the top of the stack. The processor then uses the address transmitted by the interrupting device to access two storage locations associated with the device. The first contains the starting address of the service routine which is sent to the program counter. The second location contains the new status word which is loaded into the status register. The processor then enters the Fetch mode and starts executing the service routine. This routine will store as many of the internal register contents as required. At the end of the service routine a special "Return from Interrupt" instruction pops the top two words from the stack, thus restoring the program counter and processor status word for the previous program. The processor can then resume execution of this program from the point at which it was interrupted.

The use of a stack in this manner allows interrupts to be "nested" to a degree limited only by the space available for the stack. This means that a higher-priority device can interrupt service of a lower-priority device, and in turn be interrupted by a device of yet higher priority, and so on. The resulting handling of interrupts is very efficient in that the highest-priority device requesting attention is always either being serviced or just about to be serviced. This method of using hardware to point to the service-routine starting address is often called "vectoring," and the new program counter and processor status word are called the "interrupt vector."

The organization of the stack has been described in terms of a fixed access point at the top of the stack, with the implication that each time a new word is stored all lower words are pushed one place down the store. Conversely, when a word is popped from the top of the stack, all remaining words are also moved one place up the store.

In practice no readily available storage system lends itself to this mode of operation. The normal store arrangement allows any word identified by the contents of the store address register to be read or written to. Each operation on a particular location takes one store cycle; thus moving a word one place down the store takes two store cycles. If there are 20 words in the stack, making room at the top for an extra word takes 40 store cycles, far too long for rapid interrupt handling. The solution to this problem is to leave all existing words in their present places, but to allow the top of the stack to move up and down as the stack expands or contracts. This procedure requires only one read or write operation to pop a word off the stack or push it on, and thus introduces only a small delay in interrupt handling. It does, however, require an extra register called a "stack pointer" which always contains the address of the top word in the stack. Thus a word popped from the stack is read from the stack-pointer address, and a word pushed onto the stack is written into the next location above the stack-pointer address. The stack pointer is then decremented or incremented ready for the next operation. When executing the pop or push instructions the change in the stack-pointer contents is made automatically by the processor. It is, however, useful to have the stack pointer accessible to the programmer. The advantage of this is that any saving of register contents required by a service routine can be done by using the stack instead of any other store locations. This procedure ensures that the contents cannot be overwritten by any other routine, and will be available for restoring at the end of the routine before returning to the previous program. The programmer is required to make the appropriate adjustment to the stack pointer each time a word is popped or pushed on to the stack.

4.7. INTERRUPT HANDLING ON THE PDP11

The PDP11 family of minicomputers employs a data, address, and control bus — the Unibus — along which all data transfers flow and to which all units of the computer are connected. Normally the processor controls the activities of the bus, acting as Bus Master and exchanging data with either a store module or a peripheral interface acting as slave.

Any peripheral device may request control over the bus, either for performing a DMA data transfer, or for creating an interrupt and forcing the processor to execute a service routine.

There are at least four separate bus request lines of increasing priority (BR4–BR7), each with its corresponding bus grant line (BG4–BG7); large machines in the range have up to 8 lines. The priority of any device depends upon the request and grant lines to which it is connected, and also on its position along the line. The bus grant signal from the processor is connected daisy-chain fashion through each interface so that, if more than one device at a given level is requesting bus mastership, the device nearest to the processor can divert the bus grant signal to ensure that no device farther down the line can create a conflict. The action is similar to that of the daisy-chained interrupt acknowledge (INTA) line used with the Nova range of minicomputers. The PDP11, however, has at least four bus request lines in addition to the top priority non-processor request (NPR) line used for DMA transfers. It thus requires an arbitration unit to resolve any conflict between different bus request lines. This unit determines which of the active BR lines has the highest priority and issues a bus grant signal only at this level. A further control, which the writer of each program segment can exert, is to assign the priority level of the processor by loading this into bits 5, 6, and 7 of the processor status word. Before issuing a bus grant signal, the arbitration unit checks the processor status and issues a grant only if the processor status is less than that of the requesting peripheral. By this means each program segment can prescribe which peripherals can interrupt it.

Having obtained mastership of the bus, a peripheral can create an interrupt, that is, cause an interrupt vector to be loaded and so cause the processor to begin execution of its service routine. Every device has two storage locations assigned to it, the first containing the starting address of the interrupt service routine, and the next word containing the new processor status word. The address of the first location is wired into the device interface and sent to the processor as the interrupt vector.

For example, the console terminal keyboard is assigned the vector address 060. Thus if the keyboard service routine starts in location 1200, and should be allocated priority level 4, the two vector locations must be loaded by an initializing program as follows:

LOCATION	TOTAL	CONTENTS
060	1200	Address of service routine
062	0200	sets priority level 4

Since the keyboard interface is normally wired to level 4 (BR4), the service routine will have greater priority than the keyboard or any other level 4 device.

The processor, when accepting the interrupt, puts the previous contents of the program counter and the processor status register onto the stack before starting on the service routine. A single instruction, return from interrupt (RTI), at the end of the routine will reverse the stacking operation and cause the processor to resume execution of the interrupted program.

The PDP11 is an asynchronous machine so that each signal after the first bus request can only be sent after the previous signal has been received. The sequence of operations is shown in Fig. 4.3, in which all lines are initially shown at logic 0 level, a logic 1 being shown by an upward shift in the line. The arrows show the dependence of the signals; the action at the head of the arrow is initiated by the action at the beginning of the arrow.

The sequence is for a successful acquisition of the bus followed by an interrupt, the individual steps being as follows:

(1) Bus Request BR5 generated by interface, received by arbitration unit.
(2) Bus grant BG5 received by interface.
(3) Select acknowledge (SACK) sent by interface.
(4) BR5 terminated by interface, received by arbitration unit.

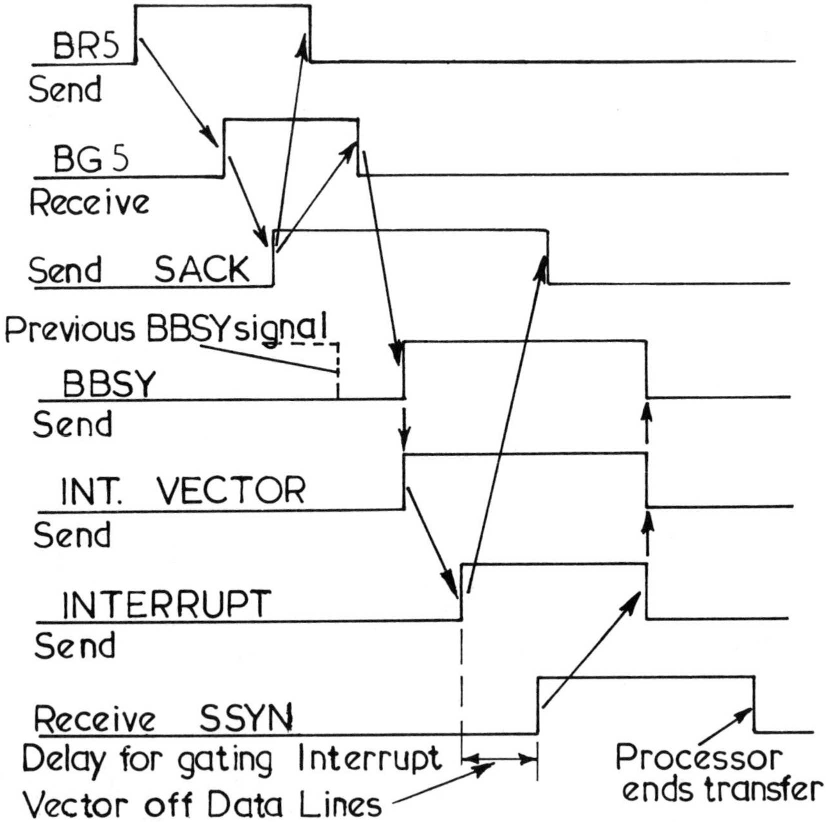

Figure 4.3. Signals at interface during PDP11 interrupt servicing

(5) Arbitration unit end BG5, received by interface.

(6) Interface waits until previous Bus Busy (BBSY) signal disappears, then issues its own BBSY, so asserting its mastership of the bus.

(7) Interface then sends its interrupt vector on the data lines (060 for the console keyboard described above), and a little later sends INTR to request an interrupt.

(8) Interface ends SACK.

(9) Processor waits about 75 ns after receiving INTR, and then gates the interrupt vector off the data lines.

(10) To signify its acceptance of the interrupt vector the processor issues Slave Synch (SSYN).

(11) Interface takes the receipt of SSYN as an indication that the transaction is over, and ends INTR, BBSY, and removes the interrupt vector from the data lines.

(12) Processor detects the end of INTR and ends SSYN, so concluding its dialogue with the interface. It then reads the starting address of the interrupt service routine from the store and the new processor status word (having stacked the previous status word and program counter contents) and starts the service routine.

The signals in Fig. 4.3 are intended to indicate only the transitions between logic levels, not the electrical waveforms. The signals tend to be rather confusing since some signals use negative logic and others positive logic.

The action described above can begin only when the current instruction has ended, since it needs action by the processor. The top priority NPR action, on the other hand, requires only bus mastership and so can occur part way through an instruction at any time that the processor relinquishes bus mastership; for example, to perform an internal arithmetic or logical operation. The action is similar to direct memory access (DMA) in earlier computers.

4.8. INTERRUPT MASKING

The flexibility of the interrupt handling is enhanced if each service routine can stipulate which devices may interrupt it and which may not.

Thus is usually arranged by using an Interrupt Enable bistable at each interface which can be set or cleared by program. A convenient method of loading the bistable is to connect each one via a gate to the data lines. Then a single instruction transfers a word from a register in the processor out to the data lines and each bit sets or clears one or a group of the device Interrupt Enable bistables. The control word which determines the state of the bistables is called a "mask."

Each service routine may require its own mask which it issues at the start of the routine before turning on the interrupt facility. As part of the register-saving process for each routine which is interrupted, the current mask may need saving (along with other registers) before starting processing in the service routine and restoring (along with the processor registers) before leaving the routine.

In some priority systems which do not have facilities for masking interrupts a similar but less flexible kind of masking can be achieved by allowing each routine to set its own priority level. Thus a low-priority routine, which during a certain phase must not be interrupted by a real-time activity, may raise its priority to exceed that of the activity during the critical phase. Since a device cannot interrupt a process of higher priority this ensures that the critical phase will not be disturbed. Since the process cannot alter the priority of any other device this arrangement is less comprehensive in scope than the method using interrupt masks.

The mask-control procedure described above is based upon the use of Interrupt Enable bistables in each interface. An alternative arrangement is to use an Interrupt-Handling module which may be plugged into the processor frame. This is connected to all device interfaces which require interrupt servicing and has the advantage of collecting all interrupt logic and storage into one module. Some interrupt-handling activities, such as loading a new mask, are thereby simplifed.

4.9. INTERRUPT HANDLING WITH MICROPROCESSORS

A physical limit imposed on the designer of all microprocessors is the restricted number of pins available to connect to external devices. This restriction, given the use of 16 address lines and 8 data lines, effectively limits the number of control lines and so the number of separate interrupt lines. For this reason early microprocessors, such as the Intel 8080, had only a single interrupt line. In order to avoid the delay which would occur in identifying the source of the interrupt by means of a skip chain, a limited form of hardware vectoring was provided.

Later microprocessors generally included several interrupt lines to simplify the task of arbitrating between several interrupts occurring at the same time.

The first actions of the 8080 in response to an interrupt request are similar to those of a minicomputer. If the interrupt line is enabled, the processor begins its response, when the current instruction has been executed, by generating the interrupt acknowledge (INTA) status bit. During the next clock cycle the data bus input signal (DBIN) appears and indicates to the peripheral interface that vector information is required. The vectoring is somewhat different from that of conventional computers, which normally expect an address. For the 8080 the interface replies by gating a restart (RST) instruction on to the data lines. This is a single-byte instruction (and so it is obeyed quickly) constructed in the format of a jump to subroutine. The destination of the jump is indicated by bits 3, 4, and 5. The values 0–7 in these three bit positions cause the processor to jump to the corresponding locations 0, 8, 10, 18, 20, 28, 30, or 38 (hexadecimal). All other bits of the RST instructions are 1's. Thus if bits 3, 4, and 5 contain the value 5, the binary instruction code will be 11 101 111, and the processor will jump to location 28, the sixth address in the list (the first address corresponds to the value zero).

Once the processor has received the RST instruction it behaves as it would for a subroutine call, that is, it places the contents of the program counter on the stack, updates the stack pointer, and then branches to the address specified in the RST instruction. If say, only, two devices requiring interrupts are connected to the processor, the first can be allocated 00 as the vector address and the second 38. This gives just over 50 (decimal) bytes of program space before the first interrupt service routine needs to jump over the second address location; this may suffice for a simple data transfer program. The second device may, of course, use any available space above the location 38 (hexadecimal).

Where several devices are connected to the interrupt line there is usually insufficient room below location 38 to hold all of the service routines required. The usual procedure then is to load into each vector location only a jump instruction; this directs the processor to the main service routine which is loaded further up the store. Thus, for example, locations 00, 01, and 02 might contain the code:

LOCATION	CODE	MEANING
00	C3	Jump to
01	00	location 0100 (hex.)
02	01	

This would cause the processor to execute a service routine starting at location 0100. The second device could set up the vector address 08; the corresponding stored instruction would be:

LOCATION	CODE	MEANING
08	C3	Jump to
09	00	location 0200 (hex.)
0A	02	

This store mapping would provide 100 (hex.) (= 256 decimal) locations for the service routine for the first device. The use of a "jump" instruction rather than a "call subroutine" ensures that the return link is saved on the top of the stack, and an RET (return) instruction pulls the link off the stack and returns control to the main program at the end of the routine. As with minicomputers, to ensure that no other interrupt can inadvertently interfere with the service routine, the acceptance of an interrupt automatically clears the interrupt enable flag inside the processor and prevents further interrupts.

The programmer has two instructions: EI, enable interrupt, and DI, disable interrupt, which can be used to specify whether interrupts are allowed or not. Generally the EI instruction is given after the initializing section of the main program and at the end of each service routine. It can, however, be given earlier in a service routine after any necessary register contents have been saved, should a high-priority device be required to interrupt the routine servicing a lower-priority device.

The 8080 is similar to a number of minicomputers in that it saves only the program counter on the stack when accepting an interrupt. Any further registers which are used by the service routine must be saved and restored by that routine. The most convenient method is to put them on the stack; a single instruction will put the contents of two 8-bit registers on the stack, or pop them off it.

The 8 different vector addresses are generally adequate to handle the interrupts for most 8080 applications, but for larger systems a Priority Interrupt Control package is available. This will accept up to 8 interrupt request signals, determine which has highest priority, and then interrupt the processor, giving it the appropriate vector address. Several packages can be cascaded to handle up to 40 separate interrupts.

Microprocessors designed after the Intel 8080 generally provided more interrupt facilities; for example the Motorola M6800 has, in addition to the maskable interrupt line ($\overline{IRQ}$), a non-maskable interrupt line ($\overline{NMI}$) which is intended for fast devices. This processor also has an interrupt which can be invoked by a program instruction — Software Interrupt (SWI). The last type of interrupt is the usual restart interrupt which is created by taking the $\overline{Reset}$ pin from +5V to earth immediately after the power is applied, and holding it at earth for a few milliseconds.

The M6800 has a simple form of fixed vectoring built into the processor by which the first instruction of the service routine is read from one pair of the following sets of storage locations:

TYPE OF INTERRUPT	**STARTING ADDRESS IN**	
Restart $\overline{Reset}$	FFFE	FFFF
Non-Maskable Interrupt $\overline{NMI}$	FFFC	FFFD
Softwave Interrupt	FFFA	FFFB
Interrupt Request $\overline{IRQ}$	FFF8	FFF9

To simplify the programmer's task the M6800 automatically saves the contents of all processor registers (except that of the stack pointer) on the stack immediately after accepting an interrupt. This involves 7 bytes in all, namely:

Accumulator A
Accumulator B
Program Counter (2 bytes)
Index Register (2 bytes)
Condition Code Register

The complete interrupt time (including other processor action) before starting the service routine is 12 cycles from the end of the instruction being executed. In some applications this delay is an embarrassment and can be reduced by using the Wait Instruction (WAI). This starts the interrupt procedure by saving all processor registers, then suspends the processor activity until either type of hardware interrupt occurs (interrupt request or non-maskable interrupt). The rest of the interrupt procedure is then executed, but as the stacking operation has already been completed only 4 further cycles are required.

The wait instruction can be given only if there is no further processor activity required until an interrupt occurs, but this situation is often found in interrupt-driven on-line systems.

At the end of the interrupt service routine a single Return from Interrupt (RTI) instruction will return the 7 bytes from the stack to the processor registers and reset the stack pointer.

The restart interrupt is a little different from the others in that it does not save the register contents, as these are entirely random immediately after switching on power. A priority interrupt controller, available as a separate package, accepts 8 interrupt request lines and, in the event of conflict, recognizes the active line which has the highest priority. This priority is then compared with the priority assigned to the current process held in a programmable mask location register. If the interrupt priority is higher than that of the current process the interrupt is signalled to the IRQ line of the processor and the vector address is obtained from an internal vector look-up table.

Interrupt controller packages can be cascaded to handle more than 8 interrupts up to a total of 64 interrupts.

Interrupts on the M6800 are normally created by energizing a control line — e.g., CA1 — on a peripheral interface adaptor. Each of the two ports on the PIA has its own interrupt request line, IRQA and IRQB. These are generally both connected to the IRQ line, working on a party-line basis. However, where an interrupt controller is used, each port may have its interrupt line connected to a separate input and be assigned different priorities.

Two other developments in microprocessor interrupt handling are worth noting; the use of multiple interrupt lines and the provision of duplicate registers. The first of these was included in the features of the 8085, a later member of the Intel 8080 family. The 8085 is program compatible with the 8080 but has a few more instructions to handle its additional facilities, which include serial input and serial output lines and more control lines. The 8085 is mounted in the same 40-pin package as the 8080, the extra lines being obtained by multiplexing the lower 8 address bits and the data bits on the same 8 lines. This modification enables 5 control lines to be assigned to interrupts. The lowest-priority line is the INT Line, which acts in exactly the same manner in the 8080 and requires a restart instruction from the interrupting device to specify one of 8 possible vector addresses. Above the INT line are three higher-priority lines which are maskable, RST5.5, RST6.5, and RST7.5, and, highest of all, the TRAP line. Each of these has a single fixed vector address. As with the 8080, a priority interrupt package is available which accepts 8 input lines and can be cascaded to handle up to 64 separate interrupt inputs.

Users of minicomputers in complex on-line applications demand powerful processors and fast interrupt servicing. The former need is usually met by a multiple register architecture, but this inevitably involves many store cycles to save all the registers after entering an interrupt service routine, and before any useful data manipulation can be performed. Thus, there is clearly a conflict between the multiplicity of registers and the need for fast interrupt servicing. The way out of this impasse is to provide two or more sets of processor registers. The main program can then use the primary register set and an interrupt can use another set of registers, so avoiding the need to save and restore registers. This facility is provided in a few minicomputers; a version of it is incorporated in the Zilog Z80 microprocessor. This is an 8-bit device developed from the Intel 8080. It executes all of the 8080 instructions, using the same machine code, and has many other instructions, some 4 bytes in length, in order to handle its extra facilities. It can also run at double the speed of the 8080 and is second sourced by several manufacturers.

The Z80, like the Motorola M6800, has both a non-maskable interrupt line $\overline{\text{NMI}}$ and a maskable interrupt line $\overline{\text{INT}}$. The $\overline{\text{INT}}$ line can be operated in exactly the same manner as in the 8080 (Mode 0) but can also be programmed to operate in two other modes. Mode 1 causes the processor to execute a restart to location 0038 (hex.) but does not require the restart instruction to be provided by the peripheral device.

Mode 2 provides a powerful interrupt response since it enables the processor to execute an indirect call to any storage location on receipt of a single byte from the peripheral. This is done by maintaining a table of 16-bit starting addresses at a convenient place in the store. When executing an interrupt service routine the processor must assemble a pointer to a particular address in the table. The upper 8 bits of the pointer are provided by the I register within the processor, which must be loaded as part of the initializing routine. The lower 8 bits of the pointer are provided by the peripheral device and, if a standard PIO peripheral package is used, they will have been loaded initially into the PIO vector register.

When responding to an interrupt in this mode, the processor pushes the program counter onto the stack, assembles the pointer, obtains the starting address from the table, and performs a jump to this address. The Z80 peripheral packages all include a daisy-chained line for interrupt acknowledgment; this ensures that only the device nearest the processor can emit the table address byte if more than one device is requesting an interrupt.

Unlike the M6800, this processor saves only the program counter; any other registers needed must be saved by the programmer. The simplest way to do this, and by far the quickest, is to swap the contents into the duplicate register set. One exchange instruction — EX AF AF′ — interchanges the contents of the accumulator and the flag or condition code registers. This is the minimum saving needed to perform any input or output. Usually other registers will be needed by the interrupt service routine, and for this a second exchange instruction, EXX, exchanges the contents of the 6 general purpose registers B, C, D, E, H, and L. By using both of these instructions at the beginning and end of an interrupt-service routine all processor registers can be saved and restored much more quickly than if they were held in some storage external to the processor. It is, of course, not possible to nest interrupts using this feature without losing data or using the stack.

4.10. MULTIPLE REGISTER COMPUTERS

Early minicomputers used only one computational register, the accumulator. Thus, saving the contents of the accumulator prior to the computing phase of service routine was a simple and rapid operation. In modern machines it is often regarded as a sign of advanced design to incorporate multiple processor registers, four, eight, or more in number.

Although arithmetic processes and some data-moving operations are thereby speeded up, a penalty is incurred at each interrupt when the contents of the central processor registers are saved before the service routine can use them. An eight-register computer requires, say, 8 μs to store registers compared with 1 μs for a single-register machine. This extra time penalty tends to nullify the speed advantage of hardware vectoring compared with the skip-chain method of interrupt identification used on earlier machines.

If rapid interrupt handling is an important requirement for a particular computer application, one rather expensive method of ensuring this is to use multiple registers. This means building into the computer several sets of central processor registers. Then, when an interrupt occurs, the processor can switch over to a second set of registers for dealing with the interrupting process, leaving the first set loaded with the numbers and program state corresponding to the original interrupted process. There is no need to store any register contents in the main store, so that transfer of control to the new service routine can be very rapid.

If the new process is itself interrupted in its turn, a further set of registers is required for maximum speed of response. Usually four sets of registers suffice; on the rare occasions when interrupts are nested to a greater depth than four the extra delay involved in saving registers in the main store can normally be accepted.

The penalty of the multiple-register scheme is the additional cost of the registers and the considerable amount of logic needed in essence to multiplex several sets of registers to the same processor.

4.11. CONCLUSION

Having considered the problem of connecting devices to a computer through a relatively short link along an I/O bus, we next consider the rather different situation when the device is much further from the computer, and the different methods of data transmission which this situation may require.

BIBLIOGRAPHY AND REFERENCES

BOYCE, J.C. *Microprocessor and Microcomputer Basics,* Prentice-Hall, Englewood Cliffs, N.J., 1979.

DATA GENERAL CORPORATION. *How to Use the NOVA Computers,* 1973.

DIGITAL EQUIPMENT CORPORATION. *PDP8/a Miniprocessor Handbook,* 1975-6.

DIGITAL EQUIPMENT CORPORATION. PDP11 Processor Handbook and PDP11 Peripherals Handbook, 1975.

ECKHOUSE, R.H. *Minicomputer Systems Organization and Programming (PDP11),* Prentice-Hall, Englewood Cliffs, N.J., 1975.

INTEL CORPORATION. User's Manuals, *8080 Microcomputer,* 1975, and *8085 Microcomputer,* 1977.
INTERSIL CORPORATION. *IM6100 12-bit Microprocessor Handbook,* 1976.
KRAFT, G.D., and TOY, W.N. *Mini/microcomputer Hardware Design,* Prentice-Hall, Englewood Cliffs, N.J., 1979.
LESEA, A., and ZAKS, R. *Microprocessor Interfacing Techniques,* SYBEX, Berkeley, Calif., 1977.
MOTOROLA SEMICONDUCTOR PRODUCTS INC. *M6800 Microcomputer System Design Data,* 1978.
VAN GELDER, M.K., and ENGLAND, A.W. A Primer on Priority Interrupt Systems, *Control Eng.,* Vol. 16, No. 3, p. 101, March 1969.
ZILOG INC. *Z80 CPU Technical Manual,* 1979.

Chapter 5

Communication Circuits and Data Links

5.1. PROBLEMS ARISING IN EXTENDED DATA LINKS

The connections between processor and peripheral devices discussed in previous chapters were along short input-output buses connected directly to the processor logic circuits. Thus the logic levels and circuit configuration (unbalanced, i.e., having one signal line and a common earth return) were chosen by the designer for maximum compatibility with the processor logic. In order to obtain maximum speed of response the data lines are operated in the parallel mode, one line per bit. These electrical conditions are satisfactory for the 10-50-ft bus lengths permitted on most on-line computing configurations. Frequently, however, data must be gathered from or distributed to devices situated much further from the computers. In this situation some interface is required on the I/O bus with an extended link to the remote peripheral. The link may be only a few hundred feet long, or may extend many thousands of miles.

In view of the extreme range of circuit length, we cannot expect the same voltage levels and signaling techniques to be suitable in all cases. Some of the questions which the designer must answer are as follows.

(a) Should the data be transmitted in serial or parallel mode?

(b) Should the circuit be balanced or unbalanced?

(c) Should direct baseband transmission be used, or is some modulation process required?

(d) What limitations do the line characteristics place upon signaling speed?

(e) What statutory restrictions are imposed on the types and availability of data circuits?

Some of the above questions can be given purely technical answers. For others, several methods are technically acceptable but cost is generally the deciding factor. The first type of link to be considered is a relatively short one of perhaps a few hundred feet.

5.2. SHORT LINKS

Links of a few hundred feet are often required for peripheral devices used in the same building as the computer. For such distances the cost of lines for parallel-mode transmission is not excessive, and this method allows a faster data rate and a simpler interface than serial transmission. However, the unbalanced low-level circuits used within computers for logic connections are not satisfactory for these longer circuits as they are too susceptible to noise voltages.

Any environment which has sufficient plant or process activity to warrant on-line computing is likely to use some considerable amount of electrical power, and the switching transients from the power circuits may induce considerable noise voltages into the data circuits. The two main methods of minimizing the effects of noise are to alter the circuit so as to diminish interference, and to increase the signal level to improve the ratio of signal to noise.

The major problem with unbalanced circuits is that the common-earth return line may have noise voltages induced in it. These then appear in each individual circuit. Furthermore, the two earths at each end of the link may have small differences of potential between them, giving rise again to circuit noise. The situation can be much improved by changing to a balanced-circuit configuration such as a twisted pair. The two lines of the circuit are physically close and little or no magnetic flux can link one wire without linking the other. Thus nearly all of the noise voltage appears as "common-mode" noise, that is equal noise voltages in both lines measured with respect to earth at the receiving end. If a receiving amplifier is used which is sensitive to the difference in voltage between the lines and much less sensitive to common-mode voltages which affect both lines equally, it can detect small signal voltages (which are differential) and reject much larger common-mode noise voltages.

Such amplifiers can be built fairly easily and generally use balanced stages such as long-tailed pairs. These inherently have high gain to differential mode signals and low gain, owing to degeneration, to common-mode signals. Negative feedback for common-mode signals only may also be introduced to improve performance. Typically an integrated circuit receiver of this kind may tolerate common-mode noise of ±3 V while operating reliably with a differential signal of 25 mV.

5.3. DIFFERENTIAL CIRCUITS

A number of different circuit arrangements can be used for line devices and receivers, but the long-tailed-pair circuit is almost universal for receivers and is one common technique for drivers. The driving circuits generally use a constant-current source, the output transistors being used to switch this into one line or the other.

The general arrangement is shown in Fig. 5.1. The output impedance of the line driver circuit is relatively high, as is the input impedance of the receiver, so that the line is matched at both ends by resistors R to minimize reflections. The two terminations are in parallel with the driving circuit, so that the sending voltage of each line to earth when carrying current is $I_0 \times R/2$. Thus the peak-to-peak voltage between lines during operation is twice this, or I_0R.

A TTL version of this in integrated form, the 75110 type line driver, has a current I_0 of 12 mA. With a line having a characteristic impedance Z_0 of 200 Ω, R = $Z_0/2$ = 100 Ω, and the driving voltage is

$$I_0R = 1.2 \text{ V p/p}$$

If the line series resistance is small, this is also the receiver input voltage. This is not very large, but if the receiver can tolerate a common-mode voltage of ±3 V a considerably greater voltage on the line may be permitted if attenuators are fitted at the receiver. If the line resistance is assumed to be 100 Ω, the received signal for the same drive current of 12 mA falls to 0.8 V p/p. This could be reduced to 0.16 V = 160

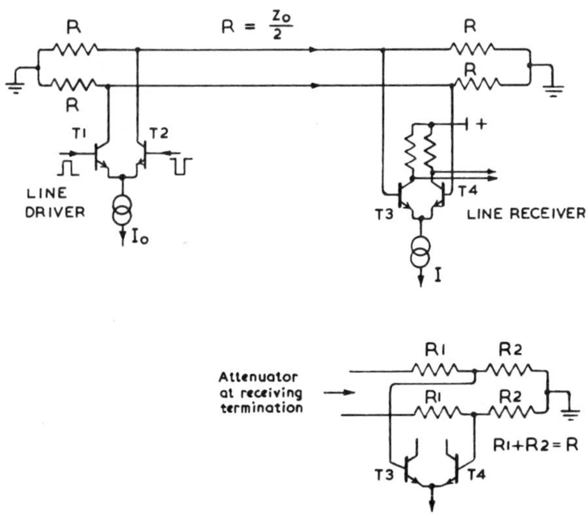

Figure 5.1. Balanced line driver and receiver

mV p/p by fitting 5:1 attenuators. This is still well above the 25 mV at which the receiver is guaranteed to switch. This will require resistors R1 = 83.3 Ω and R2 = 16.7 Ω for the same line impedance. If these values are accurate, the line will now tolerate 15 V common-mode noise, giving 3 V noise at the receiver input terminals.

Where larger driving voltages are required, low-impedance driving circuits can be used, having output stages similar to those of TTL gates. These are essentially unbalanced stages, so that to obtain the differential driving conditions which the long-tailed pair provides it is necessary to use a special driver with two complementary outputs, or couple a single output driver to one of the lines and feed the other from an inverter stage. The output impedance of a typical TTL driver is generally less than the characteristic impedance of the line, so there is a mismatch at the line-driving point. However, if there is appreciable line attenuation this is of no great consequence if the receiving end of the line is properly terminated. This kind of driver has an output level of just over 3 V for logical 1 and 0.4 V maximum for logical 0. Thus the voltage swing into a 100-Ω load (half of the characteristic impedance) is typically 3.1 V, the difference between the 1 and 0 voltages falling in the worst case to about 1.9 V. Consequently the peak-to-peak driving voltage is typically 6.2 V, and 3.8 V in the worst case.

This is a significant improvement on the voltage swing available from the long-tailed-pair driver, and the driver propagation delay is less than 20 ns. The maximum operating speed of the link is generally more dependent upon the line characteristics than upon the driving- and receiving-circuit delays. For distances up to a few hundred feet the line should not degrade transmission unduly when working at typical DMA speeds of 1 word/μs. At speeds greater than this some increased losses arise from the skin effect in the conductors, but the major contribution will arise from dielectric loss in the insulation. Thus longer cable lengths will normally require some amplitude equalization to restore the severely attenuated high frequencies, and perhaps some phase equalization to counteract the increased phase delay at high frequencies. With these correcting measures a computer-computer link has been tested at 1 MHz when working over about 2800 ft of twisted-pair multiway telephone cable. This was intended for audiofrequency use only, and at higher frequencies a major limitation was the crosstalk between pairs due to capacitative and inductive coupling.

Although the integrated circuit line drivers and receivers will operate at over 10 MHz, there is no general need for data rates much in excess of 1 MHz, corresponding to the maximum speed of DMA data transfers. The exceptional case is a line which is operated in the serial mode for economy in cable costs. For a 16-bit word size this may involve a bit rate of almost 20 MHz for maximum DMA transfer rate. The cable for this duty must be low loss and preferably coaxial, and may need equalizing.

5.4. OPTICAL ISOLATORS

Although the use of balanced circuits and differential line receivers will enable reliable data transmission to be conducted with a considerable common-mode interference voltage present, data circuits which pass near heavy electrical plant may experience interference voltages beyond the scope of these remedial measures.

The only satisfactory solution is then complete electrical isolation between the transmission line and the computer interface. This can be provided in several ways, of which the simplest in concept is transformer coupling. Unfortunately a conventional logic signal requires the transmission of the d.c. component of the signal, thus ruling out simple transformer coupling. The only way transformer coupling could be used is to adopt some modulation process in which all signals are balanced with respect to earth and thus contain no d.c. component. Two possibilities are amplitude modulation of a high-frequency carrier, or a phase-encoded scheme such as that used on nine-track magnetic tape systems. This uses a pair of pulses of opposite polarity to encode each bit, say positive first for 1, negative first for 0. However, both of these methods involve rather complex decoding or encoding circuits.

A simpler arrangement in practice is to use an optical isolator. This consists of a light-emitting diode mounted near a silicon phototransistor. These are available in a six-pin dual-in-line package, and have a breakdown voltage between input and output of up to 2500 V. Apart from data transmission via light the only coupling between input and output is a direct capacitance of 0.5-2 pF. The maximum data rate is mainly determined by the bandwidth of the phototransistor and is in the region of 150-200 kHz. Bandwidths of at least 10 MHz can be obtained by using a photodiode detector in place of the phototransistor, but this requires additional amplification of the output signal.

The optical isolator is much the simplest form of common-mode isolation to install as it involves only a small dual-in-line package, and its voltage rating is adequate for all normal circumstances. The bandwidth is a disadvantage only if DMA data rates are required; it is adequate for any keyboard or display system likely to be connected to a computer.

5.5. LONGER LINES

For links over a few hundred feet in length, the cost of providing one twisted pair per bit together with one or more control pairs makes the cost of cable a major consideration. It is generally cheaper to introduce some extra logic and storage at each end of the line and to use fewer pairs by changing to a series-parallel or a fully serial transmission mode. Thus a 16-bit word may be transmitted as two 8-bit bytes over an eight-pair cable, as four 4-bit bytes over a four-pair cable, etc. The optimum arrangement depends upon the data rate required and the line bandwidth, but it is frequently a series-parallel system.

An exception to this arises when the device itself is designed to transmit or accept serial data. It is then usually convenient to use serial transmission and convert from parallel to serial and back at the computer interface. A widely used example of this arrangement is the teleprinter, which was originally developed as a telegraph instrument operating serially over a single-line circuit. For reasons of compatibility this mode has been retained when teleprinters are used as console instruments and for remote links to on-line computers.

Early teleprinters used a five-element code and thus had only 30 possible character codes, excluding all 1 or all 0 elements. This was insufficient to allow all the alphabet, the decimal digits, and punctuation symbols to be uniquely encoded. For transmitting telegrams this difficulty was overcome by using two characters for many of the codes, selected by a previous ''letter-shift'' or ''figure-shift'' non-printing code. Such an arrangement is slow but tolerable for plain-language text, but most awkward for computer use when an identifier such as V5 A1 requires the transmission of eight characters; four for printing, two figure shifts, and two letter shifts.

In order to simplify coding by using only one character to each code combination, a seven-element code was introduced, now standardized internationally and generally known by the original title of the ASCII code. This allows both upper- and lower-case alphabets to be represented as well as figures, nearly 30 punctuation and other symbols, and other control codes. This ASCII code is often extended to an eight-bit code by adding a parity bit, and provision for this is made in the use of eight-hole paper tape with teleprinters.

In some systems where parity checking is not considered necessary, an eight-bit code is assembled by taking the standard ASCII code for the seven least significant bits, and a 1 for the most significant bit.

5.6. TELEPRINTER LINKS

The standard teleprinter used for computer control and remote operation uses an 11-element code: one start bit, eight information bits, and two stop bits. It operates in an asynchronous or start-stop mode, so that after receiving the two stop bits the mechanism halts and waits for the next start bit. This has the practical advantage that the difference in data speeds at the two ends of the link does not have any cumulative effect. The sending and receiving stations are put into step at the beginning of each character, and need merely remain in step for a time corresponding to nine elements (one start and eight information elements).

The element rate is 110 per second and represents a rate of 10 characters per second. The highest frequency of transmission corresponds to an alternating series of 1's and 0's, giving a 55-Hz rectangular wave. If the third harmonic is transmitted in addition to the fundamental, in order to retain some semblance of the rectangular waveform, the line bandwith required is only 165 Hz. The electrical line conditions are generally chosen to suit this slow data rate and allow relatively long lines; bipolar signals, that is equal positive and negative voltages to represent 1 and 0, are normally used.

Many teleprinter links are operated in duplex mode, that is, data can be sent in both directions simultaneously. This kind of working can be obtained over only two wires by using bridge or balanced circuits, but these are critical to adjust and more reliable working can be obtained by using separate circuits for each direction of transmission.

Serial transmission standards exist for teleprinter circuits, the first of which was established long before the introduction of computers. It is still used today on account of its wide tolerance of line resistance, external interference, and other line imperfections. The transmitting voltages are −80 V for the quiescent state and the stop pulses, and +80 V for the start pulse. Some series resistance is usually included at the transmitter to limit possible short-circuit currents. The line current may be around 20 mA if it feeds the receiving teleprinter directly or substantially less if a receiving relay is used. By computer standards this is a very large signal level, but it has the advantage that the terminals can tolerate the resistance of many miles of line without degrading the accuracy of the data transmission. Furthermore, a few volts of noise or interference will have no effect on the transmission, whereas it would completely ruin a data link operating on low-level signals of 1 or 2 V.

On many remote teleprinter circuits attached to computers 80 + 80-V working is used, but the 160-V power supply required is not of use elsewhere in the computing system and is somewhat inconvenient for transistor driving circuits. Such a high transmitting voltage, although advantageous for long links, is not necessary for short teleprinter circuits, for example in the same building as the computer. For these circuits a 15-20-V supply is adequate and the adoption of this much lower voltage simplifies the design of transistor driving circuits. A further advantage is that these circuits can be arranged to deliver a constant line current independent of the line resistance, subject to an upper limit of line and receiver resistance. This eliminates one adjustment required in the 80 + 80-V system in which a series resistance in each receiving circuit must be adjusted to give a specified line current. The lower voltage mode is often called a "20 mA-current-loop" system.

The 20 mA-current-loop circuit, although not an internationally recognized standard (as is, for example, the V24 interface) is widely used for connecting teleprinters and VDU's to minicomputers. It is the usual arrangement for PDP8, PDP11, and Nova computers and is suitable for links of up to several hundred yards in length. Theoretically, bipolar circuits should afford a better signal-to-noise ratio than unipolar circuits such as the 20 mA loop, but since the latter operates at a relatively high-signal level, noise problems do not in practice arise.

The two signals levels are:

logical 1 = 20 mA current = Mark
logical 0 = no current = Space

The source should ideally be a constant current generator, but in practice many interfaces use a transistor voltage switch in series with a current limiting resistor. This is a somewhat crude form of current regulation, but it is adequate if the line resistance is small compared with the other resistances in the circuit.

The normal arrangement comprises two or three pairs of wires. The two pairs are required for the transmitting circuit and the receiving circuit. Viewed from the computer these are, respectively, computer output to the printer and computer input from the keyboard. Where a teleprinter includes a paper tape reader, an extra pair of wires is used for the reader relay. This enables the computer to control the paper tape transport.

Although the circuit conditions for the 20 mA loop connection are fully specified, there is no standard arrangement for the power supplies, which can be at either end of each circuit. The normal arrangement for computer links is that the teleprinter is passive and the circuits are energized from the computer interface. A typical arrangement is shown in Fig. 5.2, in which a transistor switch controls the current sent to the printer magnet and a standard TTL package is used to sense the state of the transmitter contacts. Since computer interfaces use a variety of voltages, both the transmit and receive circuits are isolated from earth.

Where the links are operated at higher speeds for fast printers or VDUs the terminal is usually connected through optical isolators to the two circuits. The terminal side of the isolators can then be connected directly to the logic circuits of the printer or VDU.

The transmission circuits between computer and teleprinter can be arranged in several ways, depending upon the application. Where data is transmitted in only one direction, for example output of system conditions to a printer or input of data from a keyboard, only one pair of wires is required. This is called the simplex mode. Some teleprinter links require both input from the keyboard and output to the printer, but not simultaneously. This enables the user to have a local copy of all messages sent from the keyboard. Such an arrangement can be provided with only one pair of wires by using the teleprinter send-receive switch, but the computer interface is much simplified if separate lines are used for sending and receiving. A common-earth return line can be used so that three wires are sufficient. This arrangement, in which transmission can take place in both directions but not simultaneously, is called "half duplex." Many

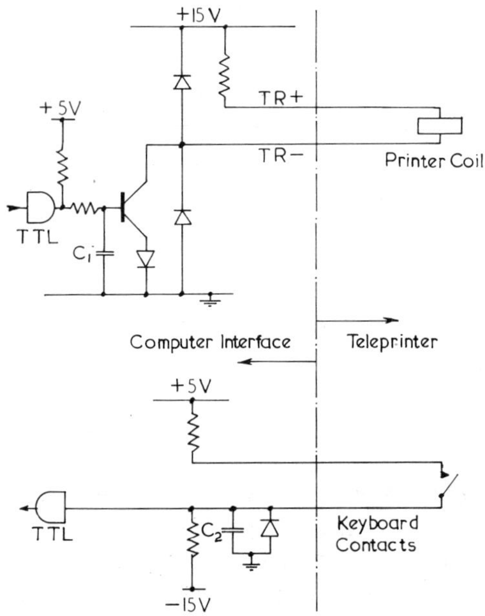

Figure 5.2. 20 mA current loop circuit

teleprinter circuits are arranged so that simultaneous transmission in both directions is possible, and are thus classed as "duplex" circuits.

For many applications it is an operational advantage for the user of a keyboard to have a local copy of all messages sent. This can be provided by a half-duplex system, but there is no check on accuracy of the data received at the remote end of the line. A more reliable system can be established with full duplex working by dispensing with a local feed from the keyboard transmitter to the receiver, and arranging the computer program so that each character which is received in the computer accumulator is immediately "echoed back," that is, transmitted back to the printer of the originating teleprinter. This introduces a small time lag which may disturb an experienced typist but has the practical advantage of checking that each separate character has been correctly received by the remote computer. This echo-back procedure requires a little extra processor time and a few more instructions in the teleprinter program but gives a valuable continuous check on the state of the circuit.

5.7. TELEPRINTER INTERFACE

The main characteristic of the interface between teleprinter and computer is the need for serial-parallel conversion and the converse. Data comes from the I/O bus, normally a character at a time, in parallel with a buffer register at the interface. There it has extra bits added to it; a start bit and a stop signal usually two elements in length. The complete character is then transmitted serially over the line at a rate, determined by the clock-pulse generator, of 110 bits/s. For this function the register is connected as a shift register, the shift pulses being supplied by the clock. The general arrangement is shown in Fig. 5.3.

In the quiescent state the clock is disabled and the first action is an IOT instruction from the computer which loads a character into the register. After this the character, with start and stop pulses added, is shifted out to line, and when the last bit has been dispatched the teleprinter output flag is set. This is connected to the interrupt line and to the skip bus. If the interrupt system is enabled, the source of the interrupt can be determined in the usual manner, otherwise the program, if time is not critical, can be held in a waiting loop until the flag is set and the next instruction can then clear the flag and load the next character into the teleprinter output buffer.

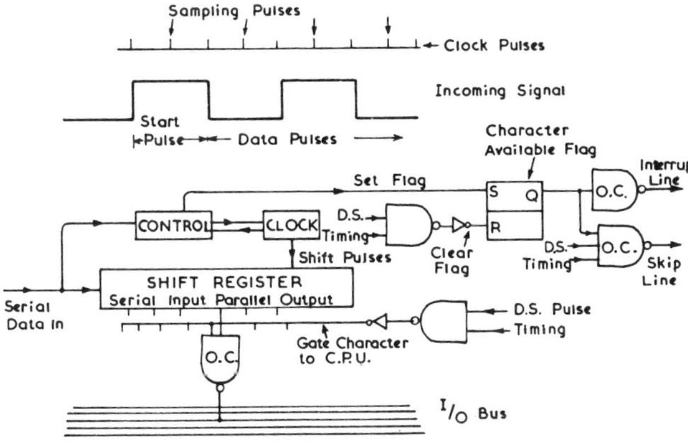

Figure 5.3. Teleprinter input interface

The receiving interface is also a shift register, but in this case the clock-pulse generator usually runs at double speed, or 220 pulses/s, with the first pulse timed from the leading edge of the start pulse. The second, fourth, sixth, etc., pulse are used to shift data into the register from the receiving line, thus ensuring that each bit is sampled at its midpoint. This helps to eliminate the effect of contact bounce and other switching imperfections at the teleprinter transmitter. The flag is set when the last bit of the character has been accepted into the register. The flag is connected to the interrupt line and via a gate to the skip line to enable the processor to test the flag. The programs to read a character and print a character are shown in Table 5.1.

5.8. CCITT INTERFACE

Where computing equipment requires a circuit over the public telephone system, an international standard for voltage levels has been defined for the link between the computing equipment and the terminal equipment which encodes and decodes the data. This is the CCITT V24 interface which uses a nominal signal level of ± 6 V, the voltage being negative for 1, positive for 0. The transmitting level must lie between 5 V (for a 3-kΩ load) and 15 V (for a 7-kΩ load). The maximum short-circuit current to any potential between ± 25 V must not exceed 500 mA, and the maximum data rate is 20 kHz.

The receiver must have maximum threshold levels of ± 3 V, and present a load of 3-7 kΩ to the transmitter. It should tolerate an input voltage of up to ± 25 V without damage. A similar specification, used in the USA, is listed as EIA RS-232 B and C. There is in addition a rather more tightly specified American standard, MIL-STD-188B, which calls for levels of 6 ± 1 V, a 6-kΩ minimum receiver load, and a data

Table 5.1

	To read a keyboard character
KSF	/Test keyboard flag, skip if set
JMP .—1	/Jump back one instruction
KRB	/Clear accumulator and flag, read contents of keyboard buffer into accumulator
	To print a character from the accumulator
TSF	/Test printer flag, skip if set
JMP .—1	/Jump back one instruction
TLS	/Load teleprinter output buffer from accumulator, clear flag, start printing cycle

rate of 4 kHz. Although the conditions are slightly different from those of the V24 standard, a single integrated circuit chip can operate to either standard; a 14-pin dual-in-line package can accommodate two drivers or two receivers.

The voltage levels for this interface are considerably larger than those used on high-speed links, and there is no provision for terminating the line in its characteristic impedance. The data rates attainable are consequently relatively slow, but this is no restriction since the basic limit to the data rate is the bandwidth of the telephone circuit rather than the computer links connected to it.

5.9. DATA LINKS ON TELEPHONE CIRCUITS

The data circuits discussed previously in this chapter were considered from a purely technical viewpoint on the assumption that the complete installation was under the control of the computer user. This is generally not the situation if the data link extends beyond the user's premises, since it may then become necessary to use lines leased from the public telephone authority. The link is then subject to a number of restrictions, since the traffic over it must be compatible with the other telephone traffic carried by the network.

For some slow-speed links, using for example teleprinters, it may be possible to lease telegraph circuits which have a bandwidth of 25-50 Hz. These are generally d.c. circuits for short links and VF telegraph circuits for longer links (this transmission technique allows 24 telegraph circuits to be accommodated on one 4-kHz telephone circuit). In most countries, however, telegraph traffic is declining and telephone circuits now vastly outnumber telegraph circuits. Thus, in the majority of situations, the only circuit available for data traffic is a telephone link. This may be a private line made available for 24 hours a day between two specified locations, or, if there is insufficient traffic to justify this, a circuit on the public switched network may be set up by a normal dialled call. When this has been established both subscribers can switch over by agreement to data transmission.

One very convenient method for occasional or mobile data terminals is the acoustic coupler which requires no electrical connection whatever to the telephone circuits. This uses a small loudspeaker and a microphone to send and receive audiofrequency signals via the telephone handset. When the call has been established by the normal dialling procedure, the handset is placed in a soundproofed box with the transmitter next to a small loudspeaker and the receiver next to a microphone. Data signals from the local terminal are turned into sound waves which are picked up by the telephone transmitter and sent down the line to the computer at the other end of the circuit. Data from the computer is converted into sound by the telephone receiver, picked up by the microphone next to it, and converted back to electrical signals for the local data equipment. This arrangement is very convenient, but owing to the additional noise and distortion introduced by the conversion from electrical signals to sound and back again the maximum data rate is less than that attainable by direct connection to the telephone line. Typical acoustic couplers can operate at a few hundred bits per second and are thus easily capable of matching teleprinter speeds.

5.10. THE NEED FOR MODULATED SIGNALS

Since many data links to computers must use telephone circuits, the characteristics of these circuits are of fundamental importance in deciding how to encode the data. Many parameters of telephone circuits have been standardized by international agreement, the important factors for data transmission being the bandwidth, the maximum permissible signal level, and the signal-to-noise ratio.

Probably the most important of these is the bandwidth, which extends from about 300 Hz to 3400 Hz. A particular feature is that no frequencies much below 300 Hz are transmitted and thus there is no d.c. component. Since the d.c. component is a crucial factor in normal data circuits, no digital device such as a teleprinter, card reader, paper-tape punch, etc., can be connected directly to a telephone line. In order to operate, say, a teleprinter successfully over a telephone line its signals must be translated from their original frequency band of 0-180 Hz or so up into the band of 300-3400 Hz which the telephone line can handle. This requires a modulation process at the transmitter and a demodulation at the receiver. The apparatus which effects the translation is called a modulator-demodulator or "modem." Since most links can operate in two directions, both processes are normally required at each end of the line.

The simplest modems are those intended for slow data rates where asynchronous or stop-start coding is used, as in a teleprinter. These are called asynchronous as there is no exact relation between the carrier frequency sent down the line and the frequency of the digital data signal. The normal modulation process used on these links is called frequency shift keying (FSK). This involves transmitting two different frequencies alternately, one to represent 0 and the other to represent 1. The CCITT recommendations for data rates of 600 and 1200 bits/s are as follows.

Speed (bits/s)	Mean carrier frequency (Hz)	Upper frequency (Hz)	Lower frequency (Hz)
600	1500	1700	1300
1200	1700	2100	1300

The mean carrier frequency is placed around 1600 Hz because if the transmission delay is measured as a function of frequency for typical telephone circuits the minimum delay usually occurs near this frequency and the curve is roughly symmetrical. In consequence the distortion of the signal will be least for frequencies centered on 1500-1700 Hz.

These circuits are operated as simplex or half-duplex circuits. Since the data transmission occupies most of the available bandwidth of the speech circuit, no other similar transmission can occur at the same time. However, there is some bandwidth unused at the lower end of the spectrum, and a slow-speed (75 bits/s) channel can be operated simultaneously, centered on 420 Hz. This is usually operated in the reverse direction from the main transmission and is used for error checking. Information in the forward channel is divided into blocks, and parity digits or other check digits are generated from each block. The parity is also checked at the receiving terminal, and if it agrees with the transmitted version no action is taken. If it disagrees, the 75-bits/s reverse channel is used to request a repeat transmission of the block.

5.11. INTEGRATED CIRCUIT MODEMS

In order to reduce the cost of transmitting data serially to or from a microprocessor via a telephone line, some manufacturers have provided a major part of the modem hardware in a single package. An example is the Motorola MC 6860 digital modem, which produces FSK signals suitable for date rates of up to 600 bauds. The frequencies used are non-standard, 1270 and 1070 Hz for the originator of the call and 2225 and 2025 Hz for the answering terminal. These frequencies are synthesized digitally from a 1 MHz crystal-controlled oscillator and require only a low-pass filter to produce a signal suitable for coupling to the telephone circuit. On the receiving side, a band-pass filter and amplifier are followed by a limiter which feeds the digital demodulation circuits. The package also contains logic and time delay generators to enable it to originate and answer a telephone call. Other packages are available which can operate at speeds above 600 bauds, and which use the frequencies recommended by the CCITT for data links on telephone circuits.

5.12. DUPLEX WORKING

Data circuits for speeds of 600 bits/s and above occupy nearly all of the available bandwidth of a normal telephone circuit, and must thus be operated in simplex or half-duplex mode over a two-wire circuit. Since a normal telephone circuit longer than about 20-30 miles is normally provided on four-wire basis, with separate go and return channels containing amplifiers, it does not add very much to the cost to extend the four-wire circuit to the customers' premises from the nearest repeater (amplifier) station. This requires an extra pair for the final section of the circuit and the removal of the hybrid transformer normally used to convert at the repeater station from four-wire to two-wire working. This procedure is applicable only to private lines connecting two data stations which do not traverse the normal switching network, but it allows full-speed transmission in both directions simultaneously.

An alternative is to restrict the bandwidth of the modulated signals so that they occupy only part of the available spectrum. This can only be arranged if the data rate is reduced. For teleprinter links, however, the data rate is fixed by the machine characteristics at nominally 110 bits/s. Thus a channel capacity of 200 bits/s is adequate and affords some margin for line imperfection. With this limitation it is possible to operate two FSK transmissions over the same circuit. The standard frequency allocation is 980 and 118 Hz for the sending frequencies, and 1650 and 1850 Hz for the receiving frequencies. These allocations refer to the terminal which originates the transmission; the other terminal receives the low frequencies and transmits the high frequencies.

The use of different frequencies allows simultaneous transmission in both directions. For this method of duplex operation it may be necessary to incorporate facilities for switching the sending and receiving frequencies if the terminal may both receive and originate calls. This provision is unnecessary for time sharing on a multiple-terminal system since the external user always dials in to the computer in order to use the service. He is thus always the originator and sends on the low frequencies, the computer modem sending back the high frequencies. On some systems the call is answered at the computer end by an operator who switches over to a modem; otherwise modems can be fitted with automatic answering facilities which, after say 10 s of ringing tone, put a loop on the circuit to answer the call and then connect it to a modem. The call can then be cleared down either by the originator or by a signal from the computer to its modem to release the line. All signaling between computer and modem, or teleprinter and modem, is effected with nominally ± 6-

V signals, according to the CCITT standard V24 as described in section 5.8.

One limitation which must be recognized when using data-transmission equipment over a dialled connection is that the full speech spectrum of 300-3600 Hz is not available. Certain frequencies, typically 600, 750, and 2280 Hz, are used for signaling, and thus tones at these frequencies alone (a condition which never arises during speech transmission) may cause interruptions to the circuit or disconnect it entirely. This is one reason for the choice of operating frequencies in the duplex FSK system described above.

A further difficulty which occurs with duplex working on dialled long-distance circuits arises from echo suppressors. These are normally provided on four-wire circuits to prevent signals traveling continuously back and forth, being reflected at the two-wire to four-wire junctions at each end. They increase the attenuation of the return path when signals appear above a preset level in the forward path, and if the transmitted level is too high could easily block the return channel when the first terminal starts to transmit. They will, of course, cause no great difficulty when the line is used in the normal half-duplex mode.

5.13. DATA ERROR RATES

An important characteristic of a data link is the error rate, that is, the average ratio of errors to the number of characters or bits transmitted. The basic characteristic of the link itself is the bit error rate; the character error rate depends upon the character size and what error-detecting or error-correcting features are incorporated. All links are subject to wide-band noise from transmission lines and amplifiers and the accumulation of small amounts of crosstalk from a number of other circuits. This does not, however, degrade the operation of a data link seriously. Most lines are liable to short bursts of induced noise caused by switching and other transients in neighboring circuits. These usually last for several bit times and their occurrence is unpredictable. As a result the basic performance of a typical data link, although acceptable for transmitting plain language, is not good enough for handling computer input and output, and it is customary to include some form of parity checking, check sums, or error-correcting coding.

For stop-start transmission each character can have a parity bit added to it; for synchronous operation, blocks of roughly 50-200 bits are used with associated check bits. When the receiver detects an error the block can be repeated. Where transmission conditions are known to be difficult, for example over a radio link, extra bits may be included to allow any single error in a block to be connected. The error rate considered acceptable for computer data links is the range of 1 in 10^7 to 1 in 10^8. These rates can only be attained over normal telephone circuits by using some form of redundant error-detecting coding.

One characteristic of the modem design which is carefully specified by telephone administrations is the level of the tone sent out to line. This must be at a level significantly below the peak level of a speech signal to avoid overloading the repeaters in multichannel carrier telephone circuits. A typical speech signal has a large ratio of peak to mean power. Amplifiers which handle several hundred speech circuits are designed on the basis of the mean level of speech with some overload margin in hand. Thus any continuous tone sent over a telephone circuit must be at a level corresponding more to the mean than the peak power. Typical transmitting levels over a 600-Ω line are around -10 dbm, or about $^1/_4$ V.

5.14. SYNCHRONOUS MODEMS

The modems discussed in previous sections use frequency-shift modulation, and thus the receiver needs no timing information to distinguish between a 1 and a 0 as the two frequencies used to encode them are well separated. However, if faster data transmission is required over the same quality of telephone circuit, more reliable results can be obtained if the receiver can use a local oscillator, locked to the oscillator used at the transmitter, in order to improve the demodulation process. If this is possible, phase modulation becomes a practicable method of communication, and has the advantage that it can be operated over a narrower bandwidth than frequency-shift modulation. For this reason, and also for its improved performance in the presence of noise, phase modulation is widely used in data links which operate at 2400 and 4800 bits/s over standard telephone circuits.

One consequence of this ‘‘synchronous’’ operation is that, since the transmitter must emit a continuous stream of bits to allow the receiving clock oscillator to be held in synchronism with it, start-stop character-by-character transmission is not permissible. Messages must be assembled into blocks and transmitted as a continuous stream of bits, with identifying or framing characters at the start of the block. The clock at the transmitting modem can be supplied either by the modem or the data terminal, but generally the modem clock is used, and a timing signal derived from it enables the data terminal to control the rate at which data enters or leaves the modem.

Since an absolute phase reference is difficult to establish, the simplest phase-modulation process is to encode data in the form of a phase shift between one pulse of carrier and the next. The CCITT has standardized a four-phase technique for 2400-bits/s circuits in which two successive bits of the message are jointly encoded as a phase advance from one carrier pulse to the next. Thus the bit pairs 00, 01, 11, 10 cause phase advances of 0°, 90°, 180°, and 270° respectively. Since two bits are encoded at once, there are only 1200 separate pulses of carrier per second for a 2400-bits/s system. This coding scheme is called alternative A and is used in the UK and some European countries. Alternative B is similar, but the phase shifts are 45°, 135°, 225°, and 315°; it is the standard system in the USA and is also used elsewhere. The characteristics of the two systems are very similar, but alternative A requires a little less bandwith, and alternative B can never produce a constant unmodulated carrier burst without a phase change, thus ensuring that the receiving clock oscillator always has a signal to lock to. At the receiving terminal the modem clock is used to gate data into the receiving register at the correct instant for ensuring minimum likelihood of error. The carrier frequency for this type of transmission is 1800 Hz, and the band required is normally 1200-2400 Hz. For satisfactory operation the attenuation and phase delay of the line should not vary too much over this range, the limits for a CCITT line to standard M102 being ± 2 dB for attenuation and a maximum delay change of 500 μs. Many telephone circuits require equalization to achieve this standard of quality.

In order to compress the bandwidth of a 4800-bits/s transmission within a normal telephone channel, three bits are encoded simultaneously, using an eight-phase modulation scheme. The carrier frequency is 1700 Hz in this case, and only 1600 carrier pulses/s are thus required. In order to ensure that the receiving clock stays in synchronism regardless of the data pattern, it is transmitted by a small degree of amplitude modulation of the 1700 Hz carrier. There is also a version of the 2400-bits/s modem which uses eight-phase modulation. This allows the transmission to be contained in a narrower band than the four-phase system, so that the line need not be so carefully equalized.

In frequency-division multiplex telephony, as widely used for trunk routes, the basic group comprises 12 telephone channels with a total bandwidth of 48 kHz. These group circuits are now being used for high-speed data transmission at 48 kbits/s using suitable modems. The next stage of frequency translation assembles five 48-kHz groups into a 240-kHz supergroup. For very fast data transmission it is thus possible to use the whole of a supergroup bandwidth offering a data rate of the order of 200 kbits/s.

The above discussion of data-transmission systems is based upon the use of internationally agreed standards for frequency division multiplex (FDM) speech circuits which are essentially analog transmission systems.

The availability of cheap medium- and large-scale integrated circuits has now made the digital transmission of speech a more economical method than FDM systems, and many telephone administrations are introducing pulse-coded modulation (PCM) digital systems for all new trunk telephone circuits. With the expansion of direct digital transmission it is likely that a greater range of digital data-transmission facilities will be available in the future. Although international agreement has been reached regarding PCM transmission standards, there is as yet no standardization of digital data circuits based upon the PCM channels. Many telephone authorities are proposing to introduce national networks of digital transmission circuits which will incorporate both data links and PCM speech circuits.

5.15. MULTITERMINAL LINKS

The teleprinter interface described in section 5.7 handles a single teleprinter. Somewhat more complex arrangements are required for handling a larger number of teleprinters. This situation often arises when small computers are required to handle lines to a number of terminals located around a factory or group of factories. In a large computer installation the small computer may only act as a "concentrator" by collecting together a set of messages from many outlying terminals and transmitting them at high speed to a larger computer. For less than three or four lines the simplest procedure is to use a number of separate interfaces, but beyond this it is more economical to consider what components of the interface can be shared.

Frequently the clock-pulse generator can be shared by two lines, and the connections to the I/O bus can be shared by all lines. Also some rationalization of storage is possible. Individual interfaces usually have transistor shift registers for the serial-parallel and parallel-serial conversion of input and output data. For a multiple-line system a common data store, which handles all data in parallel mode, can be used.

For a system comprising four to eight lines a simple method of sharing an I/O interface is to use the spare bits in a full word to identify the channel. Thus, for example, with a 12-bit word, the character with parity bit occupies 8 bits, leaving 4 bits which can be used to identify the channel. For duplex working each channel requires separate send and receiver buffers. As soon as a character has been received a flag is raised and a complete word is transferred from the data interface to the accumulator, the data bits being the eight least significant bits. The program must then extract the channel identity from the four most significant bits and jump to the appropriate routine.

Alternatively the computer can exercise greater control over operations and issue an instruction which can examine all flags simultaneously, or select a particular channel, test its flag to discover whether a character has been assembled ready for input, and if so read it into the accumulator. While reading in a character the computer can check the parity and remove the parity ready for transmission over a faster link or for internal storage.

For an installion with more lines (up to 80 or 100), a multiplexer switch is used to connect the control circuits to each line in turn. Each line is allocated a status register and a data register in a small store associated with the multiplexer. When a character has been assembled for input a flag is raised to initiate a transfer to the computer. In the reverse direction a flag is raised after each character has been sent out to line to call for the next character to be transferred out of the computer.

Although this operation has been described in relation to teleprinter links, the same essential procedure can be used for any stop-start data transmission such as a paper-tape reader with appropriate changes to the character size and clock rate. For example, one asynchronous data-communications multiplexer available for the Nova range of computers can be set for a range of clock frequencies from 75 to 9600 Hz. In this unit the clock rate is five times the bit rate, so that each incoming bit can be sampled five times. In order to distinguish between a genuine start pulse and a short noise pulse, the receiver only begins a cycle of operations when three successive samples have all been starting pulses. Thereafter, succeeding bits are sampled every fifth pulse, thus sampling at the middle of each bit and minimizing the chance of error due to contact bounce, etc.

The 16-bit word allows more information to be coded along with the character being transferred. For example, the input instruction specifies which of the four accumulators shall receive the information. The multiplexer transfers to this accumulator a full 16-bit word, bits 8-15 of which contain the received character. Bit 0 is set if the receiver is ready to transmit a character to the processor, and is subsequently cleared. Bit 1 is set if the transmitter buffer has loaded its character into its shift register and is free to accept another character from the processor. The remaining six bits, nos. 2-7, specify the number of the channel concerned in the transfer. The computer is normally interrupted whenever a character has been received or a transmitter has loaded its shift register and so is free to accept the next character.

Most multiplexers operate with what is called "double buffering." This means that on input, for example, a word is assembled serially in a shift register and then transferred in parallel to another register before being sent to the computer. As a result the computer has a complete character time to respond to the particular channel concerned, accept its incoming character, and store it away. Without the double buffering the time available would be only about half a bit time, if the channel is receiving a continuous stream of characters, because the "character available" flag is usually raised about halfway through the last bit-time of the character.

5.16. SYNCHRONOUS MODEM OPERATION

The transmission of data through a synchronous modem differs from that through an asynchronous modem because stop-start operation is not used. Since the stop and start bits are not required for synchronizing the transmitter and receiver, they may be eliminated, thus allowing more data to be transmitted. There still remains the need to subdivide the continuous stream of bits into characters.

This is normally done by sending a special pattern of bits at the start of every message which the receiver can detect and synchronize to. The transmitters and receivers can be set up to deal with a range of character sizes, typically seven to nine, and when the appropriate adjustments have been made the receiver automatically subdivides the bit stream into characters. If the terminals are adjusted, say for 8-bit characters, each group of 8 bits will automatically be recognized as a character at the end of the synchronizing pattern. The general pattern of the complete message also includes a header which indicates its destination and routing. A typical format is as follows.

SYNC SYNC SYNC SYNC	}	Group of four synchronizing characters
SOH	/	Characters denoting start of heading
Header		
STX	/	Characters denoting start of text
Text of message		
ETX	/	Characters denoting end of text
Check data		

A typical SYNC character for an 8- or 9-bit operation is 226_8. Many data links are set up so that a group of SYNC characters is sent at the start of a message and a continuous train of SYNC characters is sent when the link is idling. The receiving terminal is usually programmed to require at least two SYNC characters at the start of a message. When these arrive the receiver is alerted to expect a message. Any further SYNC characters are disregarded, but as soon as the last one has been received all further bits are divided into groups of eight and treated as characters. This procedure ensures that the counter in the receiver which ensures that each successive group of 8 bits is correctly identified as a character has time to synchronize to the incoming bit stream before any information is received.

The message format shown above includes some check data or check sums which will normally detect any single error which has occurred in transmitting the message. Alternatively, or in addition, a parity bit may be encoded with each character sent out and checked at the receiver.

5.17. SERIAL COMMUNICATION INTERFACES FOR MICROPROCESSORS

Minicomputers used in control applications frequently have a teleprinter or VDU attached for entering commands and displaying system conditions. In such applications the processor has many tasks to perform, and the teleprinter is arranged to require a minimum of processor attention, typically by using interrupts to request a further byte of output or to signal the arrival of a byte from the keyboard. Although economical in processor time, this method requires a substantial quantity of hardware — of the order of 50 packages — and the complete interface board costs as much as a microprocessor development kit.

At the other extreme, microprocessor systems are usually designed to perform as many tasks as possible by software, using a minimum of hardware to reduce the overall cost. Where a microprocessor can devote a considerable proportion of its time to teleprinter activities, it is possible to dispense almost entirely with special interface hardware. Thus, for output, a port with only 1 bit connected to the teleprinter is needed. The character output for asynchronous operation comprises one start bit (0), 8 data bits, and 2 stop bits (1).

The 8 data bits are held in an accumulator and rotated, so outputting each bit in turn. The start bit can be produced by clearing the carry bit and rotating this to the output first. A delay loop is used to produce the appropriate data rate. The sequence of operations is as follows:

(1) Set counter to 11 (= OB hex.) to check the number of bits transmitted
(2) Clear carry bit
(3) Load 8-bit character into accumulator
(4) Rotate accumulator bit left, bringing the previous carry bit into the bit DO position
LOOP (5) Output bit DO to teleprinter
(6) Jump to delay loop
(7) Rotate accumulator right, bringing first data bit into position DO
(8) Set carry bit for stop bits
(9) Decrement counter
(10) Jump back to LOOP (5) if the counter is non-zero

The teleprinter is connected to the least significant bit DO of an output port. A similar process can be used for assembling a character from the keyboard, but a little more activity is required at the beginning of the program. The processor must either be held in a waiting loop, from which a logical 0 on the input line will release it, or it must be connected so that a logical 0 will create an interrupt. It must then enter a delay loop corresponding to the duration of half a bit and sample the input line again. If still logical 0, this can be assumed to be a genuine character and not a noise pulse. Thereafter, the input line is sampled at intervals of 1-bit time (9.09ms for a 110 bit/sec. circuit) and the character is assembled by reversing the procedure for output. This process gives maximum tolerance for bit timing, as it samples the data in the middle of the nominal bit interval.

The input and output will normally require two lines of a parallel I/O port but a few microprocessors, such as the Intel 8085, have a serial input and a serial output line connected to pins on the processor. For these no I/O port is needed, only level-changing circuits to match the MOS levels of the processor to either current loop or V24 signal levels.

The procedure described above is satisfactory if the microprocessor is otherwise lightly loaded and can be allowed to spend much of the time attending to serial data transmission. If, however, processor time is critical or interrupts are used some alternative scheme is required. Software generation of serial characters cannot be used if the processor is liable to interrupts, as one of these may occur during a delay period and so the timing of delays would become unreliable.

The usual alternative is a hardware solution using a special serial interface package designed for the purpose.

Assuming that asynchronous operation is used, there are many options which may be required; these are all available by programming the package. Typically, these could be:

(a) 5, 6, 7 or 8 bits per character
(b) Parity bit or not
(c) Odd or even parity
(d) One or two stop bits
(e) Clock division ratio
(f) Create interrupt when ready, or not

The package usually incorporates what is described as ''double buffering,'' that is, an additional register in addition to the shift register which performs the serial input or output. Thus, on output a word loaded into the data register is automatically moved to the shift register as soon as the previous character has been transmitted. Simultaneously a TBMT (transmitter buffer empty) signal is sent back to the processor. The double-buffer feature then allows a complete word transmission time for the processor to detect the signal, extract the next word from the store, and send it to the serial interface data register.

An early design of package used for serial data was the UART (universal asynchronous receiver–transmitter) which handled only the serial-parallel data conversion and required a peripheral package to connect it to the microprocessor bus. Later designs included interface hardware and could be connected directly to the bus. An example of these is the Motorola 6850 ACIA (asynchronous communications interface adaptor). This has the following connections to the processor:

(a) 8 data lines
(b) 3 chip select lines and one register select line. These are usually connected to the address lines in accordance with the addresses assigned to the ACIA.
(c) a chip-enable line normally connected to ^{8}2 clock for timing data transfers
(d) the R/W line for selecting the direction for data transfer
(e) the $\overline{\text{IRQ}}$ line so that if a character has been received or the transmitter buffer is empty an interrupt can be generated to service the ACIA

Signals to the data terminal and modem if used are:

(a) serial transmitted and received data
(b) request to send ($\overline{\text{RTS}}$) to the modem
(c) clear to send ($\overline{\text{CTS}}$) from the modem
(d) data carrier detect ($\overline{\text{DCD}}$) from the modem
(e) transmit and receive clocks from external sources

The two directions of transmission can operate at different speeds if required; the clock supply is normally obtained from a crystal oscillator and divider and runs at 16 times the data bit rate (e.g., 1,760 Hz for 110 bits/sec.), but can be programmed to operate at 64 times bit rate, or at the bit rate by inserting appropriate bit patterns into control register bits CR0 and CR1.

The ACIA contains a control register and a status register in addition to the two data registers used to send and receive data. Interrupts can be programmed to occur when the transmit buffer is empty, when the receive buffer contains a character, or when the $\overline{\text{DCD}}$ signal from the modem indicates that the circuit has been broken as the data carrier has disappeared.

The status register contains information about error conditions. For example: if the received character contains a different number of data bits from the number expected (framing error), a parity error (if parity checking is used), or receiver overrun, which occurs if a new word is received before the previous word has been read from the receive data buffer.

The ACIA is designed only for asynchronous communication. A different package, the SSDA, is available for synchronous operation. The Intel Corporation adopts a policy of providing a single package for both synchronous and asynchronous working, the 8251 USART (Universal Synchronous/Asynchronous Receiver/Transmitter). This has four registers accessible from the processor: for control (write), status (read), transmit data, and receive data. One control pin, normally connected to address line AO, selects either control/status pair or the data pair to be connected to the data lines. Selection between the write or read action of each pair is performed by the Read $\overline{\text{RD}}$ or Write $\overline{\text{WR}}$ control lines from the processor.

After a reset, the first byte sent to the USART establishes the mode, the character length and (for asynchronous working) the number of stop bits. Thereafter, command bytes can be sent to control the modem signals, followed by data transfers.

Other packages used in communications systems are the Intel Synchronous Data Link Controller 8273, which relieves the processor of much work involved in establishing and checking transmission protocol, and the Motorola Modem, which provides much of the hardware (apart from linear amplifiers, filters, and line coupling transformers) for a modem.

5.18. CONCLUSION

The discussion of data links in this chapter has been mainly concerned with teleprinter circuits, but the same general considerations apply to links for other devices such as visual display units (many of which include a keyboard similar to that of a teleprinter). Computer-computer links are generally operated over synchronous circuits in order to use the maximum possible data rate.

Throughout the chapter we have assumed that at the remote device data is originated in a digital form, and that output from the computer is also in digital form. In many on-line computer systems, particularly those concerned with process control and data logging, many of the inputs will be in the form of analog signals, and some outputs will need to be in analog form. For these situations we require devices to convert signals from analog to digital form and back again. These devices are considered in the following chapter.

BIBLIOGRAPHY AND REFERENCES

BACON, M.D., and BULL, G.M., *Data Transmission,* Macdonald & Co., London, 1973.

BRITISH POST OFFICE, *Handbook of Data Communications,* NCC Publications, Manchester, 1975.

COATES, R.F.W., *Modern Communication Systems,* Macmillan, London, 1975.

CYPSER, R.J., *Computer Architecture for Distributed Systems,* Addison-Wesley, Reading, Mass., 1978.

DIGITAL EQUIPMENT CORP., *Communications Equipment Handbook,* 1970.

HEBDITCH, D.L., *Data Communications: An Introductory Guide,* Elek, London, 1975.

HELD, G. *Data Communications Components,* Hayden Book Co., Inc., Rochelle Park, N.J., 1979.

KARP, H.R. (ed.), *Basics of Data Communications,* McGraw-Hill, New York, 1976.

KIRSTEIN, P.T., Data Communication by Packet Switching, *Electronics and Power,* Vol. 19, No. 20, Nov. 15, 1973, p. 503.

McGLYNN, D.R., *Distributed Processing and Data Communications,* Wiley-Interscience, New York, 1978.

MORRIS, D.J., *Introduction to Communication Command and Control Systems,* Pergamon Press, Oxford, New York, 1977.

PETERSON, W.W., and WELDON, E.J., *Error Correcting Codes,* (2nd ed.), M.I.T. Press, Cambridge, Mass., 1972.

STUTTARD, B., A Data Modem: An Application of L.S.I., *Electronics and Power,* Vol. 20, No. 9, May 1974, p. 364.

THORBURN, F.W., A Transmission Control Unit for High-Speed Computer-to-Computer Links, *IBM Journal of Res. & Dev.*, Vol. 14, No. 6, Nov. 1970, p. 614.

VILIPS, V.V., *Data Modems, Selection and Evaluation Guide,* Artech House, Dedham, Mass., 1972.

WICHMAN, B.A., and DU CROZ, J. A Program to Calculate the GAMM Measure, *Computer Journal,* Vol. 22, No. 4, p. 319.

Chapter 6

Signal Processing

6.1. DIGITAL CODING

In any on-line computer system concerned with monitoring, data logging, or control, many inputs, and perhaps some outputs, will be in analog form. It is then necessary to convert the analog signals (generally in the form of electrical voltages) into digital signals so that they can be fed into the processor. Also, since the only output from the computer is in digital form, the converse operation, conversion from digital to analog form, is necessary for any output device such as a cathode-ray-tube display which responds only to analog signals.

Before considering the conversion mechanism it is helpful to discuss the different methods which can be used for representing in digital form an analog signal. The first consideration is the radix of the digital code. Within computers this is always two, but since many analog-to-digital converters (ADC) are used in bench and indicating instruments to display readings to a human operator, binary-coded decimal outputs are normally used for these applications. Most converters used for computer input will operate in binary code, but some decimal-coded instruments have digital outputs available to feed a computer, data logger, or teleprinter. In these circumstances a binary-coded decimal signal will be sent to the computer and must be converted into pure binary form before performing any arithmetic. In the remainder of this chapter we consider only binary-coded numbers.

With this proviso, there are three number systems in use: unipolar binary, offset binary, and 2's complement binary. The first of these caters only for signals of one polarity, usually positive. The maximum signal amplitude is usually taken as 10 V, to match the analog computing and signal-handling modules now generally available. The main exception here is in signals for very fast ADC's. These may involve bandwidths of over 1 MHz, and thus in order to obtain reliable signal transmission the lines must be terminated in their characteristic impedances to avoid reflections. With coaxial cables having impedances of 75-80 Ω, a 10-V signal involves about 1.25 W dissipation and is quite unacceptable. For such cases a 1-V maximum signal is standard, and the extra gain is provided in the converter.

The analog and digital zeros correspond for the unipolar code, and the full-scale signal of 10 V corresponds to 2^N, where N-bit coding is used. Since the largest number that can be encoded with N bits is $2^N - 1$, there is no digital code for 10 V and the largest voltage that can be coded is:

$$10 \text{ V} \times \frac{2^N - 1}{2^N}$$

Thus for a 6-bit system the largest voltage, represented digitally by 111 111, is:

$$10 \text{ V} \times \frac{63}{64} = 9.84375 \text{ V} \quad \text{or} \quad 9.844 \text{ V to the nearest millivolt}$$

This form of coding can be modified to include signals of both polarities by offsetting the zero to -10 V and doubling the voltage range. The digital zero then corresponds to -10 V, and most significant digit to 0 V, and the largest digital value ($2^N - {}^1$) to:

$$\left(10 - \frac{20}{2^N}\right) \text{V} = 10 \left(1 - \frac{1}{2^{N-1}}\right) \text{V}$$

Thus for a 6-bit number 100000 represents 0 V, 110000 represents +5 V, and 111 111 represents:

$$10\left(1-\frac{1}{32}\right)\text{V} = 10 \times \frac{31}{32}\text{ V} = 9.6875\text{ V} \quad \text{or}$$

9.688 V to the nearest millivolt

This form of coding is called "offset binary."

The final form of coding uses the 2's complement notation almost invariably adopted within the processor. The digital zero then corresponds to 0 V, the most significant or sign digit to −10 V, and the next most significant digit to +5 V. Accordingly, 010000 represents +5 V, 110000 represents −5 V, and 011111 represents the greatest positive voltage which is:

$$10 \times \frac{31}{32} = 9.6875\text{ V} \quad \text{or} \quad 9.688\text{ V to the nearest millivolt}$$

The three codes are compared in Table 6.1.

The unipolar binary code is easiest to implement in A-D and D-A converters. The offset binary code can be handled by using a unipolar converter and a buffer amplifier on the analog side to change the signal excursion and offset the zero. This needs a gain of 2 for D-A conversion and $^1/_2$ for A-D conversion. Many converters can be switched or connected for either coding, but must of course use offset binary when handling bipolar voltages. For example, if an A-D converter working in offset binary code is used to provide input data to a computer, the computer

Table 6.1. Comparison of 6-bit Codes

Digital value		Analog voltage		
Octal	Binary	Unipolar binary	Bipolar offset binary	Bipolar 2's complement binary
0	000 000	0.0	−10.0	0.0
1	000 001	+0.1563	−9.688	+0.312
20	010 000	+2.5	−5.0	+5.0
37	011 111	+4.844	−0.312	+9.688
40	100 000	+5.0	0.0	−10.0
60	110 000	+7.5	+5.0	−5.0
77	111 111	+9.844	+9.688	−0.312

program can be arranged to convert the readings into the normal 2's complement notation by the following operations, assuming that 6-bit numbers are used:

$N_2 = N_o + 40_8$ for negative voltages

$N_2 = N_o - 40_8$ for zero or positive voltages

N_2 and N_o are the digital values in 2's complement and offset binary codes respectively of the input analog voltage. For a 12-bit word, the operation for negative voltages must produce 1's in the seven most significant bits, and must thus be:

$$N_2 = N_o + 7740_8$$

The operation for zero and positive voltages need not be changed as the word is normally filled with zeros in the positions not loaded by the ADC.

Considering the two arithmetic processes involved in computing N_2, the first operation involves a single arithmetic addition and the second can be performed equally quickly by using a subtract instruction if this is available. If not, the logical operation

AND 37

(the 37 being an octal number) will eliminate the most significant binary digit but leave the remaining five digits.

The same instructions can be used if the conversion is required to change offset to 2's complement notation, but interchanged so that subtraction is performed for negative voltages and addition for zero or positive voltages. Most A-D and D-A converters handle 8-12 binary digits, so that the constants 40 and 37 in the above example need modifying to suit the number of digits produced by the converter.

6.2. DIGITAL-TO-ANALOG CONVERSION

Since D-A conversion is simpler than the converse process, and in practice is often involved in it, we consider this technique first. Nearly all D-A converters use a current-summing process in which each digit of the input controls the current flowing into a summing junction, as shown in Fig. 6.1. The most significant bit controls the switch S_1 which connects the current sink I either to the summing junction for a 1, or to earth for a 0.

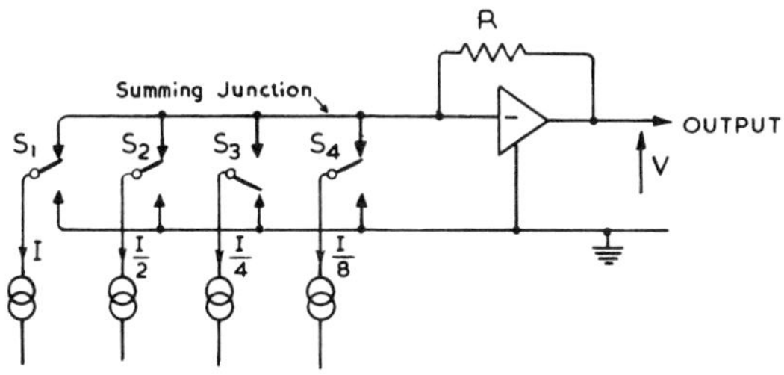

Figure 6.1. Principle of current-summing D-A converter

Successive digits control currents $I/2$, $I/4$, $I/8$, etc. The total current reaching the summing junction, I_s, causes an output voltage:

$$V = I_s R$$

The amplifier shown is a high-gain operational amplifier. The converter is unipolar, normally set up so that the output for the most significant digit, IR, is exactly half-scale, or 5V in a 10-V system. For example, if $I = 2$ mA, $R = 2.5$ kΩ. The maximum output voltage when all N input digits are 1 is:

$$V_{max} = IR\left(2 - \frac{1}{2^{N-1}}\right)$$

$$= 5\left(2 - \frac{1}{2^{N-1}}\right) V \qquad \text{for a 10-V system}$$

This arrangement can be modified to operate with 2's complement coding, producing a bipolar output, by doubling the value of R and deriving the current I, which represents the most significant digit, from a positive rather than a negative supply. The remaining bit currents as shown in Fig. 6.1 are derived from a negative supply and thus operate as current sinks. For bipolar 2's complement operation, the current I must be provided by a current source connected to a positive supply. It will then produce a negative voltage at the output of the operational amplifier, whereas all other currents produce positive output voltages.

For offset binary coding the current sinks are all left as in the diagram, but an additional bias current equal to I is injected from a positive current source and, as before, the resistor R is doubled. A digital input of all zeros will then give an output representing only the bias current, that is, full-scale negative output.

The currents *I*, *I*/2, *I*/4, etc., can be derived from a negative voltage reference by using a set of binary weighted resistors R_1, $2R_1$, $4R_1$, etc., where:

$$R_1 = \frac{V_{ref}}{1}$$

However, when more than six to eight digits are involved the ratio of the largest resistor to the smallest becomes excessive and the ladder network shown in Fig. 6.2 is more convenient. This requires only two values of resistor.

The change-over shown in Fig. 6.1 can be performed by diodes, or by bipolar or field-effect transistors. A technique convenient for integrated circuit D-A converters is to use external precision resistors for determining the currents, the current-summing transistors and the long-tailed-pair current switches being fabricated on a single chip which handles four digits. A 12-bit converter can then be assembled from three chips with a 16:1 current attenuator between chips. This allows the same four resistor values to be used with each chip.

The resistors *R* and 2*R* used in the ladder network of Fig. 6.2 can be less than 1 kΩ and thus more convenient for high speed D-A converters than circuits using large resistors fed from a voltage reference source. Also, current sources can be switched rapidly, so that for fast conversion the arrangement of Fig. 6.2 combining the two is widely used. With a suitable wideband amplifier a conversion time of considerably less than 1 μs can be obtained; for example, one manufacturer quotes a settling

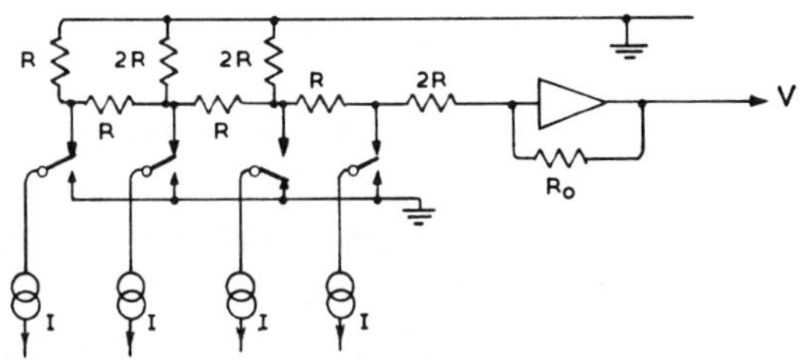

Figure 6.2. Digital to analog converter using ladder network

time of 100 ns to within 0.01% of the final value for a 12-bit converter.

The development of CMOS integrated circuits has enabled a novel form of DAC to be constructed in which resistors are replaced by capacitors. The circuit is similar to that of Fig. 6.1 but instead of summing currents at the junction (each current being generated by connecting a binary weighted resistor to a reference voltage), the junction sums charge. The binary weighted resistors which produce I, I/2, etc., are replaced by capacitors C, C/2, C/4, etc., which direct charges CV_{ref}, $^1/_2\, CV_{ref}$, $^1/_4\, CV_{ref}$, etc., to the summing junction. The output voltage is given by $Q = C_0 V_0$, where:

$$Q = a_1 CV_{ref} + {}^1/_2 a_2 CV_{ref} + {}^1/_4 a_3 CV_{ref}, \text{ etc.}$$

The constants a_1, a_2, a_3, etc., are either 1 or 0 depending upon the digital inputs which determine the switch positions. For clarity, the switched transistors which discharge the capacitors prior to conversion have been omitted from Fig. 6.3, which shows the basic circuit of a 4-bit capacitor DAC.

6.3. OTHER TYPES OF D-A CONVERTER

A method of A-D and D-A conversion widely used in general instrumentation is to convert indirectly using time as an intermediate variable.

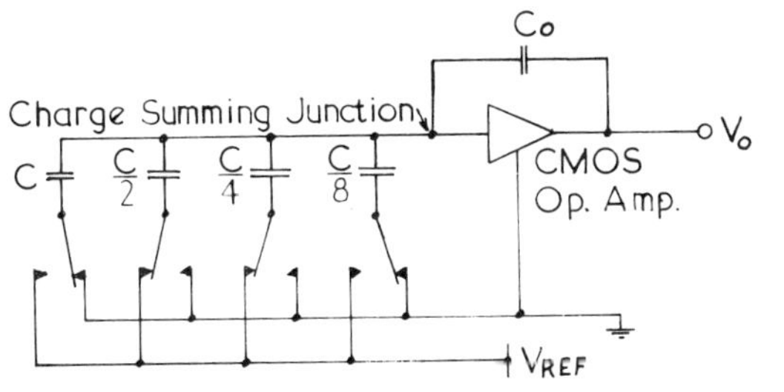

Figure 6.3. Weighted capacitor D-A converter

For D-A conversion this involves producing an accurate time interval proportional to the digital input and connecting a reference voltage to an integrator circuit for this interval. The final output voltage of the integrator circuit will be proportional to the time interval and thus to the digital input. The usual way of performing the initial conversion is to use a down-counter, initially loaded with the digital value and driven by a precision oscillator.

After the digital value has been loaded and the integrator reset, a gate connects the oscillator output to the counter and, simultaneously, a further gate connects the reference voltage to the integrator. When the contents of the counter fall to zero the oscillator is disconnected and the integrator is switched to "hold"; its output will then be proportional to the digital value previously loaded.

This type of converter is fairly simple to produce since there are few precision elements required, but it is inherently slower than the current-summing type previously described. However, where the output changes only slowly it would be adequate. Where fast conversion is required, for example to produce a rapidly changing analog voltage for deflecting a cathode-ray tube, it is unable to operate quickly enough.

6.4. A-D CONVERSION

A variety of A-D conversion techniques have been used, but for fast conversion only a few arrangements prove adequate. The fastest is the fully parallel or "flash" converter, in which all digits are produced simultaneously. This requires $2^{N}—^{1}$ voltage comparators to encode N binary digits, and is thus usually restricted to three or four digits. The development of MSI linear and digital circuits may make converters able to handle more digits available in the future.

The general arrangement is shown in Fig. 6.4a. The logic network needs a set of gates to examine the outputs of two adjacent comparators. If these are, say, 1 for N and 0 for $N + 1$, the incoming signal lies between $(N/8)V_{ref}$ and $[(N + 1)/8]\ V_{ref}$. A set of OR gates is then needed to energize the appropriate bit lines on the output side in order to encode N in binary form. As shown, the output will be 000 for all input voltages from 0 to $V_{ref}/8$, 001 for inputs from $V_{ref}/8$ to $V_{ref}/4$, and so on.

This is the way in which A-D and D-A converters are usually set up. It is equivalent to using a high-resolution converter and truncating the lower-order bits to produce a 3-bit output. For some purposes it could be argued that the procedure which represents the analog voltage most accurate is round-off rather than truncation. In order to produce this kind of encoding, a bias or zero offset of $V_{ref}/16$ is needed. Then all inputs

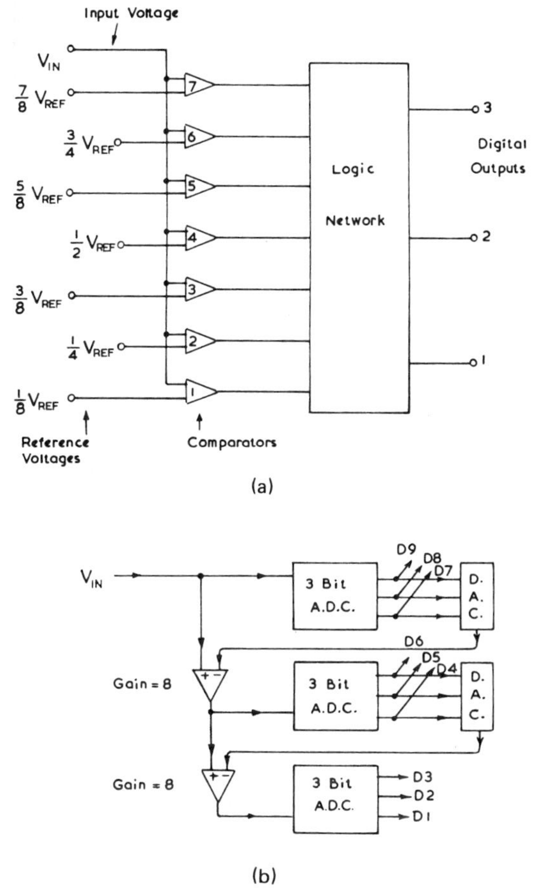

Figure 6.4. Parallel A-D converters: (a) 3-bit parallel ADC; (b) 9-bit series-parallel ADC

below $V_{ref}/16$ will produce an output of 000, all between $V_{ref}/16$ and 3 $V_{ref}/16$ will produce 001, and so on.

The circuit shown in Fig. 6.4a handles only unipolar signals, but if the voltage-divider chain which supplies reference voltages to the comparators is returned to $-V_{ref}$ instead of to earth, it will handle bipolar signals and will produce an offset binary-coded output. Using fast digital elements and fast comparators, a conversion time of around 20 ns for 3 bits is attainable.

As mentioned above, the amount of logic and the number of comparators required is an exponential function of the number of binary digits encoded, and therefore of the resolution. For this reason three to four digits are a practical limit for a fully parallel ADC. Greater resolution with only a linear increase in hardware is possible, however, by using a series-parallel arrangement as shown in Fig. 6.4b. In this scheme the 3-bit circuit of Fig. 6.4a is used with the digital outputs connected to a DAC. This produces a quantized output V_1 corresponding to the nearest multiple of $V_{ref}/8$ below V_{in}. In this application no bias is added to V_{in} before conversion. The difference between V_{in} and V_i is multipled by 8, giving it a maximum possible value of V_{ref}, and passed on to a similar 3-bit converter, whose residue is in turn passed to a third converter. Clearly the second converter cannot produce an accurate output until the first converter has settled. Thus the three converters must operate sequentially, and some timing mechanism is required to prevent the computer sampling the output until the converters have finally settled. This can be done by using a monostable which is triggered by the "start conversion" pulse, and produces a "conversion finished" output pulse after a delay set to the longest conversion time the converter is found to require.

Although the series-parallel arrangement has been described in terms of a 3-bit parallel module, other sizes of module can equally well be used. If a slightly slower conversion is acceptable, a 2-bit module is rather more economical of hardware and is fast enough for many requirements.

Since A-D conversion is a more difficult and usually a more complex operation than D-A conversion it generally takes rather longer. Fast A-D converters readily available from several sources have conversion times around 0.8 μs for 8 bits and 1 μs for 10 bits. Special-purpose converters are available which can operate at 4-5 MHz sampling rate, and the advent of digital television links has created a demand for conversion rates of up to 30 MHz.

6.5. SERIAL A-D CONVERTER

The series-parallel converter uses a considerable amount of hardware, and where extreme speed is not required a more economical method of conversion is the serial arrangement. This uses a digital register connected to a DAC. The control logic inserts a 1 into each stage of the register in turn, starting with the most significant bit. If the DAC output is greater than the analog input the 1 is cancelled; if not it is left and the control unit moves to the next stage. The same procedure is followed for this and other stages. When a 1 has been tried in all stages of the register the conversion is finished and the result can be gated from the register into the computer, usually via the I/O bus.

The control unit requires some logic to provide set and reset signals for the register, and often includes a shift register containing a single 1 and 0's in all other stages. The 1 is initially placed in the most significant stage and copied across into the register. After each comparator decision the timing system emits a shift pulse which transfers the 1 to the adjacent stage, and the process is repeated.

This serial process is often called a ''successive approximation'' conversion, and is in such general use that integrated circuits are now available, for example Motorola MC14559 and MC14549 and Advanced Micro Device AM2502, which contain all of the storage and logic associated with the process. The addition of a clock supply, a comparator, and D-A converter completes the A-D conversion unit.

For microprocessor applications where conversion time is not a major consideration a more economical form of successive approximation conversion can be arranged by using the processor itself as the storage and logic element. By using a D-A converter designed for direct connection to the data lines of the microprocessor, the only other hardware needed is a comparator whose output is connected to a control line or an input data line of a PIA. If any scaling or offsetting of the analog input is required an operational amplifier will also be needed.

Assuming that an 8-bit conversion is required, the first stage in the process is the generation of the immediate operand 80 (hexadecimal). A copy of this is made in a processor register and is output to the DAC. If the resulting DAC output is greater than the analog input, the 80 is subtracted from the register contents and shifted right to produce 40. This is added to the register and the result output to the DAC.

Should the DAC output be less than the analog input, the subtraction operation is bypassed and the next procedure is the shift right. The above operations are repeated until the original 80 has been shifted right 8 times and reduced to zero. In order to allow the DAC and comparator time to settle before sensing the comparator output, NOP (no operation) instructions may be inserted between the output to the DAC and the instruction which senses the comparator output. Although this process is slower than a completely hardware ADC it costs significantly less and is therefore a preferred method for many high-volume microprocessor applications where there is no need for fast conversion. For example, many temperature measurements in domestic appliances and industrial processes involve considerable masses of material which have a large thermal inertia; there is thus no point in sampling temperature too frequently.

6.6. TRACKING A-D CONVERTER

The successive approximation converter generally has a "status" or "busy" output which is logical 1 during conversion and returns to 0 when conversion has finished and the digital output is available to the processor. The processor is either held in a waiting loop during conversion, or allowed to continue some other processing and interrupted when the busy signal changes from 1 to 0.

Programming is simpler if no delay is required and the A.D. converter can be read at any time without delay. This is possible if a tracking converter is used, that is, a converter which is continuously monitoring the analog signal and adjusting its digital value to follow or "track" its variations. This is usually based upon an "up-down" counter which has an uninterrupted clock supply and whose counting direction is determined by a comparator. The counter is connected to a D-A converter whose output is compared with the incoming analog signal.

If the DAC output is the lower, the counter increments; if it is the greater, the counter decrements. Thus the contents of the counter will follow the varying analog input and, when it remains constant for a time, the counter will "dither," that is, successively increment and decrement about the true value. If the counter clock is synchronized with the processor clock, it is usually possible to ensure that, at the data-reading clock phase, the counter contents will not be changing.

With this type of ADC no "start conversion" signal is required but a compromise is needed between resolution and slewing rate. For an N-bit counter with a clock frequency of fHz the time to change by full-scale voltage $\hat{V}$ is $\frac{2^N}{f}$ secs. Thus the maximum slew rate is $\frac{V \cdot f}{2^N}$ V/sec. For a fast TTL counter operating at 25MHz, a 12-bit converter with a range 0-10V would have a slew rate of $\frac{10 \times 25 \times 10^6}{4096} = 0.061$ V/μs. This corresponds to a sinewave of amplitude 5V and a frequency of only 1.94kHz, since the maximum slew rate of a sinusoidal signal of amplitude $\hat{V}$ and frequency f is $2 \pi f \hat{V}$ volts/sec.

Should a reduced resolution of 8 bits be acceptable, the same counting rate would provide a slew rate of 0.244 V/μs, and the limiting frequency for a 5 volt sinewave which could be tracked would rise to 7.77kHz.

6.7. SAMPLE-AND-HOLD CIRCUITS

When considering the operation of the serial converter we have assumed that the input voltage remains constant, at least within plus or minus half a step during the conversion process. Since each stage of the register is tested once only with no subsequent retest, any significant change during the course of the conversion can produce serious errors. If the analog voltage is changing only slowly, no error may occur, but this requirement puts a very severe limitation on the rate of change of the analog signal.

When the 1 signal arrives at the far end of the shift register the conversion is complete, and a "finished" or "data ready" pulse is issued. This can be used in the computer interface to set the ADC flag, or the Done bistable. The program must then read the register contents into the accumulator, thence into the store, and clear the flag. It can then request a further conversion.

The converter described above is assumed to operate on unipolar signals. If bipolar offset coding is required the same converter can be used, but must be preceded by a linear amplifier with a gain of $^1/_2$ and a zero offset of 10 V. This will compress the input range of ±10 V to 0-10 V. In some converters there is no input amplifier but the zero offset can be introduced when required. This gives alternative input ranges of 0-10 or ± 5V. By modifying the current source for the first bit in the DAC, which feeds the comparator, and changing the first-stage logic, the serial or "successive-approximation" ADC can also be arranged to give 2's complement coding. Many commercial packaged ADC's can provide unipolar, bipolar offset, or 2's complement coding as required.

For example, with an input signal of amplitude V and angular frequency ω the input may be represented by:

$$v = \hat{V}\sin \omega t$$

The rate of change is:

$$\frac{dv}{dt} = \omega\hat{V}\cos \omega t$$

which has a maximum value of $\omega\hat{V}$ V/s

For an 8-bit encoder with a 0-10 V input range, the least significant bit correspondents to a step of:

$$\frac{10}{2^8 - 1} \text{ V} = \frac{10}{255} = 39.3 \text{ mV}$$

Thus if the input must change less than this amount during the conversion time of, say, 20 μs, the maximum rate of change permissible is:

$$\frac{dv}{dt} = \frac{0.0393}{20} \text{ V/μs} = 1965 \text{ V/s}$$

For a sinusoidal signal of 10 V p/p, or 5 V amplitude, the maximum frequency is given by:

$$\omega\hat{V} = 1965 \text{ V/s}$$

whence

$$\omega = \frac{1965}{\hat{V}} = \frac{1965}{5} = 393 \text{ rad/s}$$

corresponding to a frequency of 62.6 Hz

Such a frequency restriction is acceptable for signals which change only slowly, for example the output of a thermocouple amplifier measuring the temperature of a bearing or steam pipe. Where the input is changing more rapidly than the calculated figure the analog voltage cannot be connected directly to the ADC, and a circuit must be used which can take a rapid sample of the signal when required and hold the sampled output constant during the conversion process. This is called a ''sample-and-hold'' circuit, and generally uses a plastic-film capacitor to store the voltage. In essence it need be no more than a switch and a capacitor, as shown in Fig. 6.5a. This has two limitations: the input must come from a very low impedance source if there is to be sufficient current available to charge C during the short period that the switch is closed, and any

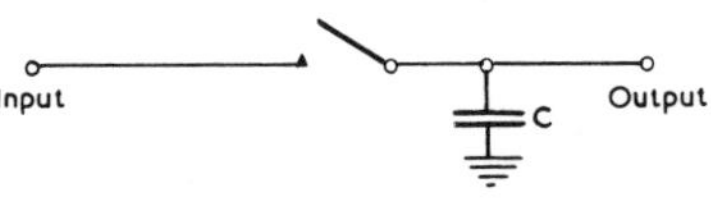

(a)

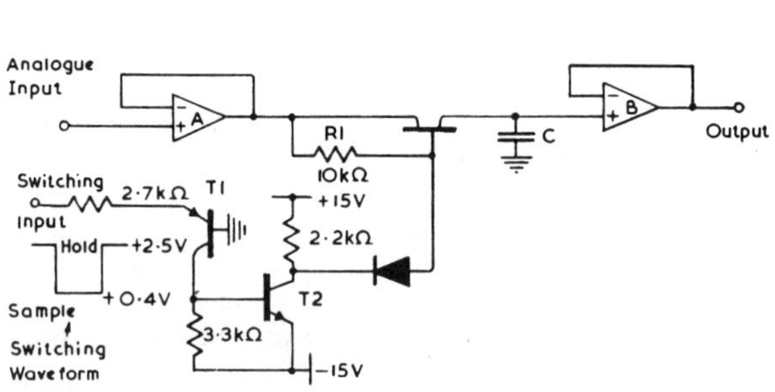

(b)

Figure 6.5. Sample-and-hold circuits: (a) elementary circuit; (b) circuit with input and output buffer amplifiers and FET switch

load on the output circuit imposed by the A-D converter will discharge the capacitor thus causing an error in the ADC input signal.

These limitations can largely be removed by using two operational amplifiers connected as voltage followers with a gain of almost unity, as shown in Fig. 6.5b. The first amplifier, using full voltage feedback ensures a low output impedance to drive capacitor C. The second also provides a low-impedance output to feed the ADC. The feedback connection ensures a high input impedance and thus only slow discharging of capacitor C. For critical requirements it may be necessary to use an FET-input operational amplifier as the output unit to ensure a very small capacitor discharge current. Alternatively, an FET connected as a source-follower can be interposed between capacitor and amplifier for the same purpose. There are several variations of this circuit, such as the use of overall feedback from the output to the first amplifier in order to improve accuracy. For maximum operating speed the FET switch can be included within the feedback loop in order to diminish its effective impedance and so speed up the sampling process. For this function junction FET's are often used as they generally have lower "on" resistances than insulated-gate FET's. The provision of a suitable voltage to control the FET switch is a little involved. The gate-source voltage for an *n*-channel FET must be about 0 for full conduction and, say, -4 V for cut-off. In the circuit of Fig. 6.5b, however, the source has the full signal voltage impressed upon it and thus the gate must be biased with reference to the signal voltage and not earth. The constraints upon the gate voltage are as follows: firstly, the gate must not become positive to the channel, otherwise the gate-channel diode will conduct, thus impressing some of the switching waveform upon the analog signal; secondly, the gate-channel voltage must not exceed the manufacturer's rating, typically 25-30 V of reverse bias.

The two states of conduction and cut-off in the circuit of Fig. 6.5b are obtained by adding a diode and resistor to the gate circuit. The resistor R_1, sometimes called the "referral resistor," allows the gate-channel voltage to fall to zero when D is reverse biased, thus turning the FET fully on and allowing the capacitor voltage to follow the input. The digital input signal for this condition is a low potential of, say, 0.4 V or less. Transistors T_1 and T_2 are then cut off and the collector of T_2 rises to $+15$ V, thus reverse biasing diode D, since the anode of D is held at signal voltage (not more than $+10$ V) by resistor R. In order to hold the sampled voltage, the digital input is raised to $+2.5$ V, thus turning on T_1 and T_2. The collector of T_2 falls to nearly -15 V and with it the cathode of D, so that D conducts and pulls the gate of the FET negative to around -14 V (-15 V less V_{ces} and one diode drop). If the FET has been chosen to have a pinch-off voltage of 4 V or less it will now be cut off even if the signal is at − 10 V, its most negative value. For any other signal level the FET will have more bias than is necessary, and at the other extreme signal level, +10 V, the gate-channel voltage attains its maximum of about 24 V. This is within the rating of most FET's but allows little margin.

A further design factor which is not evident from the circuit diagram is the charge stored in the diode D. When the FET is biased off, the diode conducts current from the output of the first amplifier via the 10 kΩ resistor, and thus stores some charge at the junction. In order to turn the FET on the stored charge must be removed, since the diode is then reverse biased. By careful design the stored charge can be made of the correct magnitude to turn on the FET, thus decreasing its turn-on time. The manufacturing control needed to meet this requirement is most conveniently obtained when both diode and FET are processed together on the same chip. These are now available with TTL compatible logic inputs and having four switches assembled in a single DIL package.

6.8. SAMPLING ERRORS

When the circuit shown in Fig. 6.5b is used for sample-and-hold operations, the digital input is normally 1, say 2.5 V, to cut off the FET and hold the sampled value. In order to take a sample the digital input is changed to 0 for a brief period to sample the input voltage and then returned to 1. In order to ensure that the sample taken is accurate, several conditions relating to the amplifier characteristics and the FET resistance must be satisfied. These all depend upon the duration of the sampling pulse, so the effect of this variable is considered first.

The normal action of any control circuit, whether driven by a computer or a simple timing device, is to generate a "sample" pulse to initiate the sampling operation on the assumption that the sample will be taken at the instant corresponding to the leading edge of the initiating pulse. In fact, all sampling systems are essentially "track/hold" circuits in which the output tracks the input while the circuit is in the "sample" mode. Thus the voltage output retained in the "hold" mode is that corresponding to the trailing edge of the sampling pulse, not the leading edge. Even if the circuit responds very rapidly, this error, called the "sampling error," will occur. Its magnitude can be estimated by using the analysis given in the previous section, but taking the time interval as the duration of the sampling pulse in place of the ADC conversion time.

Assuming as before a sinusoidal input signal given by

$$v = \hat{V} \sin \omega t$$

the maximum rate of change of voltage is:

$$\frac{dv}{dt_{max}} = \omega \hat{V} \text{ v/sec}$$

Consequently the maximum voltage change which can occur during a sampling pulse δt is:

$$\delta v = \frac{dv}{dt} \delta t$$

$$= \omega \hat{V} \delta t \text{ V}$$

This is the sampling error attributable to the finite width of the sampling pulse.

Taking as an example the same 8-bit ADC as considered in section 6.6, with a 0-10 V input range, the voltage corresponding to half of the least significant bit is 19.7 mV. This is the maximum sampling error permissible if the output is to be correct within $\pm ^1/_2$ bit.

If the width of the sampling pulse is

$$\delta t = 100 \text{ ns} = 10^{-7} \text{ s}$$

the maximum frequency of the input signal is given by:

$$\delta v = \omega \hat{V} \delta t$$

or

$$19.7 \times 10^{-3} = \omega \times 5 \times 10^{-7}$$

The amplitude of this sinusoidal signal is taken as 5 V, giving a total variation of 10 V p/p. Thus:

$$\omega = \frac{19.7 \times 10^{-3} \times 2}{10^{-6}}$$

$$= 39.4 \times 10^{3} \text{ rad/s}$$

or

$$f = \frac{\omega}{2\pi} = 6.26 \text{ kHz}$$

In addition to the sampling error caused by the finite duration of the sampling pulse, other errors may arise if the amplifiers cannot respond quickly enough or if amplifier A cannot provide sufficient current to charge the storage capacitor.

For large changes in output voltage, the limitation on amplifier response is generally quoted as the ''slewing rate,'' or the rate at which the output changes when the input signal is large enough to cause non-linear operation. The amplifier is then generally working in a current-limited regime, with a roughly constant rate of change of output voltage. In the present example the minimum acceptable slewing rate corresponds to a full-scale change of output voltage during the sampling pulse, a rate of

$$\frac{2\hat{V}}{\delta t} \text{ V/s.}$$

In practice we shall design for a rate of 20-30% greater than this to ensure that the amplifier leaves the non-linear regime before the end of the sampling pulse.

In the case of the 8-bit converter the limiting slewing rate for amplifier A, when loaded with the storage capacitor C, is:

$$\frac{2 \times 5}{10^{-7}} = 100 \text{ V/}\mu\text{s}$$

Thus we would specify a slewing rate of, say, 120-140 V/μs. Integrated-circuit operational amplifiers are now available with quoted slewing rates of around 300 V/μs.

The amplifier in Fig. 6.5b must provide charging current for the storage capacitor C, which may be large when the present sampled voltage differs considerably from the voltage of the previous sample. In the worst case the capacitor voltage may need to change by the full-scale voltage ($2\hat{V}$) during the sampling pulse. This requires a mean current given by:

$$I_{\text{out}} = \frac{CV}{t} \quad \text{for a change } V \text{ in time } t$$

$$= \frac{2C\hat{V}}{\delta t} \quad \text{for the sampling circuit}$$

In the example used previously, $2\hat{V} = 10$ V, δt; = 100 ns, and taking $C = 1000$ pF gives:

$$I_{\text{out}} = \frac{10 \times 1000 \times 10^{-12}}{10^{-7}} \text{ A}$$

$$= 100 \text{ mA}$$

Since this is the mean amplifier current a suitable design would provide say 130-150 mA initially so that the final settling of the output voltage would take place with the amplifier working in the linear regime and not the current-limited regime. With this magnitude of output current the on-resistance of the FET should be in the region of 20 Ω, otherwise the charging time constant of this resistance and the storage capacitor will introduce too much delay.

A final source of error in the output voltage arises from switching "spikes" or "glitches" which are caused by capacitance coupling of the FET gate signal to the channel. This occurs through the unavoidable gate-channel capacitance, and it can to some degree be diminished by a neutralization process in which the complementary switching signal is also coupled via a small adjustable capacitor to the channel of the FET.

At the cost of more complicated switching the circuit of Fig. 6.5b can be given greater accuracy by overall feedback from the output of amplifier B to the input of amplifier A during the "sample" phase. This allows the output signal to track directly the input signal, rather than doing so in two operations in cascade.

There is an additional source of error in the "hold" mode due to the discharging of the storage capacitor through the FET and the input circuit of amplifier B. If the total discharge current is I_L, the rate of change of output voltage is given by:

$$\frac{dv}{dt} = \frac{I_L}{C} \text{ V/s}$$

If the total leakage in our example is 10^{-7} A, then:

$$\frac{dv}{dt} = \frac{10^{-7}}{10^{-9}} = 100 \text{ V/s} \quad \text{or} \quad 100\mu\text{V}/\mu\text{s}$$

This drift will equal the increment of 1 bit (39.4 mV) after a time of:

$$T = \frac{\delta v \times C}{I_L}$$

$$= \frac{39.4 \times 10^{-3} \times 10^{-9}}{10^{-7}} \text{ s}$$

$$= 39.4 \times 10^{-5} \text{ s}$$

$$= 394 \ \mu\text{s}$$

This calculation is based upon a small total leakage current of 10^{-7} A, the major component of which is the input current of amplifier B. This can to some degree be balanced out by supplying an external current, but it is difficult to make this alter in the same manner with temperature as the amplifier current.

The calculated time of 394 μs before the output drifts by 1 bit is much greater than the conversion time of a typical ADC, and a considerably larger capacitor leakage current could be tolerated with a conversion time of say 20-30 μs. If, however, longer holding times are required, the leakage current must be decreased. This generally requires that amplifier B should have an FET input stage.

6.9. ANALOG MULTIPLEXERS

Analog-to-digital converters cost much more than the logic circuits required at a typical interface, particularly if they have a small conversion time. Consequenty in data-logging applications and other situations where perhaps several hundred analog voltages must be sampled and digitized the expense of a separate ADC for each input would be prohibitive.

With some penalty in the rate of sampling the cheaper solution of a single ADC connected in turn to each input voltage is normally preferred. The sampling rate is then determined by the total time needed to switch to the next input, sample the voltage, and convert it to a digital quantity. Thus a relatively fast converter might require, say, 10 μs plus 2 μs settling time for a switch and sampling circuit, making 12 μs in all. The maximum sampling rate would then be just over 80 kHz.

If, however, there is one ADC per input, or at least 12 if there are more than 12 inputs, their conversion periods can be overlapped to produce 1 sample/μs, the full speed of a typical DMA channel. The very expensive arrangement of one converter per channel is thus rarely used, and most converters are preceded by some switching network. This is called a "multiplexer" and is in effect a multipole switch which can connect the ADC to any one of the input circuits. The control of the multiplexer can be arranged in several ways.

One possibility for data logging is to sample at fixed intervals of time, using a constant-frequency pulse train. When each pulse appears the multiplexer steps on to the next input which is then sampled and converted. The pulse train is usually locked to real time, and not synchronized to the computer clock waveform. Thus the program must either be kept in a waiting loop until conversion is finished and the data is ready for transfer, or the computer can be given a background task which is interrupted each time a conversion is finished and a data transfer is required. The particular channel connected at any moment is usually controlled by a counter, followed by a set of decoding gates, each of which energizes the appropriate input switch when the counter contains its channel number. In order that the program can keep track of the switch position, it is necessary to have some provision for clearing the counter so that the sampling always starts at channel 0.

Another procedure often used is to omit the timing pulses but drive the counter from the "A.D.Convert" instruction. Then each request for a conversion ensures that after sampling the required input the multiplexer moves to the next input ready for the next sample. Again it is necessary to start with the multiplexer in a known position to enable the program to keep track of the current switch position.

The most versatile arrangement is the second of the above procedures, with, in addition, the provision for the multiplexer counter to be read or loaded by the program. This enables the program to read the analog signals in any order, not merely sequentially, and also to step round the signals rapidly until some anomaly is discovered, and then to identify the channel by reading the contents of the counter.

As an example one multiplexer available for the PDP8 computer series has a maximum capacity of 64 unbalanced inputs, and is controlled by a 6-bit channel-address register which is connected as a counter. It is assigned the device code 54 and by using this in conjunction with each of the three IOP pulses three different control instructions can be assembled. Those normally used are as follows.

(1) ADCC (6541). This uses IOP 1 and clears the channel-address register to zero.
(2) ADSC (6542). This uses IOP 2 and transfers the contents of the accumulator (bits 6-11) to the channel-address register.
(3) ADIC (6544). This uses IOP 4 and increments the channel-address register. After reaching 63_{10} the next address will be 00.

A somewhat later machine, the PDP9, uses the same general arrangement but the "clear channel address" instruction is replaced by a "read channel address" instruction which copies the contents of the channel-address register into the least significant six bits of the accumulator, thus allowing the program to identify the current channel number.

In the Nova range of computers a similar set of instructions is provided, with provision for an 8-bit channel-select register (256 inputs) and a 16-bit data register. These are connected as the A and C registers of the interface respectively, and the device code allocated is 21. Thus the instruction

```
DOAS        2        ADCV
```

sends a channel number previously loaded into bits 8-15 of accumulator 2 into the channel-select register (register A), and sends a start signal to initiate conversion. The mnemonic ADCV is altered by the compiler to 21, the device code of the multiplexer. The instruction

```
DIA         3        ADCV
```

will clear bits 0-7 of accumulator 3 and copy the contents of the channel-select register into bits 8-15. Bits 8 and 9 of the instruction can also specify what function the multiplexer and converter perform.

The third instruction allows data to be read from the converter output buffer, the C register. For example

```
DIC         1        ADCV
```

will copy the contents of the converter buffer into accumulator 1. There is provision for extending the sign digit of a negative value to the left if, as is usual, the ADC output comprises less than 16 bits. By including extra coding in bits 8 and 9 the same instruction can be used to increment the channel-select register after the data transfer and start another conversion.

The above instructions, by setting 01 in bits 8 and 9, can issue a "start" signal on the I/O bus which initiates a conversion. If the timing of the conversion is important an external timing clock can be used. The interface will then start conversion at the clock pulse following the start pulse.

If a large number of points must be examined quickly the program control of A-D conversion may be rather slow. For such situations a data scanner can be used which automatically samples each channel in turn and sends the digitized value directly to the store via a data channel. The timing is usually controlled by an internal clock, and the scanner needs a channel counter, a channel register, a 15-bit address counter to provide the address to the main store, and a word counter to check the total number of words transferred. The scanner must be initialized by program, being given the starting channel number, the final channel number, the starting address in the main store, and the 2's complement of the word count. The automatic scanning sequence is started by sending an I/O pulse from the processor in place of the usual start signal. When the scanning sequence has finished the scanner may be arranged to cause a program interrupt. This transfers control to a program which uses the data which has been read and then initializes the scanner for a further sequence.

6.10. ANALOG SWITCHES

Although a number of devices have been used for switching analog signals, only two are now widely used, one electronic and one electromechanical. The most efficient switch in the sense that it has the lowest "on" resistance and the highest "off" resistance is a mechanical device. Since the switch setting must be controlled by digital signals some form of relay is required. The most suitable device is the reed relay, which has its contacts sealed in an inert atmosphere inside a small glass tube. At the low voltages and currents involved in multiplexing a life of around 10^9 operations is typical. Such a device is essentially slow since the operating time is about 1 ms and a similar period may elapse before the contacts have ceased to bounce.

Where faster operation is required an FET can be used, with a gate-control circuit similar to that shown in Fig. 6.5b for sample-and-hold switching. Although in principle multiplexers can be made with a large number of inputs, it is customary to limit the number of inputs to one switch to 32 or 64 in order to avoid crosstalk from the other channels to the selected channel. If the multiplexer has to cope with a greater number of inputs two-level switching is more satisfactory.

Whatever type of switch is used it is essential that two different inputs should never be connected together. This calls for a driving circuit which ensures that the switching is always "break before make." This can be ensured by inserting a delay in the make operation and ensuring that the break operation proceeds at full speed.

For some special applications it is necessary to sample a number of signals simultaneously. This requires a separate sample-and-hold circuit for each signal, all actuated by the same sampling pulse. After the samples have been taken, the analog multiplexer can connect each in turn to the ADC.

The switching arrangements discussed above all provide a direct connection through the analog switch to the sample-and-hold circuit or directly to the ADC. Where a signal has superimposed upon it a large common-mode noise voltage this direct connection may not be permissible since the ADC or the input amplifier of the sample-and-hold circuit might be damaged. Some method of substantially reducing the common-mode voltage reaching the ADC is needed.

A technique which has been used in such situations with relay switching is the "flying-capacitor" arrangement. This requires two switches, a multiway two-pole switch which selects the pair of lines carrying the wanted signal, and a second two-way two-pole switch which connects a capacitor alternately across the incoming signal and then across the ADC input. If the input capacitance of the ADC is small compared with the transfer capacitor and the ADC input resistance is large, the signal value stored on the transfer capacitor will be an accurate sample of the signal. This method can cope with common-mode signals of the order of 200-300 V, the working voltage of a typical relay.

Some reduction in the number of switching elements can be obtained if each pair of switches can be controlled separately, as shown in Fig. 6.6. Here all switches are initially open. In order to sample channel 2,

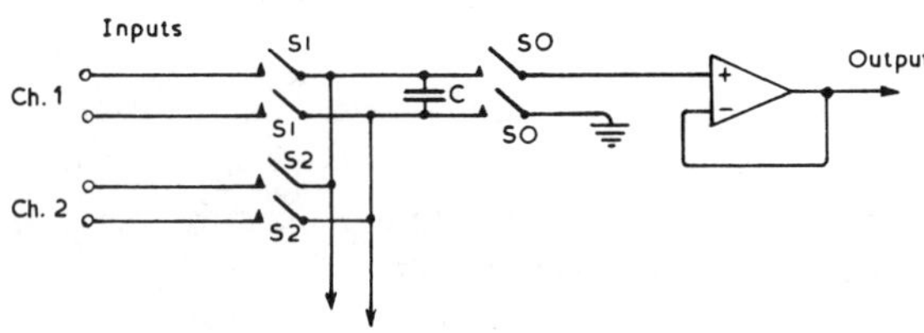

Figure 6.6. Flying-capacitor multiplexer

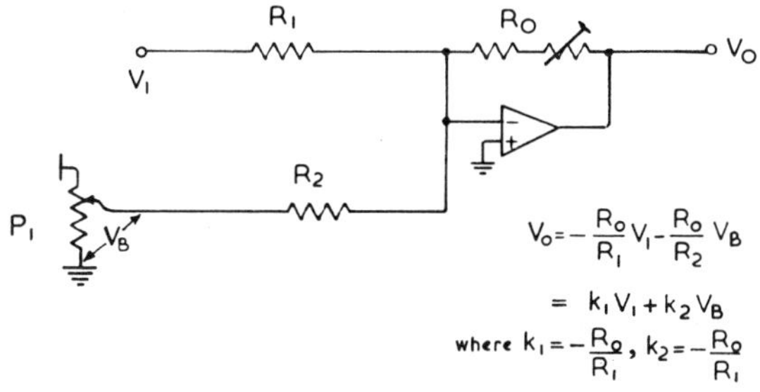

Figure 6.7. Scaling and zero adjustment of analog signal

say, switches S2 are closed for long enough to charge up capacitor C. Switch S2 is then opened, and S0 closed to connect C to the output amplifier. This arrangement is best suited to inputs having a fairly low source resistance, as the charging time of the transfer capacitor C may be prohibitively long if the source resistance is large. In such cases the signals may require a low-output-impedance amplifier at the far end of the line.

6.11. ANALOG SIGNAL PROCESSING

Measuring transducers often produce voltages which are too small for the normal ADC and may have a zero offset. In order to produce a digital signal which correctly represents the physical quantity being measured it is then necessary to scale the voltage (multiply it by a fixed quantity) and shift the zero.

This can be performed by a single high-gain direct-coupled amplifier (usually called an operational amplifier) as shown in Fig. 6.7. Assuming infinite amplifier gain and high input impedance, the output voltage V_0 is given by:

$$V_o = -\left(\frac{R_0}{R_1} V_1 + \frac{R_0}{R_2} V_B\right)$$

Here V_1 is the input voltage and V_B the bias voltage controlled by potentiometer P1. Part of R_0 may be made adjustable to trim the gain $(-R_0/R_1)$ and P1 is used to adjust the zero. Several signals can also be summed in this circuit by connecting them via suitable input resistors to the junction of R_0 and R_1.

Once this circuit has been set up, the only variable input is V_1, and the output V_0 is a linear function of V_1. Sometimes it may be necessary to produce an output proportional to the product of two variables. This might arise, for example, when logging the flow of liquid through an open rectangular duct. The easiest quantities to measure are the depth of the liquid and its velocity. The product of these two quantities is then proportional to the volume flowing per second. For this situation packaged electronic multipliers are available which will typically accept two input signals in the range 0-10 V and produce full-scale output for two full-scale inputs. Thus if the input signals are V_x volts and V_y volts, the output V_z is given by:

$$V_z = \frac{V_x V_y}{10} \text{ V}$$

The accuracy of these devices when carefully set up is typically 0.25%; thus if greater accuracy is required it is necessary to adopt the slower process of digitizing both quantities and multiplying the digital values by program after they have been transferred to the processor. The same multiplying unit can be used to generate the square, or (with an extra amplifier) the square root of a variable.

For some purposes a logarithmic characteristic is required. This is generally obtained by using a diode or transistor as the feedback element of an operational amplifier, taking advantage of the exponential relation between current and voltage in a semiconductor junction. Other non-linear relations can be obtained by using a diode non-linear function generator.

In all of these instances the characteristic could be obtained by using digital processing in the computer, but the analog signal processing has the advantage of greater speed since it requires no program to implement it.

The multiplexer circuits previously described were concerned solely with switching one of a number of inputs to an A-D converter. This implies that all of the inputs include amplifiers where necessary to bring all signals up to the same level. With a large number of inputs this may be an expensive procedure, and one solution is to switch at low level and use a single amplifier after the multiplexer. This imposes more severe constraints upon the zero error and other inaccuracies of the multiplexer, and for small signals such as those from thermocouples necessitates relay switching for maximum accuracy. Even with this provision thermal e.m.f's caused by the use of dissimilar metals in the low-level circuit may be troublesome.

A further problem arises when inputs differ in magnitude, thus needing different amplifier gains to bring them up to the standard level to match the ADC range. At the cost of extra switch elements it is possible to use what is sometimes called a "programmed" amplifier. This incorporates several feedback resistors, the appropriate one to give the required gain for each input being selected either by program from the computer or by a prewired multiway switch which is ganged to the multiplexer switch. With the latter arrangement, as the multiplexer switch selects each input the additional switch bank simultaneously adjusts the amplifier gain by switching in the appropriate feedback resistor.

Alternatively, the gain may be selected by program. For example, one low-level analog input facility which can be used on the PDP11 computer, the AFC11, accepts inputs in blocks of 32 channels up to a total of 1024 differential inputs. The channel which is to be examined is selected by a 16-bit word which is loaded into a channel-address-gain-select register in the interface. Bits 0-10 of this word are used to select the channel, and bits 12-14 select the gain. The gain is adjustable in steps from 2 (control inputs 111), in a 2, 5, 10 sequence up to 1000 (control inputs 000). Field-effect-transistor switches are used to adjust the gain so that the amplifier will respond quickly. This interface uses three registers, the chanel-address-gain-select register mentioned above, a 16-bit data register which stores the output of the A-D converter before sending it to the processor, and a 3-bit control and status register. The latter indicates the three separate states of Busy, Done, and Interrupt Enable.

6.12. DIGITAL MULTIPLEXING

Some situations occur in on-line systems where a number of digital outputs are required. If there are only a few of these it may be convenient to allocate a separate device-select code to each one and operate them as separate interfaces. Otherwise it is more economical to multiplex them through a single digital-output interface. This procedure is particularly convenient if the data rate is well below the maximum capacity of the I/O bus.

In general this requires a set of registers, one for each output channel, which are up-dated in turn from the I/O bus. Also required is a channel-address register. In order to effect a data transfer two IOT instructions are required, the first to load the required channel number into the channel address register and the second to transfer the data. The channel-address register is loaded from the I/O bus. Its output is connected to a decoder so that each channel number loaded energizes one of the output lines. This is connected so as to gate data from the I/O bus into the register feeding that channel when the appropriate device IOT is issued.

The general arrangement is shown in Fig. 6.8. This has provision for loading a new channel address each time an output transfer is made. Other possible arrangements could be to use the IOP pulses to allow either a data transfer to a device register, or a data transfer followed by incrementing the channel address register. In the latter case only the first transfer would need to be preceded by a transfer of the channel address required, so long as the channels were addressed sequentially. Then each subsequent transfer would increment the channel address ready to load the next register.

A simple program to load data sequentially into a set of *N* output registers is shown in Table 6.2. It uses PDP8 code, in which the two numerical instructions are input-output transfers. The first digit must thus be 6. The next two digits indicate the device-select codes, 35 for the channel-address register and 36 for the data registers. The last digit is 2, signifying that the timing pulse IOP2 is used to gate information from the data lines to the various registers. The program will make *N* data transfers, the first one to channel *M*. It assumes that some previous

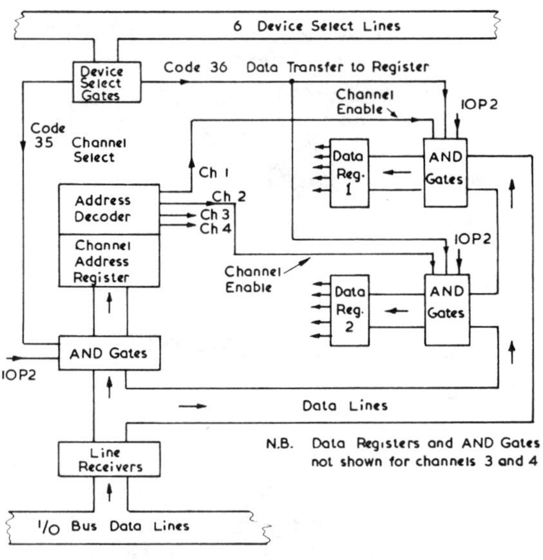

Figure 6.8. Digital multiplexer on I/O bus

Table 6.2. Program to Load into Output Registers

	CLA		
	TAD	(—*N*)	/ Load complement of block size
	DCA	COUNT	/ Store in location COUNT
	TAD	(*M*)	/ Load no. of first channel examined
	DCA	CHNO	/ Store in location CHNO
START	CLA		
	TAD	CHNO	/ Load channel number
	6352		/ Transfer to channel-address register
	CLA		
	TAD I	DATA	/ Load next data word
	6362		/ Transfer to selected deviced register
	ISZ	CHNO	/ Increment channel number
	ISZ	DATA	/ Increment data address
	ISZ	COUNT	/ Increment count, skip if finished
	JMP	START	/ Not finished, go to next word

instructions which loaded the data into the store have planted the address of the first data word in the location DATA, and that the data words are stored in contiguous locations.

The channel-address register shown in Fig. 6.8 cannot be incremented, so that a new channel number must be loaded into it for each data transfer. Since the program uses indirect addressing to fetch the data word, the ISZ DATA instruction could be avoided by holding the data-word address in an auto-index register. Also by adding to the hardware, so that the channel-address register could be used as a counter, the ISZ CHNO instruction would not be needed for sequential transfers into the device registers.

In addition to the extra hardware, an extra step in the instruction is needed to increment the channel-address register after each data transfer. This could conveniently be organized by making the instruction issue an IOP4 pulse and using it for the incrementation. Since the IOP4 pulse occurs just over 1 μs after the IOP2 pulse which times the data transfer, the extra step takes significantly less time than fetching and executing the ISZ CHNO instruction.

Allowing for the use of IOP2, or IOP4, or both, three instructions could be issued causing the actions shown below.

6362	(IOP2)	Load device register
6364	(IOP4)	Increment channel-address register
6366	(IOP2 & IOP4)	Load device register, then increment channel-address register

The above arrangement, although often used, necessarily up-dates the device registers one at a time. For some applications it is necessary for all of the registers to be up-dated simultaneously. Typical of these are CRT displays in which the registers feed directly to DAC's which control the deflection voltages. In order to meet this requirement double buffering can be used, with two data registers per channel. The first registers in all channels are loaded one at a time from the I/O bus, and then a final instruction transfers data from the first register in each channel to the second register simultaneously. In effect this delays up-dating the output or second registers until all data have been transferred from the processor, and then up-dates them all together.

In this section we have examined multiplexers which are used to output data, but almost identical arrangements can be used to multiplex input data. Furthermore, it is not necessary for data to consist of, say, 16-bit words only. In many control situations it is necessary to sense and control a number of separate on-off functions, each of which can be assigned to a single bit in a data word. Although for convenience these separate signals are usually grouped together 16 at a time, in order to assemble a complete word they can be read, output, and manipulated individually. Thus the output interface may provide 16 sets of relay contacts which may be individually opened and closed by program. On the input side, a similar set of relays can be used. The computer senses the state of the contacts, and the driving circuit inputs data by energizing the relay coil, say for a logical 1, and disconnecting it for 0.

This arrangement has the advantage that there is no need to have a common connection between all input circuits as there would be if the computer sensed only voltage levels. Where the inputs may come from a variety of sensing and control devices, as in a large chemical plant or a power station, it is generally impossible to common together one side of all the incoming circuits, otherwise the signals would suffer from excessive noise and mutual interference.

In addition to handling standard logic signals which are directly coupled, it may be convenient to use only short pulses for input signals which can be transformer coupled and so eliminate common-mode interference. Each input pulse is then connected, usually through a Schmitt trigger to standardize its amplitude, to a storage bistable. In order to allow the computer to react to the arrival of a pulse, all bistable outputs are usually connected to an OR gate which energizes the interrupt line. The computer can then either check each bistable separately to find which is set, or more easily read the entire word of, say, 16 bistable outputs into the accumulator and by shifting decide which bit has been set. Each Accumulator Rotate instruction will move one bit of the word into the link or carry position which can then be tested to determine whether it has been set. This is quicker than using a mask with an AND operation to isolate each bit of the word in turn. If the program is required to start with the least significant bit in the word a rotation right is needed to bring this bit into the link position. A PDP8 program which will test each bit in turn and jump to the appropriate service routine is shown in Table 6.3. This includes a count of 12 to test each bit in the 12-bit word. The starting addresses of the 12 service programs to attend to the devices which set each of the 12 bits are assumed to be loaded into the store in location SERV + 1 to SERV + 13.

Here the position of the bit which is set, calling the least significant bit no. 1, is indicated by the contents of the location LOOP, *N*, say. When a 1 is found, the contents of LOOP are added to the address SERV so modifying it to give the location of the starting address of the service routine required, in this case SERV + *N*.

This program provides for reading a data word from only one input register, thus limiting the interface to only 12 inputs. If more inputs are needed the interface needs more data registers and a short word-select or word-address register. The program then needs an extra IOT instruction to load the word-select register before reading the data word, and a further loop to read in and test a data word from each of the interface registers in turn, in a similar manner to the program given for outputting data words in Table 6.2.

Table 6.3. Program to Test Each Bit in a Data Word

	CLA		
	DCA	LOOP	/ Clear location to count no. of bits tested
	TAD	(−14)	/
	DCA	CNT	/ Stores -12_{10} (-14_8) in CNT for loop counter
	IOT		/ Reads word from input register to ACC
	CLL		/ Clear link
START	RAR		/ Shift least significant bit into link
	ISZ	LOOP	/ Increment LOOP
	SNL		/ Skip if link is set
	JMP	START	/ Otherwise return for next bit
	DCA	TEMP	/ Store contents of ACC
	TAD	SERV	/ Load base address
	TAD	LOOP	/ Modify address
	DCA	ADDR	/ Store temporarily
	TAD	TEMP	/ Restore contents of accumulator
	ISZ	CNT	/ Increment loop counter, skip if all 12 bits tested
	JMP I	ADDR	/ Jump to service routine
	Rest of program		

6.13. REMOTE MULTIPLEXERS

The multiplexers described in previous sections are connected directly to the I/O bus or the DMA channel of the computer and are thus close to it. Multiplexers, generally digital, are sometimes remote from the computer and connected to it through a telephone circuit. A typical application would be to collect together the information from a number of slow data channels, such as teleprinter circuits, and assemble it into a single fast data stream at 2400 or 4800 bits/s.

Such remote multiplexers may contain at minimum little more logic than would be needed for a multiplexer attached to the computer. At the other extreme they may undertake a considerable amount of processing, parity checking, code translation, etc., and incorporate a standard small computer.

The main advantage of remote multiplexers is the saving in the cost of telephone lines which they allow, and in some cases the saving of central-processor time which is possible if parity checking and other tasks can be handled by the multiplexer rather than by increasing the burden on the central processor.

A typical application is in a teleprocessing system such as that used by banks, finance companies, or insurance companies to provide data links to each branch office. Each branch terminal may be connected to a local multiplexer serving the connurbation, thus requiring only a single link from the multiplexer to the head-office computer, rather than one for each branch office.

6.14. WAVEFORM GENERATION

The low cost of microprocessors allows them to be used as an inexpensive method of generating waveforms of prescribed shape with controlled timing. This is a requirement in many control applications where a particular velocity — or displacement — time profile may be needed. It is usually performed by storing a set of ordinates and sending these successively to a D-A converter. For a limited number of cases a polynomial may be used to compute the ordinates, but generally it is much quicker to store the data needed.

The timing of the waveform can be altered by controlling the interval between data transfers, by using a software delay loop, or a counter-timer package. Alternatively, an external pulse can create an interrupt which outputs the next ordinate, so allowing the waveform to be varied in speed by a voltage-controlled oscillator. Another variant is similar to a driven oscilloscope time base in that a single external pulse can create an interrupt which executes a program to output a complete cycle of the waveform. The program given in Table 6.4 generates a parabolic waveform using an 8-bit D-A converter connected to a Motorola M6800 via a PIA. In this program the timing of the waveform is controlled by a set of thumb switches which are read into accumulator B as each ordinate is output, and decremented to zero to determine the duration of each step of the waveform.

The index register is initially cleared and subsequently incremented after each transfer to point to the next ordinate. It is also used as a counter. The program arbitrarily has 16 ordinates and, when the contents of the index register have reached 16 (= 10 hexadecimal), it is cleared and the waveform is started again.

The same approach could be used for a waveform of any shape, with any number of ordinates.

LOC	DATA CODE	DECIMAL VALUE
0040	00	0
41	01	1
42	04	4
43	09	9
44	10	16
45	19	25
46	24	36
47	31	49
48	40	64
49	51	81
4A	64	100
4B	79	121
4C	90	144
4D	A9	169
4E	C4	196
4F	E1	225

6.15. TRANSDUCERS

The earlier sections of this chapter were concerned only with processing electrical signals in various ways. In many control applications, the original source of data is a non-electrical state or quantity, and the final control must be exercised on some non-electrical variable.

Microprocessors in particular are increasingly being incorporated into non-electrical devices such as fuel pumps, cash registers, washing machines, machine tools, etc. In all of these applications, transducers are necessary in order to convert various physical states or quantities into

Table 6.4. Program for Parabola Generator

LOCATION		PROGRAM INSTRUCTION	CODE	COMMENT
0010		LDA A # 04	86	Set up bit pattern
11			04	for Control Register A
12		STA A CRA	B7	Load into Control
13			80	Register
14			05	
15		COM 8006	73	Set DDRB for
16			80	data output
17			06	
18		LDA A # 24	86	Set up bit pattern
19			24	for Control Register B
1A		STA A CRB	B7	Load Control
1B			80	Register B
1C			07	
1D	START:	LDX # 0000	CE	Clear Index
1E			00	Register
1F			00	
20	STEP:	LDA A X,40	A6	Fetch next ordinate
21			40	
22		STA A PB	B7	MOVE to PB,
23			80	(DAC)
24			06	
25		LDA B PA	F6	Read switches
26			80	into ACC B
27			04	
28	LOOP:	DEC B	5A	Decrement ACC B
29		BNE LOOP	26	Repeat if not zero
2A			FD	
2B		INX	08	Increment Index Reg.
2C		CPX # 0010	8C	Compare with 10 (hex.)
2D			00	$= 16_{10}$
2E			10	
2F		BNE STEP	26	Repeat the step if
30			EF	not equal
31		BEQ START	27	Restart waveform if 16
32			EA	ordinates have been output

electrical signals for computer input and to reverse the process for output. Ideally all input transducers should generate digital signals which can be connected directly to an input port or interface, but a number of measurements, for example that of temperature, cannot be treated in this way, since the only convenient transducers generate an analog voltage. This may need amplification before it is passed to a D-A converter and thence in a parallel form to the processor.

The term transducer should strictly be applied only to devices which convert one form of energy into another, and so, for computer input, they must abstract energy from the object being measured in order to generate electrical energy. This loading may cause serious errors in measurement, and in such situations the measuring system must be arranged so as to cause no loading whatever. In position measurement, for example, an optical sensing device will satisfy this requirement. Such sensing devices are often included in the category of transducers.

The table on the next page gives a list of some common forms of transducer suitable for computer input:

It will be seen from this table that many measurements, notably those of force, pressure, and temperature are inherently analog in nature and need subsequent A-D conversion. Some control functions, however, can be exercised adequately if a signal can be obtained when a quantity reaches a certain value. Thus, if temperature needs controlling within a coarse band, it may be sufficient to use an on-off sensor which signals when a particular temperature has been reached. The heat input can then be reduced until the temperature falls below the target value, when it is increased again. Similarly, a tank which is being emptied by some process and replenished under computer control may need only two level sensors. When the liquid reaches the top sensor, the input rate is reduced, and when it falls to the lower sensor the input rate is increased. In these situations simple level sensors can be used rather than measuring systems which give a continuous indication of the value of the process variable, and which are usually much more expensive.

In the table, the proximity and level sensors are devices with a single binary output which indicates when the variable being measured has reached a prescribed value.

Most of the transducers are linear devices, producing an output proportional to the change in the input variable. In some cases the phenomena are inherently non-linear as, for example, the relation between fluid speed (which is proportional to flow rate) and pressure differential across a venturi. The pressure differential is proportional to the square of the speed, and an advantage of a computer interfaced measurement is that the computer can be used to extract the square root to any required degree of precision. Also, measurement of temperature by resistance thermometer involves a quadratic relation between temperature and resistance. The computer can be used conveniently to add a small correction to the basically linear relation between temperature and resistance.

Thermistors are also used for less accurate temperature sensing, and exhibit an exponential characteristic:

$$R_T = ae^{\frac{b}{T}}$$

Table 6.5. Types of Input Transducer

POSITION	
Coded plate	Digital
Moiré fringe plate	Digital
Linear variable differential transformer	Analog
Potentiometer	Analog
Capacitance sensing	Analog
PROXIMITY SENSORS — digital outputs	
Capacitance — senses any solid or liquid	
Inductive — senses any metal	
Optical — senses any opaque or reflective object	
FORCE	
Strain gauge bridge	Analog
Piezoelectric crystal	Analog
Variable reluctance sensor	Analog
PRESSURE	
Diaphragm + strain gauge	Analog
Diaphragm + displacement sensor	Analog
Diaphragm + variable reluctance sensor	Analog
Piezoelectrical crystal	Analog
FLOW	
Venturi + pressure difference sensor	Analog
Rotor + magnetic sensor	Digital
Vortex counter	Digital
Piston displacement	Digital
ROTATIONAL SPEED	
Tacho-generator, voltage output	Analog
A.C. tacho-generator, frequency output	Digital
Magnetic pickoff	Digital
Optical sensor + optical disc	Digital
LEVEL OF LIQUID	
Float + position sensor	
Capacitance sensor	
Ultrasonic sensor	
TEMPERATURE	
Platinum resistance thermometer used up to 600°C.	Analog
Thermocouple with suitable material usable up to 1700°C.	Analog
Thermistor used up to 300°C.	Analog

where a and b are constants. Their extremely non-linear characteristic restricts the temperature range over which they can conveniently be used, but within this range a computer program can be employed to interpolate between known calibration points.

Output transducers generally fall into fewer categories than input transducers. Many output transducers involve the control of a.c. mains supply to a motor, contactor, relay, heating element, lamp, etc., and for all of these a triac is generally used as the switching device. A triac is a bilateral solid-state switch which requires a current of the order of 100 mA to establish conduction. Once conducting, the device stays in a low-resistance state until the current through it falls to a (small) value roughly similar to the trigger current needed to establish conduction. Typical values of trigger and holding current for a 25A triac are 100-200 mA.

The triac can be used either as a simple switch, in which case a trigger current pulse is applied at the beginning of each mains half-cycle, or as a proportional controller, in which the current in the load can be reduced by delaying the firing pulse with respect to the mains zero crossing.

A crucial requirement in any such trigger circuit is complete electrical isolation between the computer interface and the triac. This can be provided either by a double-wound pulse transformer or by an optical isolator.

For the control of low power d.c. supplies, for example, the reference voltages for automatic test equipment, a D.A. converter followed by a d.c. amplifier can be used. However, the higher power levels required for d.c. motor drives are usually controlled by a switching device in order to achieve economy in power and to use the controlling device most effectively. Where the supply comes from a.c. mains, thyristors, in a single-phase or three-phrase configuration, are generally used as controlled rectifiers.

Where the supply is d.c., thyristor chopper controllers can be used, but this requires a commutating thyristor to switch off the load current in addition to the load-carrying thyristor. For moderate loads and particularly for high-frequency operation, transistor switches may be more economical as they do not require extra commutating components. They are now available in a Darlington (double emitter follower) configuration which has a typical overall current gain of 1,000 or more.

In addition to d.c. motor drives, low-power actuators may use stepping motors, which require a sequence of pulses to be generated by the processor. They have the advantage of moving through a precise angle for each cycle of driving pulses, so that no shaft position encoder is needed to check the position of the load.

6.16. CONCLUSIONS

Having considered the ways in which information can be processed and modified in its transfer between the attached devices and the processor, we examine in the following chapter some typical applications of on-line computing systems. As a preliminary, some proposals for establishing a standard interface between computers and external devices are examined, and their characteristics compared with those of typical I/O bus highways.

BIBLIOGRAPHY AND REFERENCES

A-D AND D-A CONVERSION

AMAZEEEN, B., et al., Monolithic D-A Converter Operates on Single Supply, *Electronics*, Vol. 53, No. 5, Feb. 28, 1980, p.15.

BLOOD, B., & KINSEY, L., 10-hs Monolithic D-A Converter keeps Bipolar Drive Circuits Hustling, *Electronics*, Vol. 52, No. 24, Nov. 22, 1979, p.140.

BROKAW, P., I^2L puts it all together for 10-bit A-D Converter Chip, *Electronics*, Vol. 51, No. 8, April 13, 1978, p.99.

FIEDLER, U.F, & SEITZER, D., A High-speed 8-bit A/D Converter based on a Gray-code Multiple Folding Circuit, IEEE J., *Solid State Circuits*, Vol. SC-14, No. 3, June 1979, p. 547.

GILCHRIST, N.H.C. A-D and D-A Conversion for Broadcast Quality Sound, *Radio & Electronic Engineer*, Vol. 49, No. 2, Feb. 1979, p.77.

GORDON, B.M., Standardizing the A.D.A.-to-Microprocessor Interface, *Electronics & Power*, Vol. 23, No. 5, May 1977, p.393.

GRAY, P.R., & HODGES, D.A. ALL-MOS A/D Conversion Techniques—An Overview, *IEEE Circuits and Systems Magazine*, Vol. 1, No. 12, 1979, p.15.

HNATEK, E.R. Microprocessor—Digital Converter Applications, *Microprocessors*, Vol. 1, No. 4, April 1977, p.227.

I.E.E.E. Special Issues on Analog Circuits, *IEEE Journal*, Vol. SC-14, No. 6, Dec. 1979.

MATTERA, L., Data Converters Latch Onto Microprocessors, *Electronics*, Sept. 1, 1977, Vol. 50, No. 18, p.81.

MOKHOFF, N., Monolithic Approach Bears Fruit in Data Conversion, *Electronics*, Vol. 52, No. 10, May 10, 1979, p.105.

VAN DE PLASSCHE, R.J., & GOEDHART, D. A Monolithic 14-bit D/A Converter, *IEEE Journal of Solid-State Crts.*, Vol. SC-14, No. 3, June 1979, p.552.

SCHOEFF, J.A., Standard Bipolar Process yields 12-bit Monolithic D-A Converter, *Electronics*, Vol. 52, No. 25, Dec. 6, 1979, p.152.

TITUS, J.A., et al., *Microcomputer—Analog Converter Software and Hardware Interfacing,* H.W. Sams & Co., Indianapolis, 1978.

TUTHILL, M., & BURTON, D.P. Low-cost A-D Converter Links Easily with Microprocessors, *Electronics*, Vol. 52, No. 18, Aug. 30, 1979, p.149.

ZUCH, E.L., Where and When to use which Data Converter, *IEEE Spectrum*, Vol. 14, No. 6, June 1977, p.38.

TRANSDUCERS

BARRETT, D.F., and BROWN, A.E., The Computer Interface of Ultrasonic Flowmeters, *I.S.A. Trans.*, Vol. 16, No. 2, p.51, 1977.

BARTOSIAK, G., Guide to Thermocouples, *Instruments and Control Systems*, Vol. 51, No. 11, Nov. 1978, p.53.

BENEDICT, R.F. *Fundamentals of Temperature, Pressure and Flow Measurements,* 2nd ed., Wiley, New York, 1977.

BIBBERO, R.J., *Microprocessors in Instruments and Control,* Wiley, New York, 1977.

DIEHL, W., and REYNOLDS, W., *Microprocessor-based Engine Dynamometer Data Acquisition System,* Proc. 5th Annual Conf. Industrial and Control Applications of Microprocessors, p.210, IEEE, New York, 1979.

EDWARDS, J.E. Flow Measurement Practice, *Chem. Eng* (G.B.), No. 344, May 1979, p.325.

ELENGO, J.J. Applying Weight Sensing Transducers, *Mach. Des.*, Vol. 51, No. 19, August 23, 1979, p.82.

HUDSON, C., A Guide to Optical Shaft Encoders, *Instruments and Control Systems*, Vol. 51, No. 5, May 1978, p.33.

I.E.E., *Digital Instrumentation,* IEE Conference Publication, No. 106, London, 1973.

KEFFER, J.F., et al., Digital Techniques for the Simultaneous Measurement of Velocity and Temperature, *Rev. Sci. Instr.*, Vol. 49, No. 9, Sept. 1978, p.1343.

MALMSTADT, H.V., et al., *Electronic Measurements for Scientists,* Benjamin. Menlo Park, 1974.

MORRIS, H.M., Pressure Measurement: A Wide View of a Wider Subject, *Control Eng.*, Vol. 25, No. 5, May 1978, p.57.

MORRIS, H.M., Rotary Tachometers Dominate the Velocity Sensing Market, *Control Eng.*, Vol. 25, No. 12, Dec. 1978, p.37.

NORTON, H.N., *Handbook of Transducers for Electronic Measuring Systems,* Prentice-Hall, Englewood Cliffs, N.J., 1969.

OWER, E., and PARKHURST, R.C. *The Measurement of Air Flow,* Pergamon Press, Oxford, England, 5th ed., 1977.

RENNEBERG, M., Trends in Thermometry, *Electron.*, No. 169, March 20, 1979, p.13.

SHEPHERD, I. Reviewing Pressure Transducer Technologies to Aid Selection, *Control and Instrumentation*, Vol. 11, No. 1, Jan. 1979, p.35.

SINHA, P.K., Electromagnetic Micrometers, *I.E.E. Conf., New Developments in Automatic Testing*, Nov. 1977, p.20.

SKELTON, M.H. Digital Tachometers Utilizing Position Encoder with 2 Outputs in Quadrature., *IBM Tech. Disclosure Bull.*, Vol. 22, No. 4, Sept. 1979, p.1313.

SLOMANIA, M. *Selecting Differential Pressure Instrumentation,* Intech Vol. 26, No. 8, Aug. 1979, p.32.

TESCHLER, L. Transducers for Digital Systems, *Mach. Des.*, Vol. 51, No. 16, July 12, 1979, p.64.

TOLLIVER, B.R. Strain Gauge Pressure Transducers, New Look for an Old Standby, *Mach. Des.*, Vol. 49, No. 25, Nov. 10, 1977, p.123.

WATSON, D. Three-chip Digital Scale Zeros Tare Weight, *Electronics*, Vol. 52, No. 24, Nov. 22, 1979, p. 146.

WOLBER, W.G. *Sensor Development in the Microcomputer Age.* 1978 Int. Electron Devices Meeting, Washington, D.C., Dec 4-6, 1978, p.12., IEEE, New York.

WOOLVET, G.A. *Transducers in Digital Systems,* IEE, London, 1977.

Chapter 7

On-Line Applications

7.1. STANDARDIZATION OF INTERFACES

A complaint expressed frequently by users of on-line computing systems and by the manufacturers of peripheral equipment for them is the variety of interface arrangements through which information must be transferred. Virtually all manufacturers of small computers have adopted different sets of control signals; some have unidirectional data lines, while others have bidirectional data lines, and there is no general agreement about the number and meaning of device flags and status bits. Thus any interface designed for a particular machine, or family of machines, will not be suitable for machines built by another manufacturer and usually not even for a different family of machines made by the same manufacturer.

This means that the user or manufacturer of devices to attach to computers may have a wide variety of interfaces to deal with. From the user's point of view the ideal arrangement would be a standard interface which would fit the I/O bus of any make of computer. This is at present an unlikely prospect, since various manufacturers have a heavy investment in the hardware and software of their current machines. The nearest approach to this is an interface, such as that for the IBM 360 series of computers, which is used not only by IBM but also by other makers of ''plug-compatible'' equipment.

The only practicable arrangement at present is to have a standard interface at one remove from the computer bus. This means that all external devices have a standard highway or data bus to plug into, with standard circuit conditions and signals. The highway then feeds into an adaptor which is coupled to the computer I/O bus. Thus everything beyond the adaptor is completely standardized and, if the computer is changed, the only hardware that needs changing is the adaptor.

This arrangement leads to a considerable reduction in the number of interfaces which must be designed. If there are N different models of computer and M different external devices, the direct connection of device to computer requires a total of $N \times M$ different interfaces. Using the principle of an adaptor and a standard highway, only M different device interfaces and N different adaptors are needed. The utopian situation of only one type of computer interface requires only M interfaces in all.

The standard highway with adaptor arrangement offers many advantages to the user. An important one is economy. Since any particular module needs only the standard highway interface, a single design can be used for all installations regardless of the type of computer to which they are connected. This means larger-scale production and lower cost. Also, modules from several manufacturers can be combined in a single system. The computer can be up-graded or changed to a different model without needing any change in the modules, thus avoiding much expense due to obsolescence.

These were among the reasons which led the committee for European Standards on Nuclear Equipment (ESONE) to define a standard data-highway system for all of the nuclear instruments and controllers which are used in nuclear research and the operation of nuclear reactors. The system was called CAMAC. Some moves towards a standard system had been made in Canada and America, but the CAMAC system has now been adopted in these countries and Europe, and it is used in at least one installation in Russia.

7.2. THE CAMAC SYSTEM

The CAMAC system specification was first published in 1969, and covered the electrical conditions, signal levels, pulse durations, meaning, and protocol of control signals as well as the mechanical size of the plug-in module and the "crate" or chassis into which they fitted. The specification ensured that units from a range of manufacturers would operate together satisfactorily in the same crate. In 1972 the specification was revised and extended to allow for multiple-crate systems and this version is the current standard.

The information highway or "dataway" in a crate is common to all modules and allows parallel 24-bit data transfers to occur between any two modules. There are two sets of data lines, one for data transfer into modules and a second for transfers from modules, together with address, function, and timing pulse lines. The dataway has 25 ports or "stations," each fitted with an 86-way edge-connector socket into which a device or "module" may be plugged. The flow of data between modules, or between a module and some external device such as a computer, is organized by a unit called the crate controller.

Although the maximum capacity of the dataway is 24 bits, many modules will not use all of them, and it is possible to use only 16 bits if the CAMAC system is interfaced to a 16-bit computer. The complete list of signal lines, excluding the two sets of data lines, is shown in Table 7.1.

Table 7.1. CAMAC Dataway Signals

Function	Symbol	
Read data	R	
Response	Q	Generated
Look-at-me	L	by module
Command accepted	X	
Station	N	
Sub-address (4 lines)	A	
Function (5 lines)	F	
Write	W	
Stroke 1	S1	Generated
Stroke 2	S2	by controller
Busy	B	
Initialize	Z	
Inhibit	I	
Clear	C	

Apart from the L and N lines, these lines are all common to all stations in the crate. The four A lines allow a total of 16 subaddresses per module, and the five function lines provide for 32 different functions in all. The particular station to be addressed is indicated by energizing an N line, and each station can request attention by energizing its L or look-at-me line. Each station has its own L and N lines to the crate controller. The full system allows for a total of seven crates so that a complete CAMAC command must specify the following.

C	(3 bits)	the crate number
N	(5 bits)	the station number
A	(4 bits)	the subaddress or substation number
F	(5 bits)	the function to be performed

There is some redundancy in the coding since a crate can accommodate only 23 normal stations as the controller needs two of the 25 slots; the remaining nine of the station number codes can be used for multiple addressing, etc. A system comprising one crate will need only a 14-bit command (NAF). This conveniently fits within a word from a 16-bit computer.

The modules in a crate are normally passive in that they obey commands from the crate controller. This may be a manually operated device for setting up, checking, and calibrating the modules. For normal operation it may be automatic sequencer which initiates a sequence of operations under the control of a program stored in a read-only store. In many installations, however, the volume of data to be gathered and the computation required to evaluate it require the use of a digital computer which can either be interfaced directly to the crate controller, or, in a multicrate system, to a branch driver which in turn can control up to seven crates.

The only independent activity which the modules can initiate comes through the L lines. These are similar in function to the interrupt lines of a computer, and the usual arrangement in a computer-controlled system is to OR all L lines together so that energizing any one of them causes an interrupt. The computer can then read in a 24-bit word which comprises 1 bit for each L line,and thus identify the module which has the highest priority amongst those requesting attention. Control of the processor can then be passed to the appropriate service routine.

The dataway in a crate is organized on a 1-μs fixed timing sequence with two successive strobe pulses, S1 and S2, which can be used, for example, to read a register and then clear it. There is also a common Q line which acts in a similar manner to the skip line of a computer. The crate controller can issue commands which test the state of a particular module, for example data ready or register overflow, and the response is signalled back along the common Q line.

The mandatory power supplies which must be provided are ±6 V and ±24 V, which cover the needs of all standard digital and analog elements. In addition, ±12 V, +200 V, and a.c. mains may be provided for some special modules.

The signal levels on the dataway are similar to those on many computer I/O buses and are compatible with TTL logic elements. The transmitted levels are +0.5 V or less for logical 1 and +3.5 V or above for logical 0. This negative logic convention is used on account of the party-line working. The drivers must be open collector units as each line has a single pull-up resistor, typically 500 Ω connected to a +5 V supply. The receivers recognize a level of +0.8 V or less as a 1 and 2.0 V or more as a 0. The standard TTL driver which can sink 16 mA is satisfactory for the module-dataway connection, but many of the lines driven by the controller energize all 23 modules simultaneously and require a more powerful driver. Power gates which can sink 100 mA are available and easily meet the requirement as the maximum current to be handled is about 50 mA.

Interfacing to the I/O bus of a small computer such as a PDP8 is relatively simple. The unidirectional data lines of the bus can be extended to the dataway, using one-word transfers for a 12-bit number, and two-word transfers for a 24-bit number. The dataway L signals are connected so as to cause an interrupt signal to the computer, and where necessary the flag test instructions from the computer can be interpreted as CAMAC test instructions, the response from the module along the Q line being extended to the computer skip line.

More complex computer architecture, such as that of the PDP11, can also be used to advantage and, for example, the individual substations within a module can be given unique addresses and used in instructions in exactly the same manner as normal store locations.

The basic concept of a unified and standard databus and interface offers many advantages to users and manufacturers alike, and the CAMAC interface is now being used for a variety of instrumentation and control applications outside its original sphere of nuclear instrumentation. Most manufacturers of small computers provide CAMAC-compatible interfaces, and proposals are in hand for developing a programming language specifically for the CAMAC system.

7.3. THE IEEE : 488 BUS

The CAMAC interface is a fast and powerful highway suitable for the large volumes of data typically handled by nuclear instrumentation and control systems, but its 24-bit data path is sometimes unnecessarily wide.

A need for a much more modest bus system arose in the early 1970's for automatic test and data collection systems. Of the various schemes suggested, that proposed by Hewlett-Packard found the widest acceptance, comprising only 16 lines compared with the 86 needed for CAMAC. It was originally called the General Purpose Interface Bus (GPIB). Of the 16 lines, 8 are used for a parallel bidirectional bus which handles both data and addresses. Three of the remaining lines are used for handshake control of data transfers and five for bus control.

The original scheme allowed for only 15 devices to be attached to the bus, but secondary addressing can be used in which the byte following the address can indicate up to 31 different actions or instructions for any particular device.

The bus signals are all TTL compatible, the maximum length of line allowed without buffers being 20 meters. Having an 8-bit parallel data highway, this standard is clearly convenient to attach to microprocessors, and several manufacturers provide interface packages which couple the GPIB lines to the microprocessor bus. An example is the Motorola MC68488.

Devices attached to the bus may be "listeners" (which receive only) or "talkers" (which transmit only), and are assigned separate addresses for these functions. In addition, some device must be in control of the bus; this was originally expected to be a programmable calculator or a hard-wired controller, but is now often a microprocessor.

The GPIB scheme was adopted for many instrumentation systems and, as more manufacturers produced apparatus compatible with it, the IEEE adopted it as an industry standard; through ANSI it was proposed as an international standard, IEC-66. It is thus often referred to as the IEC bus.

The bus handshake protocol is somewhat more complicated than that of some other buses because, although this is unusual, several devices as "listeners" may be receiving data from a single source or "talker." This requires that the Master device must wait for all of the listeners to conclude each stage of the process before proceeding to the next stage. The mechanism for this is the wired —OR arrangement by which each interface can hold a handshake bus low by means of an open-collector driver. The signal for the next stage to begin is a logical one on the bus, obtained only when every driver connected has been turned off. This effect is produced by a pair of resistors connecting the bus to earth and +5V (typically 3.3k Ω to +5V and 6.2kΩ to earth).

The timing for a data transfer is shown in Fig. 7.1. The first action is that Data Valid (DAV) is changed to 0 by the Master device, assumed here to be writing data to slave listening devices. The devices previously addressed then indicate their readiness by turning off their drivers on the NRFD (Not Ready For Data) line. When the last driver is turned off, the NRFD line changes to logical 1 and this causes the Master to put the data on to the data lines. After a short delay for any ringing to die away, the Master releases the DAV line which changes to 1 as a signal to the listeners to gate data from the data lines into their data registers.

To indicate that the data has been captured, the listening devices first change the NRFD line to a logical 0, then, when the transfer is over, release the NDAC line to logical 1. The transition will occur only after the last listening device has concluded, and it is sensed by the talking device to indicate the end of the data transfer. It then returns DAV to logical 1 and removes the data from the data lines. If there is more data to be transferred, the process to transfer the next byte can now start.

The five bus management lines have the following functions:

Attention (ATN) If this is 0, the information on the data lines is treated as an interface command comprising 5 address bits and two function bits. A logic 1 indicates that the information is data.

Interface Clear (IFC) This is an initializing signal which sets all registers and devices into a known quiescent state.

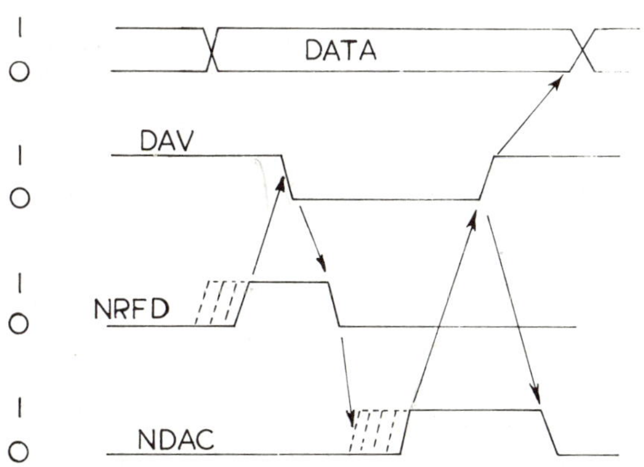

Figure 7.1. IEEE/IEC Bus handshake signals

Service Request (SRQ) This is used to indicate that a device requires attention, and the current sequence must be interrupted to attend to it. When the controller is a microprocessor this signal normally creates an interrupt which polls the devices to find which requires service.

Remote Enable (REN) Many instruments used with the GPI bus have front panel controls to allow them to be used alone, not connected to the bus. The REN line enables the instrument to be operated either through the front panel controls or via the GPI bus.

End or Identify (EOI) The EOI line can be used by a talker to indicate the end of a multiple-byte data transmission, and by the bus Master to conduct a poll of devices.

Before a data transfer can occur, the controller must issue commands to the device required to talk, and to all of those required to listen. This is done by driving a 0 onto the ATN line and issuing successive commands to the other talkers and listeners and, if necessary, preceding these by "untalk" and "unlisten" commands to disable the interface involved in the previous transfer.

There is no separate ATN line to each device, so that after an SRQ signal the controller must poll all devices to discover the source of the request.

7.4. THE BS 4421 : 1969 INTERFACE

The CAMAC dataway is a "party-line" synchronous data highway, resembling many small computer I/O or multiplexer buses, and thus is easily connected to them. At a lower level of complexity it is useful to have some standard interface which operates between a single transmitter (the source) and a single receiver (the acceptor). This kind of star or radial connection was used between early computers and their peripherals, and is a convenient arrangement for simple data-collection and data-transmission systems. It is the operating mode of the British Standard 4421 : 1969. Since many applications were expected to include stop-start or asynchronous devices such as teleprinters, paper-tape readers, etc., the interface is also asynchronous, using the handshake principle for the control signals. The maximum attainable data rate depends upon the logic delays and the propagation time of the line.

Data is transmitted in 8-bit bytes in the parallel mode, using signals compatible with the CCITT V24 standard, or EIA RS-232C. At the transmitter these should be between 5 V and 11 V for any load resistance between 3 kΩ and 7 kΩ, a positive voltage denoting logical 1 and a negative voltage logical 0. The cable specified for the connection between source and acceptor is either a screened 18-way cable using unbalanced circuits sharing a common-earth return, or a 34-way twisted-pair cable in which each circuit has its own return line.

Each link operates in only one direction, so that a bidirectional data channel needs a source and acceptor interface at each end. The interfaces are connected to a plug (acceptor) or socket (source), so that in the event of a fault each source many readily be looped to its adjacent acceptor. This allows each section of the link to be isolated and tested separately.

One disadvantage of the BS 4421 is that lines which have characteristic impedances in the region of 100-300 Ω generally cannot be correctly terminated because the receiver impedance is specified as lying between 3 kΩ and 7 kΩ. Consequently fast data rates cannot be transmitted, since the receiver signals would be blurred and liable to error from reflected signals. Fast data rates can be transmitted reliably only when the lines are correctly terminated, at least at the receiving end. This requires a smaller signal level if the transmitted current is not to become excessive. The most convenient circuit arrangement is then to transmit a standard current along the line, using a correct termination at the receiving end, as shown in Fig. 5.1. The twisted-pair option allows the line to be operated in a balanced-circuit configuration. British Standard 4421 is currently under revision, and the new version is expected to include alternative signal levels for current-drive operation, thus matching the integrated-circuit line drivers and receivers now available.

Although BS 4421 specifies only an 8-bit parallel-data transfer, there are several similar interface arrangements which use the same control signals but vary the format of the data. The changes reflect the way in which the data is originated, but since the control protocol is standard these variants can be connected readily to a BS 4421 system. Typical signal formats include 8-bit serial transmissions, and 16-bit and 24-bit parallel transfers to suit computers with 16 and 24 bits per word. Other variations allow for signalling that a program interrupt is required.

7.5. MICROPROCESSOR BUS STANDARDS

When small microprocessor-based computing systems became available a major sales feature was their flexibility, which allowed a range of store units, peripheral interfaces, etc., to be attached to them. In order to make this a simple operation, one firm, MITS Inc., decided to adopt a standard bus configuration with sufficient lines and spare ways to cope with any anticipated development such as more complex processors and 16-bit data paths. This scheme was of benefit to both users and manufacturers and was so widely adopted as to become almost an industry standard in the form of the S-100 bus.

The original design was intended for use with the ''Altair'' kit and was thus convenient for coupling to the Intel 8080 family of microprocessors. It was deliberately made so that most 8-bit and 16-bit processors could be interfaced to it, but in doing so some features were not fully specified.

In view of its wide acceptance, the IEEE agreed to draw up a more detailed specification of the bus signals and protocol, in order to ensure full compatibility between all units built to the standard, even if these come from different manufacturers. This allows the user to assemble a microprocessor system from a set of S-100 boards chosen to meet his particular requirements without being confined to the products of one manufacturer.

The S-100 bus permits data transfers between a master which controls the bus and a slave which is addressed by the master. In all, 16 data lines are provided; for 8-bit systems these are divided into 8 Data Out lines and 8 Data In lines, and for 16-bit systems they form a single bidirectional bus.

There are 16 address lines, 38 control lines, 8 interrupt lines, and 16 spares. The power supply voltages, ± 8 V and ± 16 V, appear oddly chosen, as they do not match those of any microprocessor. It is intended that a regulator should be fitted on each board for each supply used, to produce stabilized ± 5 V and ± 12 V sources. Although bound to increase hardware costs a little, this approach will reduce excessive voltage drop in interboard wiring and cross-coupling.

A criticism of the S-100 bus is that the $+8$ V and -16 V supplies are connected to adjacent pads on the connector, so that any attempt to remove or insert a board with the power connected can momentarily give the wrong supply and damage all packages connected to it. Also the clock lines which carry waveforms with fast edges are located near slower signals and can induce considerable noise voltages in them.

More boards are now made to the S-100 standard than to any other standard, although there is a similar bus, the S-50, defined by South-West Technical Products Corporation for 6800-based systems.

Some microprocessor manufacturers have introduced standard buses for their multiple-board systems, but these are generaly suitable only for a very limited range of microprocessors. For example, the 86-way Multibus designed by Intel for their 8080 family, cannot easily be used with the Z80 or with the M6800.

Another bus system designed specifically for a single family of microprocessors is the LSI 11 bus which is a reduced version of the Unibus used with all PDP11 minicomputers

Excluding 15 spares, the LSI 11 bus has more control and power lines than the Unibus, but saves 18 lines by multiplexing data and address on the same set of lines. This inevitably reduces the transfer rate across the bus, but it can still easily handle the maximum processor data rate. In addition to the manufacturers of the LSI 11, Digital Equipment Corporation, nearly 20 other manufacturers now make boards compatible with this bus. The use of this bus is likely to increase as more powerful processors, such as the LSI 11/23, come into use.

7.6. ON-LINE APPLICATIONS

Having considered the separate components of an on-line computing system in previous chapters, we conclude by taking a broader view of a few complete installations. A class of applications which may include analog and digital inputs and outputs, data transmission, and a wide range of peripheral devices can be grouped under the headings of data logging and control.

In the simpler systems the sole function may be data logging, with the computer having no control over the plant or operation. Although this arrangement may be justified in certain situations, it generally involves sacrificing some of the computer's potential benefit. Since the computer is used to collect all of the important data about the operation of the plant or process, it can easily scan the data as it is is acquired for any abnormality and initiate some corrective action. This may be a visible or audible warning to the plant operator, or a printed teleprinter message in a non-critical application which involves long time constants. If the plant or process involves short time constants there may be no time for human intervention. Unless some form of automatic control is used the computer must start corrective action immediately the disturbance is recognized, without waiting to refer the situation to a human operator. Even if automatic control is available, the computer system may be arranged to take emergency action as a back-up to the normal control.

If sufficient reliability can be assured, it is of course cheaper to dispense with the automatic-control system and use the computer alone. This procedure has been followed in some chemical plants. Most early computer-control systems were arranged to alter the set points of existing analog control loops in the plant. Once the users were satisfied with the effectiveness and reliability of computer control, later installations dispensed with the many expensive analog loops and exercised direct control over valve and other control settings.

In a complex plant several stages of computer operation may be required. Initially it may be necessary to use the machine purely for data gathering during a study to determine the plant chararacteristics and if possible to form a model of the plant's behavior. Various control algorithms may then be tested on the model before being used on the actual plant.

7.7. DATA LOGGING

The simplest of these applications is that of data logging. This involves scanning a large number of analog signals, converting them into digital form to store in the computer, performing a similar scan on a set of digital inputs, and printing out any abnormal condition. Usually, even if all variables are within their normal range, the computer prints out regular reports on the state of the system and any required statistical data. The analog inputs may come from a range of instruments and transducers, from thermocouples which generate only millivolt-level signals to instruments incorporating electronic amplifiers which deliver a standard output in the range of 0-10 mA. All of these inputs need to be converted to a uniform range of 0-5 V or 0-10 V before being presented to the A-D converter. For the current-drive signals this requires only a precision terminating resistor; for low-level voltage inputs a programmed amplifier may be required.

The digital inputs may represent individual binary signals such as the state of switches, contactors or on-off valves, numerical values in binary or BCD coding, or serial signals such as pulse trains from flow meters, etc. These need conversion to standard logic levels either electronically or by means of intermediate relay switching, or, in the case of pulse trains, by using some counting device which accumulates the total number of pulses received and which can be reset periodically.

An almost essential digital input is a "real-time clock." This allows the computer to determine the elapsed time in hours, minutes, and seconds since it was initialized. For many purposes only relative time is needed to allow certain actions to be implemented at fixed intervals. Where the system is required to synchronize with other real-time activities, for example in a computer-controlled television switching center, the correct local time may be required, however. The real-time clock is often driven from the mains frequency which is usually held at its nominal value within a few seconds a day. If this is not sufficiently accurate a crystal oscillator can be used as a frequency standard.

Real-time clocks are available in a variety of formats. Amongst the simpler of these is the KW11-L clock available for the PDP11 series of computers. This has a 2-bit status register through which it is accessed, one bit being set by program to enable the clock to cause an interrupt, and the second bit causing a processor interrupt. When the interrupt is enabled, interrupts are caused every 16.7 ms (60 Hz mains) or 20 ms (50 Hz mains). By using a preset counter decremented at each interrupt, events can be programmed to occur at any interval which is a multiple of the power-supply period.

If shorter time intervals than this are required, or more exact timing than the power supply can provide, the programmable version of this clock can be used. This includes a 16-bit counter, a buffer register for setting the counter, and a 9-bit status register. The counter can be operated to count either up or down, and it can be loaded automatically from the buffer register after each count if required. When the clock interrupt is enabled, an interrupt is caused either by an underflow or an overflow of the counter. Two bits of the status register allow program selection of one of four count rates, 100-kHz or 10 kHz (crystal-controlled) mains supply frequency or an external source.

The real-time clock for the Nova range of computers is intermediate in facilities between the two previous options. Four operating frequencies are provided, mains supply frequency, 10 Hz, 100 Hz, and 1000 Hz, the last three being crystal-controlled. Once the clock frequency has been set by a DOA-, RTC instruction and the Interrupt Disable is clear, setting Busy will cause the next clock pulse to set Done and thus cause an interrupt. Thereafter it is only necessary to set Busy before the clock pulse is due to ensure that subsequent clock pulses will also cause interrupts.

A somewhat wider range of timing intervals is provided by the Hewlett-Packard Time Base Generator, available as an option for their small computers. This provides a crystal-controlled train of pulses with provision for selecting the interval between pulses by program. This interval can be changed in decade steps from 100 μs to 1000 s, and is normally used to cause a regular series of interrupts.

With all of the real-time clocks described, the action of the clock is merely to cause an interrupt at specified time intervals. Should it be necessary to perform operations at particular times of the day, a short program is needed which typically up-dates periodically three registers in the computer's main store. These contain the current time in hours, minutes, and seconds, and can be read by any other program which handles particular peripheral systems or is required, for example, to print out a summary of the system's operation at regular intervals. Such a program will need initializing facilities to allow the operator to type in local time after the computer has been switched on, thus presetting the hours, minutes, and seconds registers.

When used solely for data logging the computer system shown in Fig. 7.2 may require only a teleprinter for output, giving a summary of the data sufficient to indicate the general trend of the readings. If much data processing is needed, the incoming data may be recorded on magnetic tape with only a minimum of checking and processing. The tape can then be processed by a larger computer off-line. The increasing speed and arithmetic capabilities of small computers now allow a considerable amount of calculation to be performed on data as it is fed into the system, including such operations as fast Fourier transforms.

Other operations may include data checking by examining the degree of correspondence between readings taken from different sensors. For example, the temperature of a large component in a power station or a chemical plant may be measured by temperature sensors such as ther-

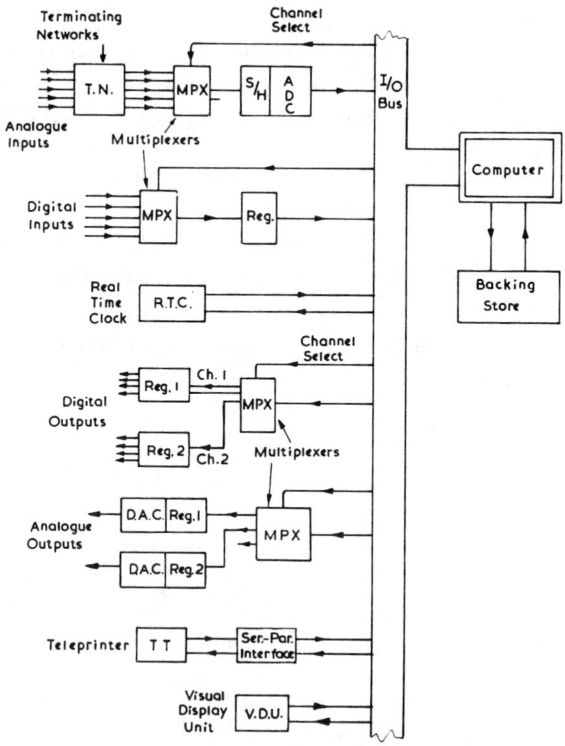

Figure 7.2. Data logging and control system

mocouples at a number of different points. There is usually a high degree of correlation between the temperature at any point and those at neighboring points, particularly if the plant operating conditions are known. It is thus possible to use interpolation methods to estimate the temperature at the sensor location from readings taken at adjacent points. This estimate can then be compared with the actual measured value in order to check the accuracy of the interpolation and if necessary to refine it. Subsequently, each time a reading is taken, the measured value is compared with an interpolated value computed from readings at other points. Any marked disparity is assumed to indicate a faulty sensor. The computer program can then print out a warning to the operator of the plant, and future readings from the faculty sensor can either be ignored or replaced by the interpolated value.

7.8. THE MONITORING FUNCTION

Although there are some situations in which a computer can record and perhaps preprocess data only, the majority of applications require the computer to monitor the data and check as far as practicable for any serious deviations from the expected values. The program can then be arranged to print out an appropriate warning to the operator and, if the computer is allowed to exercise control over the plant, to initiate some action to restore the operating conditions to normal.

This monitoring action is usually performed by assigning low and high limits for each plant variable. As each variable is read, it is compared with the limits and if it is within them no action is taken. Should the variable be outside the limits, a control signal is sent out to bring the variable within the limits. Sometimes extra limits are set, outside those just mentioned, for emergency action. If the variable is found to be outside the emergency limits it is a sign that the normal corrective action is incapable of restoring conditions as quickly as required, and emergency action, often involving a complete shutdown, is essential.

The emergency limits are generally set by considering the safety of the plant or operators, and both these and the normal control limits may need to be under the control of the plant manager so that they can be altered from time to time. This is usually done by keyboard input, with program facilities for printing out any such adjustable parameters on request.

7.9. COMPUTER CONTROL OF PLANT AND PROCESSES

The control activities of an on-line computer may vary very widely. A fairly simple action is that in which the computer is required to instruct the controlling elements of the plant to take up a series of predetermined dispositions. Examples of this are the control of the guide rollers, feed speeds, roll adjustments, etc., for rolling a range of different sections of steel. The computer may here control various feedback loops in order to position parts of the mill, but the settings have been decided by previous experience. Sometimes the same situation of plant being required to set up a range of adjustments may occur, but the time of some actions cannot be determined exactly in advance and a human operator provides the time information. Examples of this are computer-controlled television switching centers. Here, although programs are scheduled exactly, some external events may cause delay or over-run, and the precise timing of some program changes must be done manually.

In a number of early computer applications to process control, for example in the chemical industry, the computer was used to adjust the set-points of existing analog control loops which regulated pressure, temperature, flow, etc., at various points in the plant. Later installations gave much more responsibility to the computer, and used direct digital control. This involves dispensing with the analog control loops, but retaining the sensors and the output device. The digital computer is then multiplexed between all of the control loops. At each loop it samples the input data and, on the basis of this and previous data, computes the output setting which will remain unaltered until the computer has attended to all other loops and returns for the next up-dating.

The analog loops frequently use what are called "proportional-integral-derivative" (PID) or three-term controllers. Essentially this means that the control signal is the sum of three terms, proportional to the error, to its integral, and to its derivative respectively. In order to approximate to the PID controller, the computer must store the coefficients and some previous sampled inputs for each variable being controlled, although the program may be the same for all variables. Although direct digital control involves much more computation, the elimination of only a few dozen analog controllers may pay for the digital processor, and with larger systems which use 100-200 control loops the direct digital control will be much cheaper.

The procedure described above is an example of "predictive" control, in which the essential features of the plant's response to a control action are known for each loop, and from a knowledge of the current error and previous data a good approximation to the control action needed for the following time cycle may be computed. This procedure is usually simple to apply to each small control loop in the plant, but in addition to this small-scale control it is usually necessary for the computer to examine the overall operation of the plant, compare the present state and the output with the target, and make larger-scale adjustments which redefine the settings for each small loop. This overall activity is usually required to optimize the plant's operation according to some weighted performance criterion. Again, if predictive methods are to be used, some model of the plant's behavior in response to input changes is needed. If this can be obtained by computation or measurement the appropriate control action can be initiated. When the plant has settled down after the ensuring disturbance its condition can once more be examined, and further action taken if needed.

7.10. EXPLORATORY CONTROL

Although predictive control is the most effective method, since it uses all known information about the plant's behavior, it can be applied only if this information is available and, by implication, if it is not subject to rapid or random change with time.

Unfortunately many complex processes have responses to input changes which cannot easily be represented by a simple mathematical model, and may also be subject to unpredictable changes due to fluctuations in inputs (for example, in fuel and raw materials) as well as working conditions such as temperature. In these circumstances it may be simpler to disregard what little is known of the plant's behavior and rely wholly on observing the plant's response to known small changes of input conditions. This is often called "exploratory" control.

The procedure for any given input control is to make an adjustment, usually a small step change in value, and observe the plant's output. If the performance of the plant is improved, a further step is taken in the same direction; if it is worsened a step is taken in the opposite direction. Once the correct direction of the change needed to improve the plant performance has been established, further steps are taken in the same direction until a step worsens the performance. No further adjustment of this input is then advantageous, and a similar process can be started on the next input variable.

Since changing one input usually alters the optimum setting for other inputs, this procedure is an iterative one and it is necessary to adjust each input a number of times before approaching the optimum settings for the complete plant. Several methods have been suggested for making the process more rapid and effective.

One is to vary two inputs alternately, making a step change in each in turn. When one variable reaches its best setting it is left for the time being, and the computer begins to adjust the next variable. Another improvement is to reduce the size of the step change when the variable is nearing optimum, and thus to make a more detailed search. One disadvantage of this procedure is its slowness. It is necessary to wait for about three time constants in order to measure the output change fairly accurately after a step change of input. If the output is subject to random fluctuations an even longer wait may be needed, depending upon the ratio of signal to noise. Since variables are handled sequentially, and a number of iterations round all of the variables may be required before reaching an optimum the complete search process is inevitably slow.

One method of measuring the response to various input changes simultaneously rather than sequentially is to assume a linear system and perturb all inputs with sinusoidal variations, each input having a different frequency. A frequency analysis of the output changes will allow each component to be identified and related to the corresponding input variable which is perturbed at the same frequency. Although this shortens the measurement phase of the search for optimum, it requires much more computation than the simple process of adjusting each variable in turn.

7.11. MATCHING COMPUTER AND APPLICATION

The selection of a particular computer configuration is a lengthy task as so many factors are involved, such as the word size needed to achieve adequate accuracy, cost, the speed of response to interrupts, the amount of main and backing store required, the suitability of I/O arrangements, etc. The particular feature we now examine is the ability of a computer to meet the real-time demand for computation.

A useful starting point is the rate at which variables need be sampled. The computer is effectively multiplexed to attend to all control loops in turn, and thus can operate only on samples of information and not on continuous data as does an analog controller. Experience with sampled-data control systems shows that the important time interval in the control activity is the dominant time constant (T_D) in the system response. If the data-sampling rate is set so that 10 samples are taken in the interval T_D and the system input is changed accordingly after each sample, the resulting control action is almost as effective as that of a continuous analog controller. In most situations adequate control is obtained if only four or five samples are taken in every interval T_D.

An alternative approach may be based upon the frequency spectrum of any signal being processed. The sampling theorem states that in order to enable a signal containing frequencies up to f Hz to be reproduced from a set of samples of the waveform, at least $2f$ samples per second are required. In practice, to allow for smoothing to eliminate the sampling frequency component, $4f$ samples per second may be used. This theorem thus gives an indication of the sampling rate needed when using the computer merely as a data-collecting system where incoming waveforms are stored and analyzed and possibly reproduced later.

Reverting to the control function of the computer, once the value of the dominant time constant T_D has been determined for each control loop, the system designer can decide the sampling rate for each loop and hence the total loading on the computer. For example, if a particular variable needs sampling N times per second and the program dealing with it contains I instructions, the total number of instructions per second to be executed for this variable is NI. Adding together all such products gives the total number of instructions per second involved in the control and data-handling function. This must always be substantially less than the machine capacity, since some extra time is needed for multiplexer switching, A-D and D-A conversion, printing the summary of plant operation, performing "housekeeping" operations, etc.

If the variables relate to fairly slow processes, say temperature changes in parts of a chemical plant, there is time for a considerable volume of calculation, but if the dominant time constants are short each variable can call for relatively little computation. If this is not adequate, the task must be partitioned and shared between a number of computers. For example, the control of a rolling mill or flying shears in a steel-making plant calls for quite rapid calculation as the steel is travelling through the plant at perhaps 30 miles/h and quick decisions are needed. In this situation a small computer would be used to control each individual machine, with data supplied in part from a single computer looking after the complete production line. Again the complete plant would comprise several such production lines, and a further computer would be processing orders and stock and allocating work to each of the production-line computers. This kind of computer hierarchy is now used at a number of large steel plants, which may contain in all 30 or more separate processors.

If we consider a relatively slow process, say 200 loops in a process plant having an average time constant T_D of 1 min, taking five samples in the interval T_D means sampling a variable every 12 s. With 200 loops a sample must be taken every 60 ms. If arbitrarily the control function is allocated 50% of the processor time, the program time per sample is on average 30 ms. Assuming that each instruction takes 5 μs, this allows on average 6000 instructions per program. Some time must be allowed for A-D and D-A conversion, register saving, etc., and thus the useful program size will be somewhat smaller. Even so, the computer is not likely to be fully loaded with such an application.

If, however, the same requirement exists for a system in which the time constants may be those of small mechanisms, say of the order of

1 s, the size of program which can be used to deal with each sample is below 100 instructions, which allows time for little but the recording of data. As an example of this the control of a mill in a steel plant may require a sample of all variables to be taken every 25 ms, compared with 12 s for the chemical plant discussed previously. Since the computer is required to handle only the mill, however, no more than about six inputs are needed, and a single output to the screw-down motors which control the roll position. Allowing for some time devoted to printing the data on each billet rolled, the computer has 15-20 ms to compute the output after each set of input samples. This allows adequate time for a fairly complex control algorithm, but the computer has no spare capacity for much additional control activity.

If a preliminary survey of this kind shows that the processor is likely to be heavily loaded, it may be necessary to investigate other faster machines. Unless these have the same architecture, however, one cannot assume that the same control task will require either the same number of instructions or the same program running time measured in machine cycles.

Where program time is important machines which have word sizes of 16 bits or more generally perform better than machines with smaller word sizes. The larger word allows a larger part of the store to be addressed directly, without the need for indirect addressing and the consequent extra store cycle. Also the word allows room to handle data transfers to and from several accumulator registers, thus speeding up computation by diminishing the number of store cycles. The larger word also allows a greater variety of instructions, and thus in general a greater amount of computation or data handling per instruction. Finally it may happen that single-length calculations are adequate on a 16-bit machine, whereas some double-length (and thus slower) arithmetic is needed on 8- and 12-bit machines.

A further variation between machines arises from differences in hardware. For example, a basic machine may have no hardware for multiplication or division; these operations are then performed by software subroutines which will be much slower than hardware. For example, a multiply operation typically takes 10-30 times longer by software. Clearly any service routine which contains many multiply or divide instructions can be made much quicker by using hardware for these operations.

In order to give a comparative assessment of computer performance, attempts have been made to assemble a typical collection of instructions, each occurring with the same relative frequency as in an average work load. By estimating the time needed for executing this standard set of instructions on all computers under consideration one can obtain some comparative performance data. Examples of these standard tasks are the Gibson mix, based upon the analysis of IBM scientific programs, the GAMM mix, also related to scientific work, and the PO Work Unit devised by the British Post Office as typical of data processing applications. Although these standard tasks have been widely used for computer assessment they are not intended to simulate on-line working, and until a suitable standard task has been devised the safest procedure is to use programs related to the particular application for estimating computer performance.

In addition to processing speed it is necessary to estimate the size of main store required. This is normally provided in increments of 4 K locations. It is usually necessary to hold all programs which are frequently needed for control functions in the main store where they are immediately available. The size of store needed is then given by adding together the number of words of data space and program space needed for all of the user's programs, plus the space needed for any standard system software such as device handlers, library programs, etc. Programs used only rarely can be held on disc or tape backing storage, and read in when needed. However, this adds a good deal to the time needed for execution, since the programs read in will over-write service routines, and after the external program has been executed the original service programs must be restored. Also, while the external programs are running the over-written programs are not accessible, and so any interrupt which needs them will involve reloading part of the core store.

Other factors which must be considered when selecting a particular configuration are the availability of options such as the following: mains failure detection and subsequent restart; real-time clock; storage protection; standard peripherals such as multiplexers, ADC, DAC, and the I/O arrangements. Nearly all small computers provide DMA facilities, but this may be a normal provision or an optional extra. Other factors are automatic priority assessment and hardware "vectoring" of interrupts. All of these arrangements speed up the handling of interrupts and thus increase the machine's power for on-line application.

A final factor is the price and availability of software. In addition to the standard compilers, loaders, editors, test programs, and debugging aids, these may include special packages to handle standard peripherals such as disc and tape backing stores, teleprinters, CRT displays, routines for general applications such as curve fittings, computation of statistical parameters, Fourier analysis, etc., and for larger systems various levels of operating system or executive.

7.12. PROGRAMMING LANGUAGES

The control of plant, machines, and processes has proved to be a major area of application of on-line computers. Success requires very close collaboration between users and system designers, and on the assumption that the user of the plant knows more about its operation and characteristics in his own application than anyone else, he is the most suitable person to write the programs for controlling it. If the only means of doing so is machine code, he will normally require specialist programmers and must supervise them as best he can. If, however, suitable high-level languages are available he can readily learn to use them, particularly if they resemble existing languages in general use such as Fortran.

Some computer systems allow Fortran to be used for much of the work, although it cannot conveniently be used for IOT operations which usually need the manipulation of individual bits. The solution is a compiler which allows subroutines written in assembly language to be linked to a Fortran main program and called by it as are other subroutines. Then only the IOT operations or any particular parts of the program where maximum speed or minimum storage space is important need be coded in assembly languages. Many compilers provided with small computers now allow this mixing of high- and low-level languages.

Another possibility is to extend an existing language to allow calls to subroutines which can perform I/O operations. This is the method adopted by Hewlett-Packard for their 2100 series of computers. The language used is Fortran, and special WRITE instructions allow the computer to set the range of, for example, a digital voltmeter, set the function (a.c., d.c., ohms, etc.), and take a measurement. A subsequent READ statement transfers the measured value from the voltmeter interface register to a floating-point variable specified in the READ statement and also copies back the range and function code into an integer variable specified in the statement. This allows the program to check that the instrument is set up correctly, and also to detect an overload which is indicated by a value of the function code not used in the setting-up process.

With this kind of extension to a high-level language there is no need to use assembly-level coding for reading and setting up standard peripheral devices for which the manufacturer provides the READ and WRITE subroutines. However, if non-standard devices are interfaced, the user must provide these subroutines in assembly language.

A more radical response to the need for a high-level language matched to process-control tasks was provided by the Digital Equipment Corporation which developed a language called Indac in conjunction with Bell

Telephone Laboratories. This has a resemblance to Fortran, and includes its arithmetic operators and output-formatting provisions. Amongst its special features are its facilities for timing some operations by means of a real-time clock and reversion to a non-critical "background" job when not busy with its control activity. All requests for service interrupt the background job and are handled according to a predetermined priority assignment.

The software package provided includes a compiler, a system generator, a library of standard subroutines, and a small executive. The programs are divided into "snaps," only one of which need be loaded into the core store at a time. The task of the executive is to monitor interrupts, either external or from the clock, decide which program to run, load this into the main store from a disc backing store, and start program execution. The processor hardware for the original scheme was a PDP8 with a 4-K main store and 64 K of disc store, but the software will cope with other configurations.

Another language which is being increasingly used for control applications is Coral 66. This was originally intended as an interservice standard language for military purposes in the UK, but its advantages for general control applications are becoming well recognized and it is also being used regularly for industrial work. It is based upon Algol 60, but has some features of Jovial and Fortran. It was designed mainly by the Royal Radar Establishment. It can be implemented at several levels, depending upon the hardware available, the lowest of which excludes floating-point numbers but allows scaled fixed-point numbers. This is particularly suitable for small machines which have no floating-point hardware. The language is designed for rapid loading, execution, and compilation, the latter being intended as a one-pass process. In order to accommodate the special features of particular machines, or speed up critical segments of program, machine-language segments can be included in a Coral program. A further advantage is that its generality makes it very suitable for writing executives as well as application programs.

A high-level language which is becoming popular for microprocessor applications is Pascal. This has many of the features of Algol, but is more powerful and simpler to use. Pascal compilers are now available for the leading microprocessors, and one particular processor, the Pascal Microengine made by Western Digital Corporation, is designed specifically to handle the language. As a step in the computing process, Pascal is translated into a lower-level language called P-code; this is used as the machine language for the Microengine.

Pascal is designed to encourage programmers to write properly structured and easily understood programs by having a block structure and requiring all variables and labels to be declared and their type specified before use. Variables are valid only within the block in which they are declared and in other subordinate blocks.

This feature prompts the user to divide programs into blocks, called procedures, each of which performs a specific task and has a simple interface to other blocks. Discontinuous jumps in the program sequence are thus kept to a minimum, but where essential they can be handled, as in Fortran, by a GO TO statement.

As in most high-level languages the unit of program action is the statement rather than an instruction as in machine code. The statement may be a single line which assigns a value to a variable, or a compound statement which includes a number of simple statements contained between the words BEGIN and END.

Two types of arithmetic values are allowed, integers and real numbers. Real numbers are expressed (as in Fortran) either as decimal numbers such as 123.456 or in exponential form as in 1.2345 E2, which represents 1.2345×10^2.

There are four arithmetic operations, addition, subtraction, multiplication, and division, represented by the operators + − * and / for real numbers. Two forms of division are available for integers; 9/4 gives the real quotient 2.25 and 9 DIV 4 gives the integer quotient 2. The other three operators apply equally to real and integer quantities.

The rules for a valid name or identifier for a variable or constant are similar to those of Fortran without the restriction to six characters. An identifier must start with a letter; the rest consists of letters or figures. Labels, however, must be positive integers of not more than four digits. Boolean variables and operators are allowed as in Fortran. When writing arithmetic or logical expressions brackets may be used freely to indicate the action required, although the same precedence as Fortran is used. This means that multiplication and division are performed first, followed by addition and subtraction.

Program control statements are more powerful than those of Fortran. The DO loop is similar, for example:

```
FOR N : = 1 TO N DO
statement
```

The statement can be either a single one, or a block of statements enclosed within the words BEGIN — END.

The IF statement is similar to that of Fortran, but specifies the action required if the condition is either true or false. As an example:

IF X < Y THEN statement 1 ELSE statement 2

A novel feature of Pascal is the facility for declaring variables to be of a type selected by the programmer. The basic language allows only one-dimensional arrays. However, a matrix can be handled by declaring that each element of an array may itself be an array. Thus the inner array may be a column of a matrix, and the outer array comprises all of the columns of the matrix.

Blocks of programs which would in other languages be regarded as subroutines are called ''procedures'' in Pascal. In addition to those defined by the user a number of predefined procedures are available for reading and printing characters or complete lines, and for assembling and reading files.

Although numerical values are input and output only in decimal notation, binary values can be handled by defining binary digit strings. Operations on individual bits in a word are necessary for microprocessor programs, but in many cases they can alternatively be handled by providing a compiler which allows the user to incorporate machine code subroutines in a Pascal program.

The interest in Pascal as a high-level language for microprocessors has prompted work in several countries to publish standards for the language. Organizations involved include the International Standards Organization, the ANSI subcommittee X3J9, the IEEE Computer Society Microprocessor Standards Committee, and the British Standards Institute.

7.13. EXECUTIVES AND OPERATING SYSTEMS FOR ON-LINE WORKING

In most of the on-line systems mentioned previously we have assumed that a fairly rapid response to external events and interrupts is required, and consequently all active programs are held in the main computer store. While this is certainly the most convenient arrangement it can become very expensive if there are several large programs. If a slight delay in response can be tolerated, a much cheaper arrangement is to hold some programs on backing store, and load them into the main store only when required. The backing store must give rapid access to the service programs and must be either a magnetic drum or disc store, generally the latter.

The total time needed to service an interrupt, provided that it has higher priority than the task it interrupts, can be divided into several phases. The first is identify the source of the interrupt and check its priority. This should take some tens of microseconds and, compared with other delays, can generally be neglected. The second phase is the saving of data and machine status relating the program which is interrupted, and the third phase the transfer of the new program from the interrupting device into the main computer store. The service program can then start execution.

The usual type of disc store used has only one head per storage surface, so that the access time includes the time needed to position the head over the correct track and then the time for the required block to reach the head (an average of half a revolution time). Typical access times vary from 20 to 70 ms. Assuming that the transfers of data to the disc and of data and new program from the disc involves a total of 4 K words, the time involved would be around 40-100 ms. The total time between receiving an interrupt and starting execution of the service program requires two disc accesses and the data transfers, and would be 100-240 ms.

There are many assumptions involved in this estimate of response time. It could be even longer if a number of tasks are resident in the main store simultaneously and these need shuffling about to make a contiguous vacant area into which the new program can be loaded. Even so, there are many control situations where delays of a second or two would be acceptable and the use of a backing store would be an economical arrangement.

If response time is important, it can be reduced by a number of system changes. Firstly, a quicker access to the backing store can be obtained by using a device with a head for each track, thus avoiding the head-positioning delay. This means using either a fixed-head disc or a magnetic drum store. Also, by some expansion of the main store, it may be possible to hold all data which may be changed from time to time in the main store, so that only unchanging program information is held on the disc. This means that no writing back on to the disc is needed and only one access is required. Also, in a system using the minimum of main storage, the monitor program or executive which organizes program interchange may not all be resident in the store. A small segment is left in to detect a call for a new program to be loaded. This first of all loads the monitor program, which can in turn locate the required program and then transfer it from the disc. The whole process can clearly be speeded up if all of the monitor program is permanently resident in the main store.

For on-line working the monitor or executive program must have rather wider capability than is needed for off-line batch computation, and special executives called real-time executives or real-time operating systems have been developed for on-line working. In order to prevent one program from causing errors by overwriting another one, some storage protection facilities are often provided for user programs. When these are loaded their upper and lower boundaries are noted and any attempt to refer outside this area, other than to the executive, is not allowed. This feature is particularly valuable when the system allows a "background" job to be run in the gaps between the activities of the on-line operations. The background is often used for program development and testing, and it is most important that it should not overwrite and thus wreck the on-line programs.

In addition to the executive, some changes are needed to the on-line programs. Those which are not permanently resident in the main store may be loaded anywhere in the store when they are swapped in from the backing store. They must be thus held in a "relocatable" form which allows all instructions to be suitably modified to produce the correct linkages to other instructions in the program.

In order to avoid interference with the executive from user programs the computer may be arranged to operate in a special privileged or supervisor mode for the executive, which has no restrictions on store access and can execute all instructions. User programs can operate only in the restricted "user" mode, with storage protection and no access to certain instructions.

In order to facilitate communication between one user program and others, there is generally a common user area to which all user programs have access for passing data and parameters. Each program has a priority assigned to it when it is loaded into the computer, but most systems allow the operator to alter this priority when the system is running. Normally at the completion of any job the executive examines all programs waiting to be run and selects the one which has highest priority. If several have the same priority they are usually allowed to share the central processor equally, being allocated in turn short periods of processor time.

Some executives also control all input-output, allowing the user to write programs which specify a channel or device number, not a type of peripheral device. The particular device assigned to that channel number must be entered before the program is run, but can be changed by a command to the executive without changing the program. When the program needs to use the channel the executive looks up the device table which shows what particular peripheral has been assigned to each channel. It then uses the appropriate service routine from its library of device-service programs.

The design of real-time operating systems is a complex process involving many aspects of computer architecture, resource sharing, and programming, and in this section we have been able only to review their main characteristics, lacking the space for a detailed survey.

7.14. VISUAL DISPLAYS

Having examined a wide range of on-line computer applications under the generic title of data-logging and control systems, we now turn in contrast to a much more specific application, namely the control of visual displays using cathode-ray tubes. There are essentially two types of display: those which can produce only a prearranged set of symbols, and those which can draw arbitrary shapes under the control of a program.

The former are sometimes called ''character'' or ''alphanumeric'' displays, and are mainly used for output of text and numerical information. The displayed material is arranged in lines (usually 20-25 at a time), each containing 40-80 characters. Most of these displays have a keyboard similar to that used in a teleprinter, and the simplest type is a direct plug-in replacement for a teleprinter. It thus does not require a computer for its operation, but its main application is as a remote computer terminal.

At present these devices cost little more than a teleprinter, and their complete silence enables them to be used in offices, banks, etc., where a noisy teleprinter would be unacceptable. They cannot produce a permanent copy but for many purposes this is no disadvantage. Since they are all electronic there is no speed restriction on the data rate, as there is with a teleprinter, and many models incorporate a switch to alter the data rate from 100 bits/s up to 4800 and sometimes 9600 bits/s.

An important characteristic of a normal cathode-ray tube is that the picture must be traced out 30-60 times per second at normal brightness to avoid flicker and the consequent visual fatigue. This was a major factor in the cost of early displays, since unless the computer feeds across the complete picture data at this rate the display itself must contain enough storage to hold all the picture data.

In most current displays, MOS shift registers are used for storage, as they are simpler, more reliable, and much cheaper than previous methods such as delay lines. Most character displays use raster scanning in which the electron beam successively scans all the working area of the tube face. This is similar to the display in a television receiver, but does not use interlacing. Each character consists of a series of dots, each formed by turning on the beam for about 0.1 μs. The spots must lie on a fixed set of points, usually on a 7×5 matrix allocated for each letter, so that the characters are a little different from the normal upper-case set used on a teleprinter. The particular dot pattern required for each letter is held in a read-only store, and once the display has been assembled the only inputs needed for the tube unit are line (horizontal scan) timing pulses and field (vertical scan) pulses and the video-frequency waveform which turns on the beam. All three signals can easily be combined in a composite "video + sync" waveform and transmitted along a single coaxial cable, as in closed-circuit television systems. Thus extra parallel displays can be connected at little extra expense.

Although this kind of "replacement teleprinter" terminal is simple and adequate for some tasks, it is much more useful if it has extra logical facilities. The first of these is an "edit" mode. This allows new text to be keyed on to the screen, checked, and if necessary altered. Only when the operator is satisfied with the data is the "transmit" key pressed, thus sending the text to the computer. In some situations fixed data is sent out by the computer and the operator can insert data only in certain blank spaces. The checks necessary to prevent the operator overwriting the fixed data can be performed by the terminal. Furthermore, parity checking and other manipulation of incoming data can be performed. Ultimately it becomes simpler to attach a standard minicomputer to the display unit rather than continue to build more and more special logic and storage units. The advantage of this scheme is that the only change needed when moving the terminal from one computer to another is in the program, not the hardware.

When the terminal has editing facilities, and performs some data checking and perhaps data reduction or code conversion, it can take some of the computing load off the central processor and is classed as an "intelligent terminal."

7.15. GRAPHIC DISPLAYS

The second type of display, which can draw any required shape, is usually called a graphic display. One version is in effect a point-by-point plotter. The CRT spot can be directed to any one of a set of points on the tube face, and the beam turned on to produce a luminous spot. The pattern required is assembled from a set of such points. The resolution of the display depends upon the interface design, the matrix of points used varying from 256 × 256 to 4096 × 4096. A common size is 1024 × 1024, corresponding to a 10-bit number for both X and Y coordinates.

The general arrangement is shown in Fig. 7.3. The computer needs to supply an X coordinate and a Y coordinate to the two registers. These produce the corresponding analog X and Y deflection voltages which position the spot, and when this has settled in its required place the beam is turned on for typically a few microseconds to illuminate the point. The time needed to plot a point depends upon the settling time of the D-A converters and CRT deflection amplifiers, as well as the beam-brightening

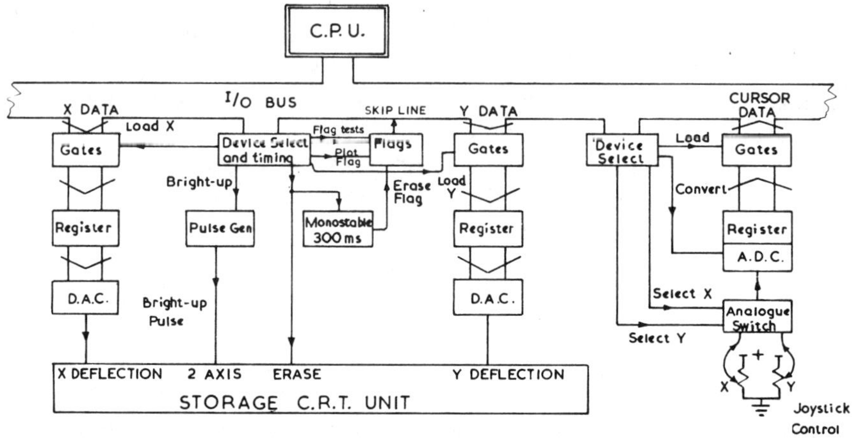

Figure 7.3. Interface for storage CRT display with joystick of cursor

time. Since the plotting time is greater than an instruction time, a flag is used in the interface which is cleared during the conversion time and raised after the spot has been brightened and data for the next point can be accepted. During the plotting time the computer is held in a waiting loop. Although the complete point-plotting operation requires three items of data, for X, Y, and Z CRT inputs, only two instructions are usually required as the Z (bright-up) instruction can be combined with the Y coordinate instruction. The arrangement shown in Fig. 7.3 assumes a binary code for Z, that is, the beam is either on or off.

For advanced graphics work, for example, producing half-tone displays with a range of intensity levels, 4-6 bits may be used to encode the spot brightness. This requires a separate Z instruction which transfers data from the I/O bus to a register and D-A converter to provide the beam-control signal.

For special purposes CRT displays are now available which give a range of colors similar to those available from a color television receiver. If only a predetermined set of colors are required, these can be digitally encoded in the *Z* instruction in place of intensity information, but if the full available range of color and luminance is needed (for example for making cartoon films from a CRT display) it is necessary to specify the drive signal needed for each of the three guns of the color tube. With a 16-bit computer this would allow 5 bits per primary color if the video information is contained in a single word. The resulting 32 levels of brightness involve some quantization error but this is acceptable.

One major factor in the use of graphic displays is the computer loading which they can cause. If the main computer is used to refresh the tube continually, little extra work can be carried out. For example, if a total of 10 μs is required for the two IOT instructions which load the interface registers, the settling of the DAC's and deflection amplifiers, and the subsequent bright-up pulse, a plot of 3000 points will require 30 ms in all. If the computer has 25% of the time for other tasks, a refresh cycle can be started every 40 ms, that is, a rate of 25 per second. At this rate the computer could not handle a second display without reducing the refresh rate to about 12 per second, which would give severe flicker.

The usual method of avoiding this difficulty is to provide the display with its own store for refreshing the picture. The complete picture data need then be fed across only once, and the main processor has much more time for other tasks. This is a rather expensive solution, since several thousand words of storage are needed. A cheaper solution is to use analog storage in the tube itself, so that the picture need be written only once on to the tube. This is the principle of the "storage" CRT in which the electron charge pattern deposited upon the target in the "write" mode is used to control the transmission of electrons from "flood" guns which produce a continuous picture. The secondary emission from the target also keeps the charge pattern maintained for up to 1 h.

An extra "erase" command is needed with the storage tube so that the screen pattern can be removed before starting to write a new picture. This process involves switching the tube potentials and discharging the target, and takes around $^{1}/_{4}$ s. During this time no further data can be fed to the tube. Thus the program can be kept in a waiting loop for this period, or allowed to continue some other task with an interrupt being signaled at the end of the erase period.

The block diagram of Fig. 7.3 requires the program to be kept in a waiting loop both during point plotting and the erase operation. This requires two monostable multivibrators which provide flag signals for, say, 10 μs during plotting and 300 ms during erasure. The interface requires a "test flag" instruction for both operations so that data transfer can be suspended until the operation has finished.

A program to plot a set of N points is shown in Table 7.2. This is used once for a storage-tube display, or repeated 30-60 times per second for a normal display. The number of points plotted is passed to the program by initially loading $-N$ into the location POINTS. The list of X coordinates is loaded into N store locations starting with location XCO, and the Y coordinates are similarly loaded starting at YCO. The program takes one X coordinate and the corresponding Y coordinate from the two lists, transfers them to the CRT interface, and causes the spot corresponding to the two values to be brightened up. This process is repeated until all points have been plotted. In order that the curve-drawing routine

Table 7.2

	Instruction		Comment
	CLA		
	TAD	POINTS	/ Load $-N$
	DCA	COUNT	/ Store in location COUNT
	TAD	XCO	/ Load starting address of X list
	DCA	TEMPX	/ Store in TEMPX
	TAD	YCO	/ Load starting address of Y list
	DCA	TEMPY	/ Store in TEMPY
START	CLA		
	TAD	TEMPX	/ Load next X coordinate
	IOT X		/ Transfer to interface
	CLA		
	TAD	TEMPY	/ Load next Y coordinate
	IOT Y		/ Transfer to interface & brighten-up point
	ISZ	TEMPX	/ Increment X address
	ISZ	TEMPY	/ Increment Y address
	IOT	FLAG	/ Test plot flag, skip if set
	JMP	.−1	/ If not set, jump back and retest
	ISZ	COUNT	/ Increment count, skip if zero
	JMP	START	/ If not, plot next point
		Rest of program	

need load the number of points and the starting addresses of the coordinate lists only once, these three items are held unchanged in the locations POINTS, XCO, and YCO. The three variables COUNT, TEMPX, and TEMPY are initially given the same values as POINTS, XCO, and YCO, but are incremented after each point has been plotted. In order to avoid holding the computer too long in the wait loop while the point is being plotted, the two instructions which increment the address pointers TEMPX and TEMPY are executed before testing the plot flag.

In addition to the three IOT instructions shown above for point plotting, a full graphics display may contain other instructions for plotting straight lines. These may either be specified in absolute terms, by giving the coordinates of the two points at the end of the line, or relatively by giving the starting point of the line and the displacement of the finishing point from it. Also at least two other instructions are needed for a storage-tube display to control the erase function and, if available, the "write-through" mode. This allows a cursor to be displayed on the screen which can be moved by the operator but is not stored with the rest of the display.

Some displays also have commands for drawing circles or arcs of circles. This can be done by gating two equal-amplitude sine waves in phase quadrature to the X and Y plates. The amplitude corresponds to the radius of the circle, and the superimposed d.c. bias to the center point of the circle. If only an arc of the circle is required, a further pair of numbers is needed to encode the turn-on and turn-off times of the CRT beam, thus controlling the length and position of the brightened arc. Generally no further figures beyond circular arcs and straight lines can be drawn directly; any more complex shape must be assembled using the point-plotting mode.

The interface layout shown in Fig. 7.5 is one of several possible arrangements. For example, some saving may be made by using only one D-A converter and multiplexing its output to two analog stores, one for each deflection coordinate. Another possibility is to split the data word into two halves, one for each DAC, and load them both simultaneously with one instruction. This produces a rather coarse matrix of only 256×256 points using a 16-bit machine, but is more acceptable with an 18-bit machine which gives a 512×512 matrix.

7.16. INTERACTIVE DISPLAYS

Although there are some applications of visual display systems which require only output from the computer without feedback from the user, the full potentiality of the display can best be realized when there is some provision for the user to control the material displayed. This may be of a fairly simple kind, for example, on a character display the ability to control the rate at which new data is presented and the old data deleted, or of a much more complex nature. This might occur in a full graphic display used for machine design, where a number of standard shapes (for example, hexagonal nuts) can be called from the store and placed where needed on the display. The user may also be able to change the size of the picture or the direction from which the object is viewed.

The ability to alter the picture on the display so that it appears to be seen from a changing viewpoint is particularly useful for architects. It enables them to gauge how the buildings they design will appear in their environment when seen from various angles. Such facilities, however, call for much software and considerable computing power.

When editing text it is necessary to indicate to the program which word or character needs changing. This process is much simpler and quicker if some kind of marker or cursor can be moved by using a keyboard or a set of pushbuttons so as to indicate the character to be edited. The cursor may be a line drawn below the character, a frame round the character, or may be indicated by making the character blink on and off repeatedly. These text-editing pointers are normally controlled by the keyboard, but some continuous manual control is often provided in graphic displays. This controls the position of a special symbol or two perpendicular lines, and can thus enable the operator to indicate to the program a specific point on the display. The point can be moved by a "joy-stick" control, which moves in two dimensions each controlling a potentiometer, or by a "rolling-ball" mechanism. This is a large (2-3-inch diameter) ball bearing free to rotate which can also operate two potentiometers which control the two coordinates of the point. Both of these mechanisms call for some manual skill not needed for other tasks and thus not likely to be developed by the occasional user.

A simpler method of indicating a point on the display is the "light pen." This is a device like a ballpoint pen attached to a cable with a small pushbutton incorporated. In order to indicate some place on the display the "point" of the pen is positioned on the CRT face and the button is pressed. The name given to this device is somewhat of a misnomer, since in fact the "pen" does not "draw" a display on the tube face, but enables the user to indicate some part of the display by receiving light from it. In operation the pen is placed over some point of the display and a button on the pen is pressed to indicate that the user requires some particular action at the point. The position of the pen is deduced by the program which checks the position of the CRT spot when the pulse from the light pen occurs. Thus for editing purposes it is convenient to use the light pen to indicate which character or line needs changing. This is usually quicker than identifying by typing in the characters adjacent to the one required, and using a program to search the file containing the displayed text for this group of characters.

The light pen can produce an output pulse only if it is pointed at a brightened trace on the tube. Thus it can easily identify any character in an alphanumeric text display. However, when applied to machine design the user may need to draw a line on a blank screen. This can be done either by brightening slightly the whole of the screen, thus providing a small but adequate pulse from any point on the tube face, or by using a standard pattern, for example a spot surrounded by a small square. The pen is pointed at the spot and moved towards the position on the tube which the user wishes to signal to the program. As soon as the pen reaches the square surrounding the point its direction can be determined by noting which point of the square it now covers. The controlling program will then move the point accordingly, and as the pen is moved the point and the surrounding square appear to follow it. If required the program can brighten up the path of the light pen, or the pen may be used to indicate two points on the display and a console command will join the points by a straight line.

A process similar to that used to "move" the spot on the display can be used to position a range of subunits on an engineering drawing. The subunits such as washers, bolts, nuts, rivets, etc., can be provided as a library of shapes in the margin of the display and moved by the light pen, being turned round and made larger or smaller by pushbutton commands.

The signal from the probe is normally a.c. coupled so that slow changes in ambient light near the display will not cause spurious signals, and if a short time constant is used the output pulse corresponds mainly to the leading edge of the light pulse. This is a more reliable signal than the trailing edge which is prolonged by the afterglow of the tube phosphor. The spot normally spends a time of the order of microseconds near any point on the tube face, so that the circuit time constant should be fairly small. This will ensure that mains frequency interference from ambient artificial light will not produce any significant signal.

Early graphic displays used a photomultiplier tube which has extremely high sensitivity but is too large to incorporate in a small probe. It is connected to the pen by a "light pipe" comprising a bundle of optical fibers. This is light in weight and transmits light efficiently, but is rather fragile. Subsequently solid-state sensors, photodiodes and phototransistors, were developed which were small enough to be built into a probe together with a preamplifier. A light flexible cable connects the probe to the display unit.

In addition to the light pen a full graphics display system has a set of pushbuttons, some of which can be programmed to control actions such as deleting a line, changing the size of the display, etc. Nearly all applications of a graphics display need some annotation, such as labelling graphs or curves and putting dimensions and other text on drawings, and consequently some facilities for character drawing are usually included.

One method is to use two separate deflection systems, the normal point-plotting one for drawing points and lines, and a minor system which is fast but covers only a small area of the screen. In order to draw a character the spot is first positioned by the normal system but not brightened, and then the code representing a particular character is used to extract from a read-only store a list of strokes and bright-up signals which the minor deflection system uses to build up the required character.

A complete drawing including titles, characters, and symbols contains a great deal of information, and if many of them are to be stored for subsequent use the computer system will need a large backing store. A full graphics system also needs a large storage space for the programs needed to control the display.

7.17. COMPUTER-COMPUTER LINKS

Links between computers fall into two main categories. The first is between processors which are near one another, generally within 50 ft or so. Here the designer is not constrained by cost or other considerations to limit the number of circuits used, and the link is often made through DMA or data channels. The second kind of link is used when the processors are farther apart and the connection must be made through the telephone administration. The expense of hiring lines and modems then forces the system designer to use only one circuit for the link in nearly all cases. The interface to the computer then involves a parallel-to-serial data conversion such as is used for a teleprinter, although generally operating synchronously and at higher data rates. The equipment has been described in sections 5.7–5.11 and will not be considered further in this section. The difference between a link to a remote teleprinter and a remote computer lies in the software and the protocol for data transfer rather than in the electrical details of the interface.

Short computer-computer links are used for two main applications. The first is to provide a multiprocessor computer system in which two or more similar processors are connected together to allow both of them access to a common area of main store and usually of backing store also. This provides a much more reliable system than if a single processor were used, since if one processor fails the other one can maintain service, perhaps with an increased response time. Computers with data highways such as the PDP11 Unibus lend themselves particularly to this kind of system.

A second important use of computer-computer links occurs in large computing systems, where it is somewhat wasteful of the fast main-frame processor to use it for slow and elementary tasks such as code conversions and controlling multiplexers for remote data links, the control of large backing disc stores, etc. It is more economical to hand over these tasks to auxiliary computers with relatively small stores but fast links to the main machine. It is much better to keep these small machines waiting for slow peripherals than to hold up the main processor.

A computer-computer link is usually arranged to handle block data transfers, so the interface requirements are similar to those for a DMA channel. This involves registers for the current word address, a word count, the data being transferred, and a status or control register. Since a normal DMA channel can operate in only one direction at a time, there is no particular advantage in arranging the link for duplex working, although it may be convenient to use a set of lines for each direction of transmission. The registers are normally loaded by program-controlled transfers with the exception of the data register which is connected to the DMA data lines. As with a DMA transfer the starting address and word count must first be loaded, and then a control word sent to the status register can begin the automatic DMA transfer.

Some machines have I/O facilities which are normally used for byte transfers, and for these two 8-bit bytes are assembled to produce a 16-bit word. This arrangement is used for the Nova 4025 interface which couples to an IBM 360 or 370 series machine. In this case the bytes from the IBM channel can either be packed as mentioned, or if the Pack Data flag is cleared, will be loaded one IBM byte in each Nova word. The transfer can be either in blocks or individual bytes.

Figure 7.4 shows a link between a PDP11 computer and a DMA channel. The main application is to enable the second computer to use the PDP11 disc backing store as a DMA channel device. For this purpose the four registers (data, word count, address, and status) are initially used to load the four registers of the disc controller via the I/O bus. They are then used in conjunction with the DMA channel. Once the disc registers are loaded, the disc controller requests a non-processor transfer on the Unibus (which has high priority) and uses this to transfer data from the disc to the interface register and so via the DMA channel to the second computer.

In addition to disc transfers, the interface can also be used for data transfers from the PDP11 to the second computer. In this example the PDP11 has much less than the maximum permissible main-store capacity, and the store of the second machine is allocated addresses which are above the main-store locations in the PDP11. This has 12 K words, so that the 8 K words of the second machine are addressed as locations 12 K–20 K. The address register in the interface contains logic in the lines which load it from the PDP11 Unibus. This modifies the high addresses 12 K–20 K to bring them into the 0–8 K range for the second machine.

In order to ensure that the program will not attempt to load the interface registers while a transfer is taking place, the word-count register has a flag connected to a zero detecting gate. Before each transfer routine is started from the second machine program the flag is tested. If the word count is zero, the transfer is allowed, otherwise the computer is held in a waiting loop.

7.18. MICROPROCESSOR CONTROL PROGRAM

This section gives an example of a simple interrupt-driven control routine which would typically be a small segment of a larger program. It deals with one PIA attached to a Motorola M6800 system, which has port A

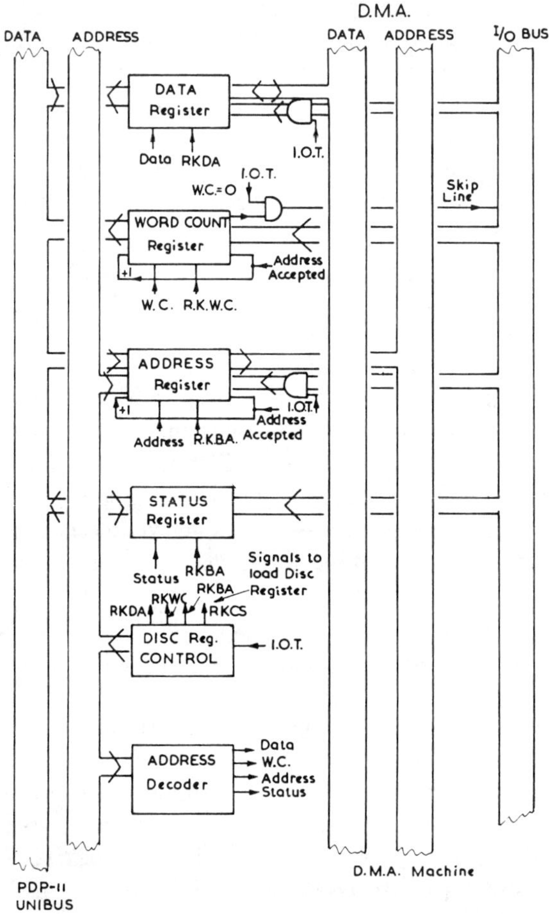

Figure 7.4. Block diagram of link between PDP11 and DMA machine

used for inputs, and port B used to drive 8 separate relays or contactors. A BCD thumb switch is connected to port A, fitted with mechanical stops to confine it to positions 1 to 8, so selecting one out of the 8 relays. The switch outputs are connected to bits 0–3 of the port. Bit 7 is connected to a separate switch which generates 0 to turn the selected relay on and 1 to turn it off. In operation the relay number is selected, and its new status, and the moment of change is determined by pressing a pushbutton connected to PIA control line CA1, so creating an interrupt. For simplicity it is assumed that no other devices can create an interrupt, and no device polling routine is included.

Port B is connected so that a logical 1 output from any bit turns the corresponding relay on. As individual bits cannot be output, only all 8 bits simultaneously, it is necessary to keep a copy of the current state of the relays in location 05, and up-date it after each alteration. The connections to the ports are shown in Figure 7.5.

The program shown in Table 7.3 can be divided into two sections; the first initializes the PIA, loads the interrupt vector address into designated locations (here A000 and A001) and then enters a waiting loop. There is no "clear interrupt mask" instruction in the interrupt routine as this is included in the waiting loop.

The interrupt service routine starts in location 0030. It uses accumulator B to generate a mask which has a 1 in the position corresponding to the relay selected and 0 in all other positions. To turn a relay on, this mask byte is ORed with the present contents of location 05, so ensuring that the appropriate bit will subsequently be 1 whatever its previous value.

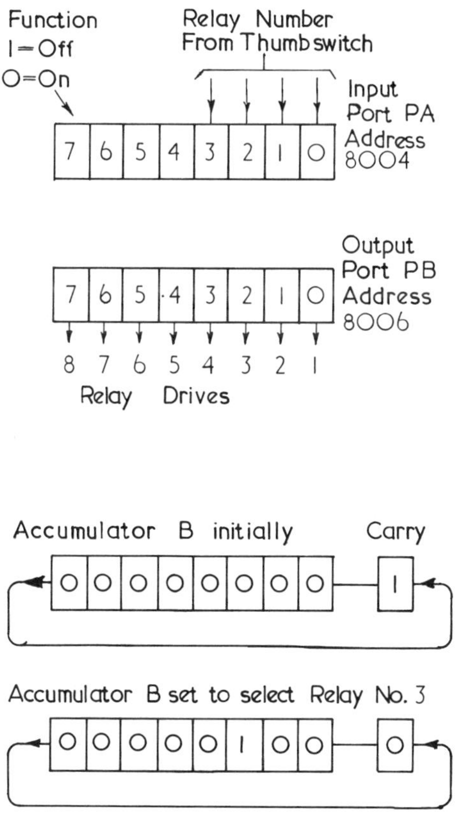

Figure 7.5. Connections to ports and use of accumulator B for relay control program

TABLE 7.3. RELAY CONTROL PROGRAM SET-UP PIA'S, INTERRUPT VECTOR, AND WAITING LOOP

LOCATION	INSTRUCTION		CODE	COMMENT
0010	LDX # 0030	CE	Load vector address into	
11			00	index register
12			30	
13	STX A000	FF	Store vector address in	
14	address		A0	A000 and A001
15			00	
16	LDA A # OC		86	Load bit pattern for
17			OC	CRA into ACC A
18	STA A CRA		B7	Store in CRA
19	address		80	
1A			05	
1B	COM DDRB		73	Set DDRB for
1C	address		80	Port B as outputs
1D			06	
1E	LDA A # 24		86	Set bit pattern for
1F			24	CRB into ACC A
20	STA A CRB		B7	Store in CRB
21	address		80	
22			07	
23	LOOP:	CLI	OE	Clear interrupt mask
24	BRA LOOP		20	Waiting loop
25	offset		FD	

The new byte, in which all other bits will be unaltered, is then output to port PB and stored in location 05.

For example, if relay No. 3 were selected the mask pattern generated would be 00000100 = 04 hexadecimal, counting from the right, as shown in Figure 7.5. The process could be achieved by complementing the bit, but this is operationally dangerous as two successive "turn on" commands would turn a relay off. The present scheme ensures that even if one command fails, the next can restore the correct state.

For turning a relay off, a similar mask byte is generated and then complemented. Thus, for the fourth relay, the mask pattern would be 11110111 = F7 hexademical. By logically ANDing this with the control byte, the fourth relay will be turned off as its control bit must end as zero regardless of its previous value. The remaining bits will not be altered as they are ANDed with a logical 1.

The mask byte is generated by a small loop of instructions which first sets the carry bit, rotates the previously cleared accumulator B left, decrements accumulator A which holds the relay number, and repeats the loop until the contents of accumulator A are zero. This shifts the bit from the carry position to the position corresponding to the relay selected. The result is the mask word for a turn-on operation, but its complement for the turn-off operation.

The type of operation needed is determined by testing bit 7 of the input port PA, most simply done by a "Branch if Minus" instruction, which branches the program down to location 41 for turn-off. For both operations the relay number is isolated from the other 4 bits read into the port by an AND # OF operation which clears bits 4–7 to 0 and leaves bits 0–3 unaltered.

INTERRUPT SERVICE ROUTINE

LOCATION	INSTRUCTION		CODE	COMMENT
0030		CLR B	5F	Clear ACC B
31		LDA A PA	B6	Fetch relay number and
32		address	80	on/off data from switches
33			04	
34		BMI OFF	2B	Branch if OFF command
35		offset	0B	to loc.
36		SEC	0D	Set carry bit
37		ANDA # OF	84	Mask off LH 4 bits leaving
38			0F	relay number in RH 4 bits
39	LOOPA:	ROL B	59	Loop to place carry bit
3A		DEC A	4A	in correct position in
3B		BNE LOOPA	26	ACC B
3C		offset	FC	
3D		ORA B 05	DA	OR ACC B with previous
3E		address	05	relay control byte in 05
3F		BRA OUT	20	branch to output, loc. 4B
40		offset	0A	
41	OFF:	AND A # OF	84	Mask off LH 4 bits leaving
42			0F	relay number in R.H. 4 bits
43		SEC	0D	Set carry bit
44	LOOPB:	ROL B	59	Loop to place carry bit
45		DEC A	4A	in correct position in
46		BNE LOOPB	26	ACC B
47		offset	FC	
48		COM B	53	Complement ACC B
49		AND B 05	D4	AND ACC B with previous
4A		address	05	relay control byte in 05
4B	OUT:	STA B PB	F7	Output relay control byte
4C		address	80	to PB
4D			06	
4E		STA B 05	D7	Store control byte
		address	05	in location 05
		RTI	3B	Return from interrupt

The initializing part of the program is similar to that for the PIA's in the parabola generator program of Table 6.4, but the control word for Port A is different, as it allows a pulse on control line CA1 (created by a pushbutton) to cause a program interrupt.

The following addresses are used:

05	Temporary storage for control byte
8004	PA and DDR A
8005	CRA
8006	PB and DDRB
8007	CRB
0030	Vector address — first instruction of interrupt service routine
A000/A001	Interrupt address for IRQ line, contains vector address

7.19. CONCLUSION

There are at present some tens of thousands of small computers in service, mostly in on-line applications. In a single chapter it is obviously impossible to give a comprehensive survey of all or even most of the functions of these computers. All that space allows is an examination of a few typical applications with a brief discussion of some design constraints. Further examples of on-line systems are described in the articles listed in the bibliography.

BIBLIOGRAPHY AND REFERENCES

INTERFACES AND INPUT-OUTPUT BUSES

ANDREIEV, N., The Search for the Standard Control Signal Bus, *Control Eng.*, Vol. 22, No. 3, p.43, March 1975.

ANDREIEV, N., Test Instruments Gain System Flexibility from IEEE Standard Interface, *Control Eng.*, Vol. 22, No. 11, Nov. 1975, p.44.

BARSOTTI, E.J., et al., *Operational Aspects of a Serial CAMAC Control System,* IEEE Trans. HS-21, No. 1, Feb. 1974, p.881.

BOBBITT, J., *A CAMAC Crate Controller Using a Microprocessor,* IEEE Trans. NS-22, Feb. 1975, p.508.

COSTRELL, L., *Highways for CAMAC: A Brief Introduction,* IEEE Trans. NS-21, No. 1, Feb. 1974, p.870.

DIGITAL EQUIPMENT CORP., *PDP-11 Peripherals Handbook,* 1975.

EL-AYAT, K.A., The Intel 8089: An Integrated I/O Processor, *IEEE Computer*, Vol. 12, No. 6, June 1979, p.67.

FALK, H., Linking Microprocessors to the Real World, *IEEE Spectrum*, Vol. 11, No. 9, Sept. 1974, p.59.

HOFFMAN, A.A.J., et al., Minicomputer Interfaces: Know More, Save More, *IEEE Spectrum*, Vol. 11, No. 2, p.64, Feb. 1975, p.96.

HORELICK, D., *The Confusing Digital Standards Picture — Are They Related?* IEEE Trans. NS-22, Feb. 1975, p.488.

HORELICK, D., *Simple, versatile CAMAC Crate Controller and Interrupt Priority Encoding Module,* IEEE Trans. NS-22, Feb. 1975, p.517.

HYDE, J., Using the Intel 8741 Universal Peripheral Interface, *Microprocessors and Microsystems*, Vol. 2, No. 4, Aug. 1978, p.236.

IEEE, IEEE Standard 488-1975. *Digital Interface for Programmable Instrumentation.* IEEE, April 1975.

KNOBLOCK, D.E., et al., Insight into Interfacing. *IEEE Spectrum*, Vol. 11, No. 5, May 1975, p.50.

LARSEN, R.S., *CAMAC Dataway and Branch Highway Signal Standards.,* IEEE Trans. NS-20, No. 2, April 1973, p.28.

LESEA, A., & ZAKS, R., *Microprocessor Interfacing Techniques,* SYBEX, Berkeley, Calif., 1977.

McGOWAN, M.J., From the S-100 to CAMAC: The Diversity of Digital Busses, *Control Eng.*, Vol. 26, No. 4, April 1979, p.31.

MITZEN, P., *The Microprocessor and its Interfaces,* 1975, WESCON Technical Session, No. 24, Paper 1.

MORROW, G., and FULLMER, H., Proposed Standard for the S-100 Bus, *IEEE Computer*, Vol. 11, No. 5, May 1978, p.84.

OPEN UNIVERSITY, *The Digital Computer TM 221. Units 9 & 10. Program-controlled input/output and event-controlled input/output,* The Open University Press, Milton Keynes, England, 1975.

PIEPER, J., & GROSSI, R.J., LSI Streamlines Instrument Interface with Standard IEEE — 488 Bus, *Electronics*, Vol. 52, No. 9, April 26, 1979, p.145.

POSA, J.G., Peripheral Chips shift Microprocessor Systems into High Gear, *Electronics*, Vol. 52, No. 17, Aug. 16, 1979, p.93.

RICCI, DiW., and NELSON, G.E., Standard Instrument Interface Simplified System Design, *Electronics*, Vol. 47, No. 23, Nov. 14, 1974, p.95.

SIGNETICS INTERNATIONAL CORP., *Interface (Line Drivers and Receivers),* 1973.

TEXAS INSTRUMENTS LTD., *Line Drivers and Receivers,* SN 55107 Series Application Report No. CA-130.

WASHBURN, J., Making Mini I/O Upward-compatible, *Electronics*, Vol. 50, No. 6, March 17, 1977, p.100.

WHITBREAD, M., Standards in Microcomputer Systems Design, *Microprocessors and Microsystems*, Vol. 2, No. 6, Dec. 1978, p.329.

MINICOMPUTER APPLICATIONS

BAILEY, S.T., Minicomputers flourish in Control Hierarchy, *Control Eng.*, Vol. 23, No. 5, May 1976, p.34.

BLACK, W.W., *An Introduction to On-line Computers,* Gordon & Breach, Science Publishers, New York, 1971.

BRAUN, J., & WHITE, G., Parallel Processing with Minicomputers Increase Performance, Availability, Part I, *Electronics*, Vol. 52, No. 14, July 5, 1979, p.125; Part II, *Electronics*, Vol. 52, No. 15, July 19, 1979, p.123.

BRIGNELL, J.E., & RHODES, G.M., *Laboratory On-line Computing,* Intertext books, Leighton Buzzard, England, 1973.

GRUENBERGER, F., & BABCOCK, D., *Computing with Minicomputers,* Melville, Los Angeles, 1973.

HARRISON T.J. (Ed.)., *Minicomputers in Industrial Control,* Instrument Soc. of America, Pittsburgh, Pa. 1978.

HEISERMAN, D.L., *Handbook of Digital I.C. Applications,* Prentice-Hall, Englewood Cliffs, N.J., 1980.

HUGHES, C.J. Computer Control of Switching, *Electronics and Power,* Vol. 23, No. 10, Oct. 1977, p.806.

MERRITT, R., Minis and Micros — Competing for Control, *Control Eng.,* Vol. 24, No. 2, Feb. 1977, p.45.

MOYA, O.E.D., and CORY, B.J., *On-Line Control of Generator Transient Stability by Minicomputer*, Proc. IEE, Vol. 124, No. 3, March 1977, p.253.

PHILLIPS, H., The Use of On-line Computer Control in Power Distribution, *Electronics & Power,* Vol. 23, No. 3, March 1977, p.225.

TUROFF, M., & HILTZ, S.R., Meeting Through Your Computer, *IEEE Spectrum*, Vol. 14, No. 5, May 1977, p.59.

URAM, R., Computer Control of Combined-cycle Power Plants, *IEEE Spectrum,* Vol. 14, No. 10, Oct. 1977, p.37

WALKER, B.S. GURD, J.R., & DRANEEK, E.A., *Interactive Computer Graphics,* Crane, Russak, New York, 1976.

MICROPROCESSOR APPLICATIONS

ALTMAN, L., & SCRUPSKI, S.E. (Ed.), *Applying Microprocessors: New Hardware, Software and Applications,* McGraw-Hill, New York, 1976.

BALLARD, D.R., Designing Fail-Safe Microprocessor Systems, *Electronics,* Vol. 52, No. 2, Jan. 4, 1979, p.139.

BEASTON, J., Second-generation Microcontrollers take on Dedicated-function Tasks, *Electronics,* Vol. 51, No. 24, Nov. 23, 1978, p.127.

BOTTARI, W., How to Design Single-chip Microcomputers into Control Systems, *Control Eng.,* Vol. 26, No. 5, May 1979, p.69.

COFFRON, J.W., *Understanding and Trouble-shooting the Microprocessor,* Prentice-Hall, Englewood Cliffs, N.J., 1980.

CROPPER, L.C., & WHITING, J.W., Microprocessors in CRT Terminals, *IEEE COMPUTER,* Vol. 7, No. 8, Aug. 1974, p.48

GALLACHER, J., Design of Modular System Applications, *Microcomputer,* Vol. 1, No. 6, Aug. 1977, p.345.

GALLACHER, J., Industrial Data Acquisition and Control Systems, *Microprocessors and Microsystems,* Vol. 3, No. 5, June 1979, p.213.

INTEL CORP,. *User's Manuals for MCS 40, MCS 48, MCS 80, MCS 85, MCS 86.*

INTEL CORP., *Peripheral Design Handbook.*

KENDLER, M.B., & LUTTE, N.P., Microprocessors Applied to Industrial Control Systems, *Electronic Eng.,* Vol. 51, No. 626, Aug. 1979, p.37.

KISTER, J., & ROBINSON, I., Development System Supports today's Processors — and tomorrow's, (M68000) *Electronics,* Vol. 53, No. 3, Jan. 31, 1980, p.81.

KOMPASS, E.J., Microprocessor-based Controller handles Analog and Digital I/O, *Control Eng.,* Vol. 23, No. 7, July 1976, p.22.

LENK, J.D., *Handbook of Practical Microcomputer Trouble-shooting,* Reston Publishing Co., Reston, Va., 1979.

LIPPMAN, M.D., & DONN, E.S., Design Forethought Promotes Easier Testing of Microcomputer Boards, *Electronics,* Vol. 52, No. 2, Jan. 18, 1979, p.113.

MARLEY, J., *Evolving Microprocessors which Better meet the Needs of Automotive Electronics,* Proc. IEEE, Vol. 66, No. 2, Feb. 1978, p.142.

MARTIN, D.G., et al., Power System Monitoring, *Microprocessors,* Vol. 1, No. 8, Dec. 1977, p. 463.

MEWIES, R.N., Triplicated Microprocessor Controlled Automatic Shut-down System, *Microprocessors and Microsystems,* Vol. 3, No. 8, Oct. 1979, p.347.

MOTOROLA, Semiconductor Products Inc., *Motorola Applications Manual, M6800.*

MOTOROLA, Semiconductor Products Inc., *Motorola Development Systems and Subsystems Data Book.*

NEIL, M., & GOODNER, R., Designing a Serviceman's Needs into Microprocessor-based Systems, *Electronics,* Vol. 52, No. 5, March 1979, p.123.

POE, E., *Using the 6800 Microprocessor,* H.W. Sams, Indianapolis, 1978.

PRAZAK, P., & MROZOWSKI, A., Correcting Errors Digitally in Data Acquisition and Control, *Electronics,* Vol. 52, No. 24, Nov. 22, 1979, p.123.

RANDLE W.C., & KERTH, N., *Microprocessors in Instrumentation,* Proc. IEEE, Vol. 66, No. 2, Feb. 1978, p.179.

RUSSO, P.M., et al., *Microprocessors in Consumer Products,* Proc. IEEE, Vol. 66, No. 2, Feb. 1978, p. 131.

TITUS, J.A., Data Acquisition System Built Modularly Around Intel 8085, *Electronics,* Vol. 49, No. 21, Oct. 14, 1976, p.104.

YEN, M.Y., Fast Emulator Debugs 8085-based Microcomputer in Rreal Time, *Electronics,* Vol. 50, No. 15, July 21, 1977, p.108.

COMPUTER EVALUATION AND ASSESSMENT

ALTMAN, L., Minicomputer Families Expand. Part 1: The New Chips, *Electronics,* Vol. 23, No. 25, Dec. 8, 1977, p.89.

BANKS, R., *Assessing Computer System Design from a Performance View Point,* Conf. Proceedings. Computer Performance-Methods of Assessment, p.19. British Computer Society, London, 1972 (gives details of GAMM Mix).

BIBBERO, R.J., *Microprocessors in Instruments and Control,* Wiley-Interscience, Englewood, Cliffs, N.J., 1977.

BURSKY, D., & BODLEY, N., Microcomputer Selection Guide, *Electronic Design,* Vol. 26, No. 11, May 1978, p.65.

BUTLER, J.L., Comparative Criteria for Minicomputers, *Instrum. Technol.,* Vol. 17, p.67, Oct. 1970.

CAPECE, R.P., Microcomputer Families Expand, Part 2: The New Boards, *Electronics,* Vol. 23, No. 26, Dec. 22, 1977, p.65.

CHRISTY, P., Minicomputer Architecture Links Past and Future Generations, *Electronics,* Vol. 24, No. 13, July 6, 1978, p.98.

DRUMMOND, M.E., *Evaluation and Measurement Techniques for Digital Computing Systems,* Prentice-Hall, Princeton, N.J., 1973.

GIBSON, J.C., *The Gibson Mix,* IBM Tech. Rept. TR00.2043, June 1970.

LUNDE, A., Empirical Evaluation of some Features of Instruction Set Processor Architecture, *CACM,* Vol. 20, No. 3, March 1977, p.143.

McKEVITT, J.L., & BAYLISS, J., New Options from Big Chips, *IEEE Spectrum,* Vol. 16, No. 3, March 1979.

MOSER, M., Designing with Single Chip Microcomputers, *Microprocessors and Microsystems,* Vol. 3, No. 3, April 1979, p.135.

MUSTON, J., Trends in 16-bit Architecture, *Microprocessors and Microsystems,* Vol. 3, No. 3, April 1979, p.129.

PENNY, B.K., The Implications of Microprocessor Architecture on Speed, Programming and Memory Size, *Radio & Electronic Engineer,* Vol. 47, No. 11, p.522, Nov. 1977.

PEUTO, B.L., Architecture of a New Microprocessor, *IEEE COMPUTER*, Vol. 1, No. 2, Feb. 1979, p.10.

POSA, J.G., Microprocessors and Microcomputers, *Electronics,* Vol. 25, No. 21, Oct. 25, 1979, p.144.

PREBBLE, N.J., and THOMAS, C.G., *A Relative Evaluation of Processor Performance against a Dedicated Real-time Application,* Conf. Proc. Computer Performance — Methods of Assessment, p.185. British Computer Society, London, 1972.

SIMMONS, G., et al., P^2 C-MOS Microcomputer Family attains N-MOS Performance, *Electronics,* Vol. 25, No. 23, Nov. 22, 1979, p.111.

SMITH, D.H., Exercising the Functional Structure Gives Microprocessors a Real Workout, *Electronics,* Vol. 23, No. 4, Feb. 17, 1977, p.109.

SUGARMAN, R., Computers: Our Universe Expands, *IEEE Spectrum,* Vol. 12, No. 1, Jan. 1979, p.32.

TURTLE, D.P., *Performance Estimation for Control Computers,* Conf. Proc. Computer Performance-Methods of Assessment, p.253. British Computer Society, London, 1972.

WILES, M., et al., Compatibility Cures Growing Pains of Microcomputer Family, *Electronics,* Vol. 24, No. 3, Feb. 2, 1978, p.95.

WILES, M., et al., Product Awareness Survey: Microprocessors, *Electronic Engineering,* Vol. 50, No. 606, mid-May 1978, p.51.

SOFTWARE AND PROGRAMMING LANGUAGES

BARDEN, W. JR., *The Z-80 Microcomputer Handbook,* Howard W. Sams & Co. Inc., Indianapolis, 1978.

BASS, C., & BROWN, D., *A Perspective on Microcomputer Software,* Proc. IEEE, Vol. 64, No. 6, June 1976, p.905.

BATE, R.R., & JOHNSON, D.S., Putting Pascal to Work, *Electronics,* Vol. 52, No. 12, June 7, 1979, p.111.

BLACK, W.W., *An Introduction to On-line Computers,* Gordon & Breach, New York, 1971.

BRUCE, R.C., *Software Debugging for Microcomputers,* Reston Publishing Co. Inc., Reston, Va., 1980.

CLULEY, J.C., *Programming for Minicomputers,* Crane, Russak, New York, 1978.

COLIN, A., *Programming for Microprocessors,* Newnes-Butterworth, London, 1979.

DAVIDOW, W., The Coming Merger of Hardware and Software Design, *Electronics,* Vol. 48, No. 11, p.91, 1975.

DUNCAN, F., *Microprocessor Programming and Software Development,* Prentice-Hall International, Hemel Hempstead, England, 1979.

ECKHOUSE, R.H., *Minicomputer Organization and Programming (PDP-11),* Prentice-Hall, Englewood Cliffs, N.J., 1975.

FREEDMAN, A.L., & LEES, R.A., *Design of Real Time Computing Systems,* Crane, Russak, New York, 1977.

GALLACHER, J., Software for Hardware Engineers, *Microprocessors,* Vol. 1, No. 3, Feb. 1977, p.169.

GRUENBERGER, F., & BABCOCK, D., *Computing with Minicomputers,* Melville, Los Angeles, Calif., 1973.

HALLIWELL, J.D., *A Course in Standard CORAL 66,* H.M.S.O., London, 1970.

INTEL CORP., *MCS-48 and UD1 41 Assembly Language Programming Manual.*

INTEL CORP., *PL/M Programming Manual.*

INTEL CORP., 8080/8085 Assembly Language Programming Manual.

ISAAK, J., Microcomputer Software Satisfies Conflicting Programming Needs, *Electronics,* Vol. 52, No. 26, Dec. 20. 1979, p.104.

JOHNSON, G.R. & MUELLER, R.A., Automated Generation of Cross-system Software for Microcomputers, *IEEE COMPUTER,* Vol. 10, No. 1, Jan. 1977, p.23.

LEE, E., When Programming Microprocessors use your Hardware Background, *Electronics,* Vol. 49, No. 14, July 8, 1976, p.93.

LEVENTHAL, C.A., *6800 Assembly Language Programming,* Adam Osbourne and Associates Inc., Berkeley, Calif., 1978.

LLOYD, M.Z., Costing Microprocessor Software, *Microprocessors and Microsystems,* Vol. 3, No. 1, Jan./Feb. 1979, p.29.

MEEK, B., *Fortran, Pl/1 and the Algols,* Macmillan, London, 1978.

MADDISON, M.S., Software as an Engineering Discipline, *Electronics and Power,* Vol. 26, No. 3, March 1980, p.237.

MOTOROLA SEMICONDUCTOR PRODUCTS INC., *Programming Manual for M6800 Microprocessor.*

OGDIN, C.A., *Software Design for Microprocessors,* Prentice-Hall, Englewood Cliffs, N.J., 1978.

ROLANDER, T., How Much Software for Microcomputer Control?, *Control Eng.,* Vol. 25, No. 1, Jan. 1978, p.54.

ROSENFELD, P., & HANNA, S.J., Developing Modular Software for the 8080A, *Electronics,* Vol. 49, No. 20, Sept. 30, 1976, p.83.

SANDERSON, P.C., *Introduction to Microcomputer Programming,* Newnes-Butterworth, London, 1980.

TEXAS INSTRUMENTS, *TMS 9900 Assembly Language Programmer's Guide,* 1975.

TURNER, R.C., *Real-Time Programming with Microcomputers,* Lexington Books, D.C. Heath & Co., Mass., 1978.

WAKERLEY, J., The Programming Language PASCAL, *Microprocessors and Microsystems,* Part 1: Vol. 3, No. 7, Sept. 1979, p.321, Part 2: Vol. 3, No. 8, Oct. 1979, p.375, Part 3: Vol. 3, No. 9, Nov. 1979, p.405.

WELLER, W.J., *Assembly Language Programming for Small Computers,* Lexington Books, D.C. Heath & Co., Mass., 1975.

WHITBREAD, M., Software Development and System Testing Techniques, *Microprocessors and Microsystems,* Vol. 3, No. 1, Jan./Feb. 1979, p.15.

WILSON, I.R., & ADDEYMAN, A.M., *A Practical Introduction to PASCAL,* Macmillan, London, 1978.

Chapter 8

System Development and Faultfinding

8.1. TEST AND FAULTFINDING ON MINICOMPUTERS

When describing interface principles and design features, little space has been devoted to testing and faultfinding. This is a necessary but fairly straightforward operation for minicomputer systems, which have write-able stores and, usually, an operator's control panel.

Generally, as each interface is attached to the computer, a specially written test program will be loaded which is then run to check the interface operation and often also to calibrate it. For example, a D-A converter would have a program to output a word set up on the control panel switches. By setting each bit separately to a 1, the output voltage generated by each bit can be measured. This allows the zero to be checked and trimmed, if necessary, and the full scale value adjusted. A final test for monotonic output and response speed can be made by using a ramp generating program which counts successively through all of the output states of the DAC. Examination by an oscilloscope — preferably with an expanded time base — will reveal any missing values or changes of slope. The sudden change from full scale to zero also provides an opportunity to measure the slewing rate.

Where more complex data transfer actions occur, tracing the program through an instruction at a time may be helpful. Timing difficulties, however, can be resolved only by running the processor at normal working speed.

In most situations a multiple-beam oscilloscope, conveniently triggered from the device select pulse, or device address decode signal, will provide all the information needed for faultfinding. This is easiest to find and use if the program is put into a loop which includes at least one data transfer to or from the interface.

The usual procedure is therefore to locate the address decode or device select pulse. If this is not present a data transfer cannot take place. Having located the decode pulse its timing can be checked by comparing it with the I/O sync or M sync signal.

Assuming that this pulse is present, examining the data lines at the same moment will indicate what data is present to load into the interface, or what data the interface has put onto the data lines.

An A-D converter can be tested in the reverse direction by putting it into a loop which continually samples a variable input voltage and displays the digital output on the CPU control panel or on some external display. By slowly increasing the input voltage from zero the converter can be checked for the correct transition levels between successive digital values. Both this and the DAC require a stable and accurate digital voltmeter to give a precise indication of the analog voltage.

The programs mentioned above merely check the operation and calibration of the interfaces. It is often possible to identify the action or set of actions which the interface will be required to perform, and to write a subroutine to produce these. The subroutine can then be tested, by a simple main program, separately from the remaining operations finally required from the complete system.

By retaining copies of these programs the stages in checking the interface operations which were initially traversed during program development can quickly be repeated for faultfinding at a later time.

Essentially the faultfinding process depends upon the use of special diagnostic programs and the tracing of signals through the interface by voltmeter and oscilloscope. The second process is possible only because interfaces are usually assembled from 20–60 or more small scale integrated circuits whose interconnections are readily available for test purposes. The only other requirement is usually an "extender board," which is a dummy board having a normal connector on one end and a matching socket wired to it on the other. This allows the interface board to be operated so that its wiring and packages are fully accessible and not, as in its working position, spaced only a few millimeters away from the adjacent boards.

When tackling a faulty system, the process of identifying where the error lies usually begins with the processor itself. Interface boards are removed or disabled and the manufacturer's test programs are loaded and run. Assuming that these run satisfactorily, each interface is connected in turn and its test program run. This procedure will generally indicate which interface is faulty or, if several are built on one board, which group is faulty. Conventional methodsd of signal tracing will then usually locate the fault, often with the help of the test program previously written for the interface.

This process of inserting a board at a time is based upon the normal "party-line" connection between the board and the computer buses.

There is an exception to this procedure in that "Intererupt Grant," "Interrupt Acknowledge," or "Bus Grant" signals are usually connected in daisy-chain fashion, passing into and out of each board in turn. Thus, in order to test interrupt actions it is necessary to bypass the connections through the board for these signals when the board is removed.

To summarize, the procedure described above for faultfinding in an on-line minicomputer system depands upon the following features:

(1) A writeable program store which allows a number of test programs to be loaded as required.
(2) An input channel which can be used for loading test programs, or a backing store which holds them.
(3) An operator's panel which allows the user to examine and modify any store location, to examine register contents, and to execute a program an instruction at a time.
(4) The facility for disconnecting device interfaces from the buses for test purposes.
(5) The ability to connect an oscilloscope or voltmeter to many accessible points within the device interface circuits.

It is a somewhat discouraging feature of microprocessor systems that in their final production version not one of these aids to faultfinding may be present.

8.2 MICROPROCESSOR TESTING

Comparing the list of minicomputer features given in the previous section with the characteristics of a typical microprocessor system gives rise to the following comments:

(1) The program store is read-only so that the only program which can be executed is that initially built into it. There is no possibility of loading or running an extra test program.
(2) There is normally no facility for loading any extra test program even if it could be stored.
(3) No operator's panel is generally provided so that there is no opportunity to examine store or register contents.
(4) The interfaces are usually connected permanently.
(5) The complete interface, apart possibly from some address decoding, is normally a single integrated circuit package, encapsulated in insulating material so that there is no access to any internal connections.

The pessimist would conclude from this list that little faultfinding can be performed on a microprocessor system other than replacing the complete printed circuit board which carries the processor, stores, I/O packages, etc.

This is an expensive replacement process, although acceptable where downtime is costly due to lost service or production. It is, however, possible to design the system so that it can be subdivided for test and replacement. One feature which contributes to this is the use of sockets to mount the processor, stores, interface packages, and clock circuit. If these can be removed individually, testing by substitution can be performed, and the cost of replacing one package when found faulty is much less than the cost of a complete microcomputer board.

The use of sockets can be supported on reliability grounds, since a processor directly soldered in to a board by flow soldering will be subjected to the heat conducted along 40 connecting pins and may consequently be overheated and have its innate reliability diminished. In any event, any PROM's used may require changing from time to time to allow for new requirements or changes in the microcomputer's environment and so will almost invariably be mounted in sockets.

Before trying to test a microcomputer it is necessary to ensure that the processor and peripheral packages are reset to the correct initial conditions. In order to ensure this it is useful to have the reset line brought out to a test point or an external connector so that any internal reset circuit can be overriden by an externally applied reset.

For some testing it is useful to be able to isolate the processor from the bus lines. This can be ensured for address and data lines by making the tristate control line externally accessible. An overriding signal on this line (usually an earth) will send the address and data lines into the high impedance state, so allowing the lines to be checked for shorts and open circuits.

The faultfinding procedures mentioned above are applicable only to production units as they are based on the assumption that the design of both hardware and software has been adequately checked. It may thus be assumed that a set of working components when correctly assembled will work as designed.

A more difficult task which usually requires much more effort and equipment is the development and testing of the system before it is put into production.

8.3. MICROPROCESSOR SYSTEM DEVELOPMENT AIDS—HARDWARE

Usually hardware and software are developed separately, but they must be brought together in the final stages, and it is usually beneficial to divide the project into individiual tasks for which hardware and software can be developed together before combining with other tasks.

For hardware development most manufacturers provide systems which comprise a microprocessor board with some RAM and one or two I/O packages, together with a port for either a serial data terminal (VDU or teleprinter) or a keyboard and display. The system is usually built in a multiboard frame which allows extra boards to be plugged in to support extra RAM and ROM, more I/O ports, A-D and D-A converters, etc. A small monitor program is generally provided either in a PROM or on a backing disc for loading into RAM when required.

The monitor program typically allows the user to perform the following:

(1) Load the program under development into part of the RAM.
(2) Examine and, if needed, alter the contents of any location in RAM.
(3) Start a program from any location in the store.
(4) Move a block of data from one part of the store to another.
(5) Execute a program an instruction at a time.

(6) Examine the contents of all processor registers when the processor is halted.
(7) Insert breakpoints in the program so that the program will run at normal speed until it reaches a breakpoint, when it will halt. Any store location or processor register can then be examined before allowing the program to continue until the next breakpoint.

Some monitors also allow any section of the store to be loaded with a specified bit pattern, and also include a direct assembler. This enables programs to be entered with symbolic addresses and labels and converts them into hexadecimal code before loading them into RAM.

A PROM programmer board may also be available so that programs which have been successfully compiled can be loaded into a PROM. This can then be plugged into a prototype microcomputer to test the operation of the program. Most manufacturers provide masked ROM and EPROM packages with the same pin connections and supply voltages. Thus, for high-volume products the program can be loaded into an EPROM for testing; if this is successful a masked ROM can be inserted in place of the EPROM for the final production version.

In the system described above the development equipment uses a separate microprocessor which is provided with the storage and peripherals that will be used on the production version. In order to test the final version, using the actual ROM, RAM, clock, and peripherals as "in-circuit emulator" may be used. This may be an additional feature of the development system, or a separate apparatus.

The emulator consists of a microprocessor similar to that of the system under test, with peripherals and its own ROM and RAM. It is connected to the system under test by removing the microprocessor package and plugging a connector into its socket. The in-circuit emulator then provides all the facilities of the development system to run the program an instruction at a time, to insert break-points, etc. In addition, it may have provision for storing any data output to a peripheral for later analysis, and for providing a predetermined stream of data for any port which is supposed to read data. Essentially the emulator allows all parts of the prototype system to be checked apart from the microprocessor package itself.

8.4. LOGIC STATE ANALYZERS

When errors occur during data transfers or interrupt servicing it is often necessary to examine a number of the microprocessor bus lines to determine the sequence of events and the stream of data which have been handled. With a typical small microprocessor there are 16 address lines and 8 data lines in addition to the control lines to investigate, so that a single or twin-beam oscilloscope is not a suitable tool for the purpose.

An instrument developed particularly for this situation is the logic state analyzer. This has 10–20 data probes which can be attached to the bus lines to capture data on the rising edge of each clock pulse. Generally a block of 250 successive bits are captured by each probe and stored in a semiconductor store. The sequence is started by a trigger pulse which can be either an electrical signal, such as an interrupt or a timing pulse, or derived from a particular bit pattern which appears on lines under test. Once captured, the data can be displayed either as a sequence of words coded in hexadecimal, octal, or binary format, or as a set of waveforms.

The display cannot usually cope at once with all the data captured and provision is made to allow the user to select which section of the data is visible, with the trigger time either marked or brightened up.

Where the program appears to jump out of the intended sequence the probes can be put on to the address lines and the sampling enabled by the Valid Memory Address (VMA) signal. The data captured will then be a list of addresses from which the microprocessor has fetched successive instructions and data. If any interface package appears to be working incorrectly, its address could be used as the trigger signal and the data lines examined for the correct signals.

Although this procedure gives a useful record of the data flow and addresses used, it is essentially a sampled system. Any short duration transients which occur between clock pulses could cause false data to be received, but would not be perceived by the display. In order to check for these, it is usually possible to operate the analyzer asynchronously. In this mode the data sampling clock is derived in the analyzer and is not locked to the microprocessor clock. By running the sampling clock 5–10 times faster than the microprocessor clock, transients which are long enough to cause a logical error will normally be sampled and stored and will be seen on the display.

Many logic state analyzers incorporate microprocessors which enable both character information and waveforms to be displayed. By putting the system under test into a loop of instructions it is possible to place the analyzer in a "watchdog" mode. It will then continuously store data but will overwrite the store so that at any moment it contains the last 250 bits of data to occur on each line being sampled. As soon as any abnormal event occurs the clock supply to the analyzer can be interrupted, so preventing any further input to the store.

The analyzer will then contain a record of all the data monitored during a period of 100-200μs preceding the event. An examination of this record will usually indicate the source of the error.

Many analyzers can store several hundred bytes of data, but may display only 25 or 40 at a time. Thus, scanning for an unexpected address or data, or the repetition of a loop of instructions or data, can be a difficult task. One method of displaying all of the data is CRT mapping. This is a process which allocates a separate position on a CRT screen for each numerical value of data. For example with 8-bit data the four high-order bits could drive a D.A. converter which feeds the Y plates and the four low-order bits could drive the X plates in the same manner. This would give a 16 × 16 matrix of 256 positions, some or all of which will be brightened as the store data is repeatedly presented to the CRT display.

For checking 16-bit addresses, two 8-bit D.A. converters would be needed, giving a matrix of 256 × 256 positions. When examining the data in this way it is easy to spot a data item or an address which is out of the expected sequence. Also, any repetition of data values or addresses, such as may occur during the repeated execution of a loop, will show up as abnormally bright spots on the screen.

8.5. SIGNATURE ANALYSIS

One of the main purposes of the mapping display described above is to compress the data being examined into a small compass which can easily be checked by inspection. Another method of achieving the same result is called "signature analysis." This allows a stream of data to be checked easily for any single-bit error. The process is similar to that used to generate the check character — normally sent after each block in many kinds of digital transmission — and uses a shift register with feedback connections.

Signature analysis was originally developed as a quick method of checking complex digital instruments, but is equally applicable to microprocessors.

Generally a 16-bit register is used. This allows a total of more than 65000 different bit patterns, or "signatures," to be recorded. In use the register is set to a standard initial condition and a prescribed number of bits fed into it from a probe connected to some node on the system under test. The register will also need access to the system clock, or will generate its own clock train which is also used by the system under test. When all the data has been fed to the register the clock supply is interrupted and the bit pattern left in it is displayed under the stimulus input to the system, on four hexadecimal displays as the signature for the node.

Of itself the signature conveys no meaning; it is used in a comparison process by first measuring the signatures at a suitable set of nodes for a standard input stimulus in a system known tobe working correctly. These form a standard "template" for the system. By measuring the signatures at successive nodes of a faulty system it is possible to locate the fault to within some particular section of the equipment. It should be noted that, however long the train of data signals, if only one bit is in error the signature obtained will differ markedly from the correct one. The test thus has a high discrimination capability.

For testing the contents of a ROM, a signature obtained by reading each bit of each word into the signature analyzer would detect an error much more quickly than a method based on trying to examine each word on a VDU screen. Also, by subsequently running a signature test on each bit of the word separately, it would be possible to identify which bit contained the error.

Also, the technique readily lends itself to automatic testing by storing a set of signatures for comparison in the computer controlling the test equipment.

Although signature analysis has been introduced in the context of microprocessor systems, the technique is equally applicable to minicomputers and their subsystems.

8.6. BUILT-IN TEST FEATURES

In many microprocessor applications the integrity of the control system is extremely important, and it is essential that any fault should be reported as soon as possible. Depending upon the degree of reliability required various schemes can be used.

One procedure which requires only a modest increase in store capacity is to include a self-test program which the processor must execute before starting its main activity. This can test that the processor executes all its instructions correctly and that the writeable store is free from faults.

Usually some degree of checking can be applied to external devices and interfaces. For example, by setting a spare output line, it may be possible to loop outputs back to inputs and so test through the interface packages to the peripheral side. Often some output action has a measuring system coupled to it and a predetermined output can be performed. The corresponding input sensor can then be read to ensure that its response lies within suitable limits. Thus, if the system is controlling some chemical process or reaction it may have a heater whose electrical input is controlled by the microprocessor, and temperature sensors to measure the temperature of the liquid surrounding the heater. The test program can then send a known power level to the heater and, after a suitable delay, check that the appropriate temperature rise has occurred.

Where mechanical motion is involved, a known signal may be sent to an actuator and the resulting displacement measured.

Where some measurement is particulary important, some degree of redundancy may be incorporated. Thus, when measuring temperature, five or more thermocouples can be used. Initially they are all read and the results compared. Should any thermocouple indicate a temperature more than, say 10° different from the average of all five, it is likely to be 50° in error and can be assumed to be faulty. The program can easily be arranged to disregard the faulty thermocouple and take the average of the other four as the correct temperature. It would, of course, be important to give some warning of the fault to maintenance.

Where reliability is paramount, for example in railway signalling and train control applications, triple redundancy schemes have been designed, in which three complete microprocessors operate in synchronism and compare results periodically. Any unit which produces a result at variance with the results of the other two either disconnects itself or is disconnected by the other two.

In these systems, as in nearly all redundancy schemes where maintenance action can be undertaken, any fault must be reported so that repairs can be started at once, even if redundancy allows the system to continue working. Only by this procedure can full advantage be gained from the redundant configuration.

8.7. MICROPROCESSOR SYSTEM DEVELOPMENT AIDS: SOFTWARE

The software development systems available for writing microprocessor programs can be divided into two classes: those which embody a processor of the same type as that for which the software is required, and those which use a different, more powerful processor, often a minicomputer or a main frame.

The systems in the first category have the advantage that, once the program has been written, it can be run in machine code form on the development system, usually with simulated peripherals. The disadvantage is that the system can handle only one type of microprocessor. In order to cope with all the tasks involved, the microprocessor needs a considerable amount of RAM, often up to 48 K bytes, with single or twin floppy disc drives which hold the set of system programs. These are transferred to RAM when used. The programs are similar in function to the system programs for a minicomputer, and would typically include a text editor, an assembler, a loader, and a file handling program together with a simple monitor program. A debugging program may also be included; this allows a terminal to be used to start the program from any initial location, to run it an instruction at a time, to examine the contents of any register or RAM location and change them if needed, or to insert breakpoints into the program. It provides control over the action of the microprocessor similar to that which the operator's panel provides in a minicomputer. Another feature sometimes included is a reverse assembler which turns machine code back into assembly mnemonic code—a considerable help when tracing a program sequence.

Peripherals used for this task include usually a VDU and keyboard, perhaps with a printer for documentation, and floppy discs, preferably with a dual drive. Also useful is a PROM programmer which can load the program into a package for insertion into the prototype system.

There is a problem with these systems in that a compilier for a high-level language, together with disc-driver programs, may require much of the available store, leaving little for the source and object programs.

Also a major constraint on all systems programs is the need to conserve storage, so that such programs generally offer fewer features than corresponding minicomputer programs.

The alternative method of developing programs is to use a standard minicomputer and its operating system. This will normally include file handling programs, a text editor, loader, and debut program. The only extra program needed is a cross-assembler, so that user programs written in the microprocessor assembly language can be translated into the machine code of the microprocessor, rather than that of the host machine. Similarly, if a high level language is used, a cross-compiler for this will be needed.

A comprehensive system may also include some special device handling utilities, for example a ROM-tape generator which produces a paper tape version of the machine code program. This can be sent to the semiconductor manufacturer to produce a masked ROM. Also, for development work, it may be useful to output the machine code program to an interface which generates a modulated audio-frequency output. This can be recorded by an inexpensive cassette recorder both for a permanent record and for transferring to a development system with a suitable interface. A popular recording standard is the "Kansas City" frequency-shift coding which uses frequencies for 1200 Hz for a zero and 2400 Hz for a one, and runs at 300 bauds. The two frequencies are easily generated by counting down the 4800 Hz clock supply (16 times the bit rate) needed for a 300 baud serial communication circuit.

The same program transfer process may be used to load a ROM simulator. This is a block of RAM into which the program is loaded; the write function is then disabled. The simulator is connected to the prototype microprocessor system by means of a multi-way cable which has a plug to insert into the ROM socket. When the prototype is started, it reads the program from the simulator in exactly the same way as it would read a ROM. A keyboard and display on the simulator, however, allow any byte of the program to be altered if necessary.

The program can thus be modified in the light of running tests before it is finally committed to a RAM.

The advantage of the minicomputer-based system is that it is not normally tied to one microprocessor; by adding another cross-assembler, programs for a second microprocessor can be developed and tested. This may also enable an existing high-level language such as Pascal to be used without the need for much extra software, since Pascal is normally translated into a standard machine-independent low-level language called P-code before being converted into a particular machine language. All that is needed for a second microprocessor is a converter from P-code to its own machine code.

Also, a minicomputer will usually have more main storage and, thus, room for better diagnostics and, in general, more comprehensive system programs that can be supported on a microprocessor system.

Although each microprocessor program is often written individually for a specific application, there are certain segments, such as device handlers and some data handling and mathematical operations, which occur frequently and may be written as subroutines. A possible development which requires no new technology would be to have a set of such routines available in ROM as a cheap plug-in item. The main program could then be reduced to a much smaller size and written more rapidly.

BIBLIOGRAPHY AND REFERENCES

BRUCE, R.C., *Software Debugging for Microcomputers,* Reston Publishing Co. Inc., Reston, Va., 1980.

COFFRON, J.W., *Understanding and Trouble-shooting the Microprocessor,* Prentice-Hall, Englewood Cliffs, N.J., 1980.

DUNCAN, F., *Microprocessor Programming and Software Development,* Prentice-Hall International, Hemel Hempstead, U.K., 1979.

ECKHOUSE, R.H., *Minicomputer Organization and Program (PDP 11),* Prentice-Hall, Englewood Cliffs, N.J., 1975.

GALLACHER, J., Software for Hardware Engineers, *Microprocessors,* Vol. 1, No. 3, Feb. 1977, p.169.

GARLAND, H., *Introduction to Microprocessor System Design,* McGraw-Hill, New York, 1979.

INTEL CORPORATION. *Intellec Series II 210 User's Guide.*

KLINGMAN, D.E., *Microprocessor System Design,* Prentice-Hall, Englewood Cliffs, N.J., 1977.

KISTER, J., and ROBINSON, I., Development Systems Support Today's Processors—and Tomorrow's, *Electronics,* Vol. 53, No. 3, Jan. 31, 1980, p.81.

LENK, J.D., *Handbook of Practical Microcomputer Trouble-shooting,* Reston Publishing Co., Reston, Va., 1979.

LIPPMAN, M.D., and DONNE, S., Design Forethought Promotes Easier Testing of Microcomputer Boards, *Electronics,* Vol. 52, No. 2, Jan. 18, 1979, p.113

LLOYD, M.Z., Costing Microprocessor Software, *Microprocessors and Microsystems,* Vol. 3, No. 1, Jan./Feb. 1979, p.89.

MOTOROLA SEMICONDUCTOR PRODUCTS INC., *Motorola Applications Manual, M6800.*

MOTOROLA SEMICONDUCT PRODUCTS INC., *Motorola development systems and subsystems data books.*

NEIL, M., and GOODNER, R., Designing a Serviceman's Needs into Microprocessor-based Systems, *Electronics,* Vol. 52, No. 5, March 1979, p.123.

OGDIN, C.A. *Software Design for Microprocessors,* Prentice-Hall, Englewood Cliffs, N.J., 1978.

PEATMAN, J.B., *The Design of Digital Systems,* McGraw-Hill, New York, 1972.

ROSENFELD, P., and HANNA, S.J. Developing Modular Software for the 8080A, *Electronics,* Vol. 49, No. 20, Sept. 30, 1976, p.83.

WHITBREAD, M. Software Development and System Testing Techniques, *Microprocessors and Microsystems.* Vol. 3, No. 1, Jan./Feb. 1979, p.15.

Index